COMMON BORDER, UNCOMMON PATHS

COMMON BORDER, UNCOMMON PATHS

Race, Culture, and National Identity in U.S.-Mexican Relations

Edited by
Jaime E. Rodríguez O. and Kathryn Vincent

A Scholarly Resources Inc. Imprint
Wilmington, Delaware

Published in cooperation with the University of California Institute for Mexico and the United States (UC MEXUS)

Scholarly Resources Inc.
104 Greenhill Avenue
Wilmington, DE 19805-1897

Sources for Illustrations

Archivo General de la Nación, Mexico City; Biblioteca Nacional de México, Mexico City; Los Angeles Times Syndicate, Los Angeles, California.

Frontispiece: © 1996 by Paul Conrad. Distributed by Los Angeles Times Syndicate. Reprinted by permission.
Front endsheet: *A New Map of America Septentrionale* (North America), based on the work of Mr. Sanson, geographer to the king of France, published London, 1669, by Richard Blome (shows California as an island).
Back endsheet: *L'Amérique Septentrionale* (North America) by Guillaume de l'Isle, published in Amsterdam, 1700.
Cover art: Brad Rowe, University of California, Riverside, Publications.

Library of Congress Cataloging-in-Publication Data

Common border, uncommon paths : race, culture, and national identity in U.S.-Mexican relations / edited by Jaime E. Rodríguez O., Kathryn Vincent.
    p.   cm. — (Latin American silhouettes)
    Some essays translated from Spanish.
    Drawn from papers presented at a conference convened under the umbrella of the UC MEXUS program Critical Issues in U.S.-Mexican Relations.
    "Published in cooperation with the University of California Institute for Mexico and the United States (UC MEXUS)"—T.p. verso.
    Includes bibliographical references and index.
    ISBN 0-8420-2673-8 (alk. paper)
    1. United States—Relations—Mexico—Congresses. 2. Mexico—Relations—United States—Congresses. 3. National characteristics, American—Congresses. 4. National characteristics, Mexican—Congresses. 5. Racism—United States—Congresses. 6. Racism—Mexico—Congresses. I. Rodríguez O., Jaime E., 1940– . II. Vincent, Kathryn, 1948– . III. University of California Institute for Mexico and the United States. IV. Series.
E183.8.M6C64   1997
303.48'273072—dc21   97-8951
                                          CIP

∞ The paper used in this publication meets the minimum requirements of the American National Standard for permanence of paper for printed library materials, Z39.48, 1984.

In Memory of Our Fathers

Luis Arsenio Rodríguez Sandoval

and

David Lloyd Thomas

Contents

Preface

RECOGNIZING THE CONTINUING IMPLICATIONS of miswritten history for relations between the two governments, and the two peoples, of the United States and Mexico, the leaders of two unusual organizations formed a partnership to investigate the issue. Dr. Arturo Gómez-Pompa, then director of the University of California Institute for Mexico and the United States (UC MEXUS) and Dr. Roger Díaz de Cossío, then director of the Programa para las Comunidades Mexicanas en el Extranjero de la Secretaría de Relaciones Exteriores, developed a two-conference program to bring together Mexican and U.S. humanists and social scientists to address the myths that abound in the recorded history of the U.S.-Mexican relationship. The conferences were equally funded by UC MEXUS and the Programa and convened under the umbrella of a UC MEXUS program—Critical Issues in U.S.-Mexican Relations—a series supported by a major grant from the John D. and Catherine T. MacArthur Foundation.

This is the fourth collection of essays to emerge from the Critical Issues Program. Contributions to this volume and its companion, *Myths, Misdeeds, and Misunderstandings: The Roots of Conflict in U.S.-Mexican Relations*, are drawn from papers presented at the fourth and fifth Critical Issues conferences: "Rewriting History: Perceptions of Mexico and the United States," held in February 1992 at El Colegio de la Frontera Norte, San Antonio del Mar, Baja California, and "Myths in U.S.-Mexican Relations," held in June 1992 at the University of California, Riverside. As were the conferences, this collection is directed toward a general audience interested in learning more about the complexities of the U.S.-Mexican relationship. The contributors and editors have concentrated less on technical details, therefore, and more on explanations of events and individual and national motives.

A number of persons and institutions contributed to the success of the conferences and the production of this volume. At the Programa in Mexico City, María Esther Schumacher and Esther González González were dedicated and efficient co-organizers of the two conferences and a great pleasure to know. Thanks to the president of El Colegio de la Frontera Norte, Jorge A. Bustamante, and his excellent staff at the beautiful San Antonio del Mar campus for hosting the "Rewriting History" conference in fine style. Josefina Zoraida Vázquez of El Colegio de México and Luis Leal of the University of California, Santa Barbara, cochaired both conferences. UC MEXUS staff members Yvonne Pacheco Tevis, Dora Velasco, and Carmen Flores Hernández provided expert conference organization.

Initial Spanish-to-English translations of some of the essays were accomplished by Yvonne Pacheco Tevis (chapter by León-Portilla), Marjory Urquidi (chapters by González Navarro, Valenzuela Arce, and Monsiváis), and Miguel R. López (chapter by Leal). Thanks to Karen Lowe and Carla Duke at the University of California, Irvine, for their assistance with the manuscript. Rodolfo Ruibal, Juan-Vicente Palerm, Carlos Morton, William F. Sater, and Christon I. Archer read parts of the volume, providing valuable suggestions for its improvement.

I am pleased that I was assigned to write this preface because it allows me to thank my coeditor, Jaime E. Rodríguez O., for the profound contributions he has made to the understanding of Mexican history, not only through his own celebrated scholarship but also by organizing the work of scholars of Mexico into an extraordinarily fine collection of edited volumes that UC MEXUS has been proud to support. We at UC MEXUS are especially grateful for his willingness to take charge of this book.

Kathryn Vincent

Riverside, California
July 1996

Contributors

Moisés González Navarro is professor of history at El Colegio de México. He is the author of numerous books and articles on nineteenth-century Mexican political, social, and labor history. He is a member of the Mexican Academy of History and has been the recipient of the José María Vigil and the Sahagún prizes for his books. His works include *Los extranjeros en México y los mexicanos en el extranjero*, 3 vols. (Mexico, 1994).

Norma Klahn is associate professor of literature at the University of California, Santa Cruz. She is the author of various studies of Latin American literature. Her works include *Los novelistas como críticos*, 2 vols. (Mexico, 1991).

Luis Leal is professor emeritus, University of Illinois, Champaign-Urbana; distinguished lecturer, University of California, Santa Barbara; and visiting professor, Stanford University. In 1991 the Mexican government honored him with the Order of the Aztec Eagle, the highest award that it bestows upon foreigners. He has published extensively on Mexican and Chicano literature. His works include *Aztlán y México* (Tempe, 1985).

Miguel León-Portilla is research professor *emerito* at the Instituto de Investigaciones Históricas of the Universidad Nacional Autónoma de México. He is the recipient of numerous prizes and honorary doctorates from Mexico, the United States, various European countries, and Israel, and is as well a member of the Mexican Academy of History, the Mexican Academy of the Language, and the National College, the most prestigious elected group of scholars in Mexico. He is the author of a score of books on pre-Columbian society, Nahuatl culture, and the history of Baja California, some of which have been translated into many languages. His most famous work is the now classic *La filosofía nahuatl* (9th ed., Mexico, 1992).

Carlos Monsiváis is a renowned man of letters—critic, essayist, novelist, political commentator, and cultural journalist for Mexico's foremost newspapers and magazines. His many works include *El género epistolar: Un homenaje a manera de carta* (Mexico, 1991).

Jaime E. Rodríguez O. is professor of history at the University of California, Irvine, and editor of the journal *Mexican Studies/Estudios Mexicanos*. He has published widely on the early nineteenth century. His works include *La independencia de la América española* (Mexico, 1996).

Ramón Eduardo Ruiz is professor emeritus at the University of California, San Diego. He has published on the Cuban Revolution and on the history of Mexican education and labor and on the Mexican Revolution. His works include *Triumphs and Tragedy: A History of the Mexican People* (New York, 1992).

José Manuel Valenzuela Arce is professor and director of the Departamento de Estudios Culturales at El Colegio de la Frontera Norte. He is the author of works on the contemporary culture of the border, particularly of Baja California. His works include *Decadencia y auge de las identidades: Cultura nacional, identidad cultural y modernización* (Tijuana, 1992).

Kathryn Vincent is assistant director of the University of California Institute for Mexico and the United States and editor of *UC MEXUS News*. She is also an independent editor and writer. Her publications include *Beyond the Basics II: More Innovative Techniques for Outdoor/Nature Photography* (with George Lepp) (Los Osos, CA, 1997).

Mexico has her men of science, her eloquent orators, her eminent researchers, her historians, her excellent novelists, and numerous poets who write in the melodious language spoken in this country.

WILLIAM CULLEN BRYANT (1872)

It is fortunate that the Yankees, except for a few rare exceptions, are persons with whom one can speak frankly. What a great country it would be if the nation were like its individuals!

MARTÍN LUIS GUZMÁN (1928)

Back to the Future: Racism and National Culture in U.S.-Mexican Relations

Jaime E. Rodríguez O. and Kathryn Vincent

> California, though a part of the republic of Mexico, has always been isolated from it, forming a distinct country, with nothing common to it and Mexico, except that the inhabitants are of the same race.[1]

THE ORIGIN OF CONTENTION between the United States and Mexico is rooted in the history of conflict between the two colonial powers that founded them. In one sense, each child-nation inherited a long-standing family feud.

Religion sharply divided the English and Spanish peoples, respectively the forefathers of the United States and Mexico. During the sixteenth century, Spain became the champion of Catholicism, and Protestant England, although not Spain's equal, became one of its most hostile enemies. The two powers engaged in conflict in Europe and in the Spanish possessions across the world.

Spain permitted no religious diversity in its American dominions. Protestants were feared not only as evil heretics but also as dangerous predators. Famous English corsairs such as Sir Walter Raleigh and Sir Francis Drake were widely regarded in Spanish America as pirates, thieves, rapists, and murderers. Indeed, countless coastal cities suffered the assaults of Protestant buccaneers, not all of whom were English, during the colonial era. Although the pirate threat declined by the eighteenth century, conflict between England and Spain continued as did their fear of and hostility toward one another.

Religious attitudes remained antagonistic as the nineteenth century began. The Spanish Constitution of 1812, one of the most liberal constitutions in Europe, did not provide for religious tolerance, a position Mexico

---

[1]John Frost, *Pictorial History of Mexico and the Mexican War* (Philadelphia: Thomas Cowperthwait and Co., 1849), 388.

1

maintained after independence. The Constitution of 1824, Mexico's first, established Catholicism as the national religion to the exclusion of all others. Thus, immigrants to Mexico, during both the late Spanish period and the early national era, entered the country with the obligation to become Catholics if they did not already belong to that faith. Subsequently, the Anglo Americans in Texas used this lack of religious freedom as an excuse to secede from Mexico. But the country's religious intolerance caused practical problems from the outset. Many foreigners who resided in Mexico after independence were Protestant, among them diplomatic and consular officials, merchants, investors, and other influential persons.

The presence of Protestants in Mexico became a serious issue in 1827 during the discussion of the Treaty of Friendship, Commerce, and Navigation with Great Britain. Good relations with that nation were important not only for economic reasons but also because Mexico needed a strong ally to counter the expanding power of the United States. Nevertheless, the Mexican Congress refused to grant religious freedom to British citizens residing in the country. It was understood that although Protestants might go about their business freely, they had to practice their religion in secret. Problems emerged, however, whenever a Protestant died: A non-Catholic could not be buried in holy ground. During the treaty debate, Senator Juan de Dios Cañedo observed that dead Protestants could not be left to rot in the streets because their corpses would constitute a health hazard. Therefore, he proposed a law permitting butchers to sell the meat of recently deceased Protestants to the public. When Congress dismissed this sardonic proposal out of hand, some in the public alleged it had been rejected because it was well known that Protestant meat was tough and salty, and not at all to the taste of Mexicans.[2]

Although many prominent individuals favored religious toleration, the Catholic church and conservatives doubted that Protestants could be integrated into Mexican society and feared that the Protestants' lax morals would corrupt the people and disrupt order. Some even believed that the criminal code would have to be strengthened to control their wrongdoing if Protestants were permitted to enter the country in large numbers. Not surprisingly, Catholic and conservative opposition to religious toleration was fierce. For example, when in 1831 Vicente Rocafuerte published a pamphlet entitled *Ensayo sobre tolerancia religiosa* (Essay on religious toleration), he was arrested for violating Article 3 of the Constitution, which stated that the Roman Catholic faith was the religion of Mexico to the exclusion of all others. His trial became a cause célèbre,

---

[2]Jaime E. Rodríguez O., *The Emergence of Spanish America: Vicente Rocafuerte and Spanish Americanism, 1808–1832* (Berkeley: University of California Press, 1975), 129–142.

particularly because Cañedo was his defense lawyer. During the trial, according to Carlos María de Bustamante, "Cañedo spoke horrible blasphemies [attacking the government and the clergy] and the spectators applauded." Despite Rocafuerte's acquittal, the issue of religious tolerance was not resolved until years later when the Constitution of 1857 introduced freedom of religion to Mexico.[3]

Many more Protestants entered Mexico during the second half of the nineteenth century, particularly during the long regime of Porfirio Díaz. Their numbers have increased substantially in this century. In recent decades, fundamentalist sects have established themselves in various areas of the nation. Many Protestants, Jews, and members of other religions now live in the country, but Mexico remains a Catholic land. Although it has been anticlerical since 1857, when the hierarchy of the Catholic Church opposed the new constitution, Mexico officially celebrates Catholic religious holidays. And every Mexican recognizes the Virgin of Guadalupe as the country's greatest symbol of nationalism. Tension between Catholics and Protestants, particularly fundamentalists, has erupted in recent years. In many ways, Catholic culture is perceived to be Mexican, whereas Protestantism appears to be not only alien but also North American. Religious conflict has been exacerbated when fundamentalist groups have refused to honor the nation's flag or the Virgin of Guadalupe.[4]

In England, anti-Catholicism was closely tied to hatred of the pope and of Spain. In the decades after Henry VIII broke with the Catholic Church, the English engaged in internal religious conflict as well as in international war with Catholic France and Spain. But as Spain became the dominant power in Europe and the defender of the Catholic faith, the English came to fear and hate all things Spanish.

The first great modern empire, Spain, threatened much of Europe: Italy, France, the Netherlands, the German principalities, and England all suffered from Spain's enormous power. The Protestant Reformation effectively used the newly available printing press to spread propaganda against the Spanish colossus. By depicting Spaniards as more ignorant, fanatical, cruel, sadistic, depraved, filthy, lazy, and evil than the people

[3]Ibid., 194–196, 203–209, quote p. 206; Jaime E. Rodríguez O., "The Conflict between the Church and the State in Early Republican Mexico," *New World* 2, nos. 1 and 2 (1987): 93–112; Dieter Berninger, "Immigration and Religious Toleration: A Mexican Dilemma, 1821–1860," *The Americas* 32, no. 4 (April 1976): 553–563.

[4]The situation in Chiapas is but one example of the issue. See George A. Collier with Elizabeth Lowery Quaratiello, *Basta! Land and the Zapatista Rebellion in Chiapas* (Oakland, CA: The Institute for Food and Development Policy, 1994), 55–66.

of any other nation or society, anti-Spanish propagandists created what has come to be known as the Black Legend of Spain.[5]

In England, the Black Legend mixed well with hatred and fear of the pope or "popery." As the Spanish Inquisition became a political as well as a religious instrument, "Spaniard" and "Catholic" became nearly synonymous. Good English Protestants despised Spaniards, who had expelled the Jews, brutally conquered the Indians in America, persecuted the Dutch Protestants, and attempted to invade England to impose the hated popish church.[6] As a final abomination, in the New World, Spaniards intermingled with the natives, creating a "mongrel" race.

"The settlers who came to America, reared in this atmosphere of intolerance, carried with them to the new land the same hatred of Popery which characterized the England of that day."[7] Despite the widely repeated myth that the English settlers came to the New World in search of religious freedom, in fact religious intolerance characterized their early settlements. Dissenting Protestants had to break away to form new settlements, where they imposed their own brand of repression. Only in Maryland did toleration of other Christians emerge from necessity. Lord Baltimore, the proprietor and a Catholic, had hoped to establish a Catholic haven there only to find his colony overwhelmed by Protestants. In 1649, to protect the few Catholics who did settle there, he passed the Act Concerning Religion, which required toleration of all Christians. Nevertheless, Maryland continued to be rent by religious conflict for the rest of the century, and in 1654 the legislature repealed Baltimore's act and introduced a law that forbade the Catholic religion.[8]

Anti-Catholic sentiment remained so pervasive in the English colonies that by 1700 only Rhode Island granted Catholics full civil and religious rights. And, as one scholar notes, it is doubtful that those statutes were upheld even there.[9] During the eighteenth century, Britain and its colonists were constantly at war with Catholic France and Spain, both in

[5]Philip Wayne Powell, *The Tree of Hate: Propaganda and Prejudices Affecting United States Relations with the Hispanic World* (New York: Basic Books, 1971).

[6]William S. Maltby, *The Black Legend in England: The Development of Anti-Spanish Sentiment, 1558–1660* (Durham, NC: Duke University Press, 1971). The English were, of course, the first to expel the Jews from their lands in the thirteenth century. They too conquered the Indians with great brutality; but, in contrast to the Spaniards, they proved unwilling to incorporate the natives into their new society in America.

[7]Ray Allen Billington, *The Protestant Crusade, 1800–1860: A Study of the Origins of American Nativism* (Chicago: Quadrangle Books, 1964), 4.

[8]Ibid., 4–6.

[9]Ibid., 7

Europe and in North America. In 1763, after the Seven Years' War, the victorious Anglo Americans still considered Catholic Quebec to be a threat, and they were ever vigilant to the dangers from the Spanish Floridas and Louisiana. Most colonies passed anti-Catholic legislation and insisted that only Protestants emigrate to their lands.

The Declaration of Independence of July 4, 1776, enumerated many grievances against King George III, among them passage of the Quebec Act, which granted religious tolerance to the Catholics of Quebec province. Ironically, the thirteen colonies were aided by Catholic France and Spain in their struggle for independence from Great Britain. As a result, for a time, Anglo-American Protestants became more sociable toward Catholics. But anti-Catholicism was too deeply rooted to expire so easily. Although in 1776 there were only thirty thousand Catholics in the newly declared nation's population of about four million, Protestants refused to grant them full rights. Virtually all of the new state constitutions denied civil rights to Catholics; many restricted office to those who "professed the Protestant Religion." One state, South Carolina, established Protestantism as its official religion. The federal Constitution of 1787, however, forbade religious tests for office holding. Subsequently, the first amendment to the Constitution guaranteed religious freedom.

The early years of the new nation witnessed continued anti-Catholic sentiment. In the 1820s renewed fears of popery afflicted the United States. Then, in 1834, a convent was burned in Boston, a community that was inflamed with fear of the increasing immigration of the Catholic Irish. Beleaguered Protestants formed organizations to defend "civilization" from the Catholic plague. Given these attitudes, both the Texas revolt in 1836 and the Mexican War in 1846–1848 can be easily explained in terms of anti-Catholicism and anti-Spanishness, now transferred to Mexico, along with the blatant desire for territorial expansion and expressions of racial superiority. In the 1850s an anti-immigrant, anti-Catholic movement known as the American, or Know-Nothing, party gained considerable strength throughout the United States. In 1856 it polled nearly 25 percent of the vote in the presidential election. By then, however, the antislavery movement was becoming the more prominent political theme.[10]

Although the Civil War changed the nature of politics in the United States, it did not end anti-Catholic and anti-immigrant sentiment. The vast waves of immigration at the end of the nineteenth and into the early twentieth century increased the size of the Catholic population as well as the paranoia of many Protestants. Despite the flood of immigrants, the United States remained culturally a Protestant nation dominated by the White Anglo-Saxon Protestant (WASP) ideal. Fears of popish control were

[10]Ibid., 10–43.

still openly expressed as late as 1960 when John F. Kennedy was forced to explain that if he were elected president, he would place the national interest before his Catholic faith. Although the country's largest single Christian denomination is now the Catholic Church, the United States, with all of its many religions, remains a Protestant culture that favors the individual, in contrast to Mexico's Catholic culture, which emphasizes the extended family.

Christian Brotherhood in the New World

As they gained independence, the United States and Mexico incorporated into their respective new nations the historic religious and cultural conflicts between England and Spain. The northern republic was an expanding, English-speaking, Protestant power with a rapidly growing population, which looked with profound suspicion and distaste upon the emerging Spanish-speaking, Catholic nations to its south. Some Anglo Americans, such as John Adams, could not overcome their distrust of what they considered to be the authoritarian and despotic heritage of Spanish Catholic culture and doubted that the new states would ever achieve representative government. In Adams's view, "The people of . . . [Spanish] America are the most ignorant, the most superstitious of all Roman Catholics. . . . [T]hat . . . a free government . . . should be introduced and established among such a people, over that vast continent, or any part of it . . . appeared to me . . . as absurd as similar plans would be to establish democracies among the birds, beasts, and fishes."[11] The religious and cultural prejudices of the United States, mixed with a strong dose of the Black Legend, easily blended into the racist bigotry that became prominent in the nineteenth century and that seemed to justify the American conquest of its southern neighbor.

The sharp lines drawn between the two countries by their religious histories and internal policies on religion were deepened by their dramatically different opinions about race, racial mixture, and slavery. Spain and England conquered and settled the lands that would become Mexico and the United States in very different ways. Whereas both monarchies had first gained ascendancy over neighboring territories in the Old World, the Spanish kings had incorporated into their burgeoning empire peoples who, although Caucasian, were perceived as belonging to different cultures—the Jews and the Muslims. Further expansion by Spain into North Africa and the Canary Islands brought other groups into the realm of the Spanish monarchy. Although the Spanish rulers ultimately imposed

---

[11]John Adams, *The Works of John Adams*, 10 vols. (Boston: Little, Brown and Co., 1850–1856), 10:145.

religious unity by force in 1492, they sought neither linguistic nor cultural uniformity. As the heirs to centuries of Muslim domination of the Iberian Peninsula, the Spanish kings conceived their universal monarchy as one composed of many lands, peoples, and cultures, not all of whom were of equal status. The Indians of America constituted one more group, albeit a special one.

The New World was organized into two legal systems: the Republic of the Indians and, for everyone else, the Republic of the Spaniards. The Indians were considered subjects of the Spanish Crown, although in a subordinate status, much as Christians and Jews had been under Muslim rule. Such distinctions were impossible to maintain, however. The worldwide Spanish monarchy was too vast and the lands it acquired were too populous for Europeans to be the largest group in the colonies. Over the years, miscegenation and economic development transformed the Viceroyalty of New Spain into a multiracial society in which Indians, legally protected but kept in a secondary status, entered the larger society as cultural and, often, as biological mestizos. Similar cultural and biological integration occurred with the Africans and Asians who were brought to colonial Mexico.[12] As a result of this history of racial and cultural mixture, Mexicans adopted *mestizaje*, or promotion of racial mixture, as their goal for integrating the nation. Still, despite Mexico's treasured policy of *mestizaje*, racial equality does not yet prevail in the country, as evidenced by the many human rights violations documented against the nation's indigenous people.

The English experience was significantly different. Although the conquest of Ireland and the subjugation of Wales and Scotland were extremely violent, they did not constitute the incorporation of fundamentally different cultures. Nevertheless, the English viewed the Catholic Irish as barbarous savages "only nominally Christian, and generally intractable."[13] They perceived North American Indians as equally wild, savage peoples who could not be incorporated into "civilized" society.[14] Thus, the Indians in the regions conquered and settled by the English Crown found themselves without a place. "The basic political aims of English colonization were the assertion of authority over indigenous land, proclaiming North America 'a vacant land,' whose occupants were not using fertile agricultural ground in useful and appropriate ways. While the Spanish

---

[12]Colin M. MacLachlan and Jaime E. Rodríguez O., *The Forging of the Cosmic Race: A Reinterpretation of Colonial Mexico*, 2d ed. (Berkeley: University of California Press, 1990).

[13]Edmund S. Morgan, *American Slavery and American Freedom: The Ordeal of Colonial Virginia* (New York: W. W. Norton, 1975), 20.

[14]Nicolas P. Canny, "The Ideology of English Colonization: From Ireland to America," *William and Mary Quarterly*, 3d. ser., 30 (1973): 575–598.

Crown officially declared all Indians its subjects and vassals in 1542, Indians collectively never became subjects of the English Crown (save in isolated instances), and did not become citizens of the United States until 1924."[15]

Anglo-American attitudes toward the Indians varied over time and place. As the tidewater regions became more settled and prosperous— "civilized," in other words—settlers came to regard the natives more benignly. "In the eighteenth century, attitudes toward the Indian were modified both because of the changing nature of American society and because of the impact of European ideas. . . . Some areas were now completely free from Indian attack or even contact, and some colonials began to appreciate the Indians from a distance. . . . This greater detachment of those on the eastern seaboard blended with the developing view of mankind emerging in the eighteenth century from the European Enlightenment."[16] The situation was quite to the contrary on the frontier, however, where whites, intent on dispossessing the natives of their lands, perceived them differently than their counterparts in the east. "Hatred of the Indians and an avid desire for their lands were common sentiments in the frontier regions. Arthur St. Clair, later to be governor of the Northwest Territory, . . . commented in 1774 from western Pennsylvania that 'it is the most astonishing thing in the world the disposition of the common people of this country; actuated by the most savage cruelty, they wantonly perpetrate crimes that are a disgrace to humanity.' "[17]

St. Clair's disgust for the greed and violence of his countrymen reflected the views of many U.S. and European intellectuals of the late eighteenth century. Such philosophies did not inform U.S. expansionist policies of the century to follow, however. Rather, the forced diversity of the American population provided a wealth of opportunity for interracial conflict and aggression. "Racial differences were dramatized in the United States, for white, black, and red were thrust together from the earliest settlements. While blacks, of course, were central to the general development of American thought on race, Indians were of particular importance in the development of American racial thought in the context of an expanding and aggressive nation. In dealing with the Indians the United States began to formulate a rationale of expansion which was readily adaptable to the needs of an advance over other peoples and to a world role."[18]

---

[15]Patricia Seed, " 'Are These Not Also Men?': The Indians' Humanity and Capacity for Spanish Civilization," *Journal of Latin American Studies* 25, no. 3 (October 1993): 651.

[16]Reginald Horsman, *Race and Manifest Destiny: The Origins of American Racial Anglo-Saxonism* (Cambridge: Harvard University Press, 1981), 104.

[17]Ibid., 110.

[18]Ibid., 100.

Americans who came into contact with Mexicans during the early nineteenth century handily transferred Black Legend concepts, such as the superstition, bigotry, and laziness of Spaniards, to their southern neighbors. While visiting Mexico City in 1822, Stephen F. Austin declared, for example, "they are bigoted and superstitious to an extreem [*sic*], and indolence appears to be the order of the day." The following year he observed, "To be candid the majority of the people of the whole nation as far as I have seen them want nothing but tails to be more brutes than apes."[19] To men such as Austin, the difference between Spaniards and Mexicans was that the latter were even more inferior because of their mixed breeding. As a writer to the *New Orleans Bee* noted in 1834, Mexicans were "degraded and vile; the unfortunate race of Spaniard, Indian and African, is so blended that the worst qualities of each predominate."[20]

Thus Americans, who justified black slavery on both biblical and racial grounds, had little difficulty in declaring whites superior to Indians and, later, to their darker-skinned Mexican neighbors. Whereas both greed and pride were high on the list of Protestant sins, the Americans of the expanding western frontier found it more comfortable to explain their occupation of others' lands by declaring the original inhabitants to be genetically unworthy of holding them. By the middle of the nineteenth century, when the Americans' desire for Mexican territory became an imperative, enlightened ideas that united humankind as one race were completely abandoned. Expansionism became an institutionalized U.S. policy supported by the presumption that the vastly superior Anglo-Saxons must prevail over all inferior races. Those who stood in the way of America's destiny were doomed to lose.

Racism as Foreign Policy

The infant nations, the United States and Mexico, each possessed a different notion of the nature of the society it wished to form. Both recognized whites—that is, Europeans—as preeminent. But at its birth Mexico consisted of a multiracial society integrated culturally and economically, to varying degrees, into a "hybrid mestizo [society] that was neither Indian nor Spanish."[21] The United States, on the other hand, from its

[19]Quoted in David J. Weber, " 'Scarce More than Apes': Historical Roots of Anglo-American Stereotypes of Mexicans in the Border Region," in *Myth and the History of the Hispanic Southwest* (Albuquerque: University of New Mexico Press, 1988), 157.

[20]Quoted in Arnoldo de León, *They Called Them Greasers: Anglo Attitudes toward Mexicans in Texas, 1821–1900* (Austin: University of Texas Press, 1983), 9.

[21]MacLachlan and Rodríguez, *The Forging of the Cosmic Race*, 3.

beginnings functioned as a nation dominated by people who excluded nonwhites from full participation in society, abhorred racial mixture, and glorified the mythical Anglo-Saxon race. As Senator Benjamin Leigh declared in 1836: "It is peculiar to the character of this Anglo-Saxon race of men to which we belong, that it has never been contented to live in the same country with any other distinct race, upon terms of equality; it has, invariably, when placed in that situation, proceeded to exterminate or enslave the other race in some form or other, or, failing in that, to abandon the country."[22]

Evaluating the role of race and culture in the history of the U.S.-Mexican relationship is not easy; as evidenced by many of the selections in this volume, scholars have no monopoly on truth but tend to approach history from their own national and/or cultural backgrounds. The debate among historians of the U.S.-Mexican relationship is hottest, however, when it comes to the role of black slavery in the determination of the Texas territory. While first Spanish and later Mexican law restricted black slavery, Mexican scholars propose conflicting reasons for this policy.

The law of the Spanish world was the most enlightened with respect to the rights of conquered peoples. Indians were recognized as integral members of colonial Mexican society in the sixteenth century and as citizens of the republic at independence. By the early nineteenth century, African slavery had been virtually exterminated in Mexico by the twin forces of miscegenation and political reform. Because independent Mexico did not rely on black slavery to provide workers for its farms and industries, it was easier for Mexicans to denounce the practice as a northern evil. But although most Mexicans abhorred slavery, some were driven to outlaw it by their dislike of having blacks, who were accompanying their Anglo owners into Mexican territory to settle Texas, as fellow countrymen. Current discussions of the international dispute over the colonization, the independence, and the U.S. acquisition of Texas frequently center on the slavery question. They conclude that expansion of the culture of slavery served as a primary motive for U.S. designs on the Texas territory, leading U.S. colonists in Mexico to repeatedly violate that nation's laws by transporting and selling slave laborers.

The emphasis on the slavery issue supports the view, which is especially prominent among Chicano even more than Mexican historians, that the United States is uniquely characterized by racism and oppression. Indeed, this theme dominated the conference from which this volume of papers was drawn as, one after another, racist episodes of recent vintage were exposed and examined. The true meaning of these events, however, can be difficult to understand. The tendency of some authors to general-

[22]Horsman, *Race and Manifest Destiny*, 8–77, quote p. 209.

ize can distort reality because Americans and Mexicans are thus depicted in rigid and simplistic terms. A nation's action is personalized and applied to every one of its citizens as if each were merely a cell in a single organism. The national stereotype erases distinctions and subtleties, both between and within the nations, about factors such as race, culture, religion, class, wealth, education, and region. Thus, depending on the writer's perspective, one is often presented with either the good or the evil Mexican or the good or the evil American, without respect for the formal and informal processes of debate and dissent that lead to foreign policy decision making in both countries.

Stereotypical thinking and vastly unequal power relations greatly complicate the interactions between Mexico and the United States. From the outset U.S. policy toward Mexico has been exploitative. The United States continues to treat Mexican leadership as tenuous, and it balances its relations with Mexico unfavorably against its other world interests. Thus, the attitude of the American public toward Mexico is generally dismissive, whereas Mexican public reaction toward the United States is usually defensive. If "life has never been easy for U.S. ambassadors in a country that has an Intervention Museum dedicated to teaching children about how the Americans have tampered with Mexico for nearly two centuries,"[23] life has been much harder for those attempting to represent Mexico's interests to a powerful neighbor whose ignorance is exceeded only by its arrogance. Indeed, many Americans are unable to grasp the simple concept that might does not always make right.[24]

Notions of American superiority often have been buttressed by the argument that Mexico is a poor backward nation whereas the United States is a rich advanced country. This is particularly true today, when the latter is the most powerful nation on earth. Although Mexico may be poorer than the United States, it is incorrect to say that it is an impoverished nation. On the contrary, relative to much of the world the region has been wealthy since pre-Spanish times. During the colonial period, the Viceroyalty of New Spain was the largest, most populous, richest, and

[23]Associated Press, *Miami Herald*, September 7, 1993. The Intervention Museum is not limited to depicting the actions of the United States; it also deals with other countries, such as France, that invaded Mexico. Of course, only the United States managed to take Mexican territory.

[24]This reality is plainly evident in the current Helms-Burton Law and in the suspension of President Ernesto Samper's visa to the United States. While the former constitutes a violation of both international law and the North American Free Trade Agreement, the latter is a breach of international protocol and an "unfriendly" action against the sovereignty of Colombia. In both instances the U.S. government, concerned only with internal political interests, threatens and intervenes in the affairs of other nations merely because it possesses the *power* to do so.

most developed part of the Spanish Empire in America. Although independent Mexico experienced a series of political, economic, and military
disasters during the nineteenth century that cost it half of its national
territory and severely reduced its potential, it nevertheless remained an
important nation. In 1990, Mexico ranked among the thirteen most indus-
trialized countries in the world. Although Mexico's per capita income of
U.S. $3,030 was about one-sixth that of the United States, it ranked first
in Latin America and was ten times higher than that of India. Thus, Mexico
is one of the wealthier and more developed nations in the world and so
enjoys a commonality with the United States that is often unrecognized.

Although both the United States and Mexico have suffered from internal conflicts over the question of race, they persist in their race-based
distrust of each other as nations. Moreover, the important distinctions
between race and culture often are blurred as both peoples tend to interpret cultural differences in racial terms. Intellectuals and writers in both
countries have frequently contributed to such misunderstandings.

Yet, in the midst of this contention, North America is changing. Neither boundaries, nor policies, nor attitudes possess the strength and rigid-
ity of the past. The economies of the United States and Mexico had become
integrated even before the North American Free Trade Agreement was
ratified. The movement of people and ideas between the two countries is
reciprocal, not one-sided as many believe. The sustained encounter of the
U.S. and Mexican cultures that takes place every day, not only in the
cities and towns of the region some call "MexAmerica" but also throughout both nations, constitutes an incredibly dynamic cultural exchange that
is never resolved. And *mestizaje* is the order of the day, not because ideologues propose or governments impose, but because millions of individuals, each in his or her own way, find biological as well as cultural and
economic intercourse to be necessary and good.

Is There a Future in Racism?

This volume reviews the representation of Mexicans and Americans
in literary, cultural, and social expression. Throughout the essays, two
stubborn and sometimes contradictory themes, racism and nationalism,
prevail. The contributions focus on particular expressions, political or
literary, of indigenous, Mexican, or U.S. culture and, especially, on refer-
ences to race, the enslavement of races, and racial mixtures.

The Universidad Nacional Autónoma de México's distinguished historian Miguel León-Portilla's delightful introductory essay on the ancient
and mythical history of the frontier known as California serves as a fitting beginning for a discussion of the shifting cultural concepts and con-

structions that have defined the United States and Mexico from the late 1700s to the present. His chapter is followed by the University of California's Ramón Eduardo Ruiz's dark exploration of the influence of race on national destiny and, most particularly, the impact of race on the construction of foreign policy by the United States. He argues that throughout its history the U.S.-Mexican relationship has been largely driven by and derived from American racial prejudice against Mexicans.

In the following chapter, El Colegio de México's Moisés González Navarro explores the related Mexican concept of *mestizaje*, the promotion of racial mixture, as a counterpoint to U.S. racism and as the cause of some U.S.-Mexican conflict. In his discussion of *mestizaje*, González Navarro introduces the theme of Mexican racist thought into the pool of perceptions that motivate not only the binational relationship but also Mexico's internal history. Together the Ruiz and González Navarro essays are an effective refresher course for those who may have forgotten just how ugly and unrelenting is the record of racial oppression in U.S. and Mexican history.

In "Mexican Cultural Identity in a U.S. City," El Colegio de la Frontera Norte's José Valenzuela Arce examines the ways in which some individuals in Mexican communities in the United States express their language and culture, and how they come together to organize for labor and community rights in an alien political and social structure. In contrast, the renowned Mexican man of letters Carlos Monsiváis, in a sharply worded essay, addresses the impact of U.S. popular culture on Mexicans in Mexico, concluding that Mexicans adapt U.S. cultural fashions in ways that suit their own social interests—that is, they "assimilate without being assimilated."

Finally, two University of California literary scholars examine the ways in which the United States and Mexico are depicted in the literature of the two nations. In her fast-paced chapter "Writing the Border," Norma Klahn reviews the nineteenth- and twentieth-century U.S. and Mexican fiction that explores the concept of the U.S.-Mexican border and the literary line between cultures and experiences that it represents. As one character after another crosses the border to enter the mysterious and forbidden world of the "Other," Klahn exposes the underlying stereotypes and occasional searches for understanding that motivate the works she critiques. In "Beyond Myths and Borders in Mexican and North American Literature," Luis Leal reviews the literature that reflects the religious and racial conflicts between Anglos and Hispanics in the Old and New Worlds, from the inflammatory essays of the colonial period to popular twentieth-century poetry and film. As the gentle and wise humanist he is, Leal suggests, in a fitting conclusion to this volume, that scholars of the U.S.-Mexican relationship would do well to study the literature that has historically influenced the development of political and cultural interactions between the two countries.

It is important to remember that the two nations have more in common than an uncertain future. Although the two peoples still differ substantially in their attitudes about religion, race, and racial mixture, they share a common Western European culture that originated in the classical world. Many observers today emphasize Mexico's Indian heritage, while noting the multiracial and multicultural nature of contemporary U.S. society. Those characterizations are true, but they overlook the fundamental cultural basis of both societies.

The independent evolution of ancient American Indian societies ended with the arrival of the Europeans. A new society was formed in colonial Mexico that incorporated aspects of both cultures as well as the influence of African and Asian immigrants. Similarly, the United States has incorporated, to a degree, the cultural traditions of its many immigrants. But the principal components of modern Mexican and U.S. society—language, law, and social organization—are derived from Europe via Spain and England. Neither is a replica of the mother country; on the contrary, both formed unique societies. Nevertheless, they share a culture based on Western civilization. In this respect it is misleading to assume that currently Mexico is being Americanized or the United States is being Mexicanized. Since the arrival of the Europeans, urban groups in both countries have sought to remain abreast of the latest developments in the world, responding to and embracing changes in cultural, social, political, economic, and artistic primacy. Unquestionably, the United States has become a leader in many areas, but it is not now nor has it ever been the sole dominant cultural force either for its own people or for those of Mexico. And because both societies are now fundamentally urban, they pursue the same general goals in their search for a better future. It is incumbent upon the two countries and their peoples to find in the commonality of their past and their present the strength and wisdom to jointly address the issues that will profoundly affect them for decades to come.

California: Land of Frontiers

Miguel León-Portilla

AMONG THE INNUMERABLE FRONTIERS with which human beings have divided their world are some conceived halfway between reality and myth, which is not to say that they are mere fantasies. Several, perhaps more than one would think, still exist today. One such frontier introduces us to the fabulous world that has been and continues to be California. Perhaps one should say "the Californias" because the first and oldest, which now some deprecatingly call "Baja," or "Lower," was part of and later violently broke away from the portion considered "Alta" or "Upper"—which shines dazzlingly today, proprietor of the magical name, without adjectives, California.

In the process of the encounter between the Old and New Worlds, amid uncontainable desires of expansionism, ancient myths often colored what was accepted as real. This perhaps not so fortuitous convergence inspired yearning for that of which the old tales spoke, mostly Mediterranean legends already mingled with Amerindian accounts about places and countries of fabulous wealth. Thus was born an imaginary geography that included Florida as the place of the fountain of eternal youth, the land of the Seven Cities, the country of El Dorado, supposed to be the richest in the world. Here, also between the mythical and the real, California appeared in the New World.

The fantasies and myths of the Old and New Worlds met and mingled in California as in perhaps no other place. The conqueror of Mexico, Hernán Cortés, wrote to Carlos V about the discoveries of two men he had dispatched to the west:

> I had, very powerful lord, some news, recently acquired, of another sea to the south, and knew from two or three parties that it was twelve and thirteen and fourteen days' journey from here. . . . And so wishing . . . dispatched four Spaniards, two to certain provinces and the other two to others, and informed of the route they had to take, gave them Indian friends to guide them.

Two Spaniards were delayed somewhat because they walked close to one hundred and fifty leagues in another direction before they arrived at the sea, where they took possession.[1]

This taking possession on the Mexican coast of the South Sea—that is, the Pacific Ocean—occurred in 1522. One year later, according to Cortés, Captain Gonzalo de Sandoval "brought news of a good port that he had found on that coast . . . and likewise brought an account of the men of the province of Cihuatan, where it is asserted there is an island populated totally by women, without any man, and that at certain times men go from the mainland and have access to them and if those who become pregnant bear women, they keep them, and if men, they throw them from their company. . . . They tell me also that this island is very rich with pearls and gold."[2]

Cihuatan means "place of women" in Nahuatl. According to indigenous beliefs, the women who died in childbirth, that is, with a prisoner in their womb, accompanied the sun on its journey across the sky, as did soldiers who perished in battle. The soldiers marched with the sun from dawn to its zenith. The women were its companions from the zenith to sunset, that is to say until it reached the west, where Cihuatan, the "place of women" and the big island very rich in pearls and gold, was located.[3] What Captain Gonzalo de Sandoval spoke of to Cortés greatly coincided with an ancient legend from the Old World that told of another great island, also populated by women and rich in coveted treasure. A celebrated book of chivalry, *Las sergas del virtuoso caballero Esplandián* (The saga of the virtuous knight Esplandián), by García Ordóñez de Montalvo, published at the beginning of the sixteenth century, which some of Cortés's men very likely had read or were reading at the time, related the same ancient myth of an island inhabited only by women. Here is the text from *Las sergas* that anticipates, by seemingly amazing coincidence, Cortés's account of the ancient indigenous beliefs:

> I would like you now to know something, the strangest thing that never in writing nor human memory has anyone been able to find: Learn that to the right-hand of the Indies there was an island called California . . . , which was populated by black women, without a man among them, and that their way of living was that of the Amazons, courageous and of ardent hearts. . . . The island itself was the strongest in the world, of rocks and fierce crags; the women's weapons were all of gold . . . for there was no other metal on all the island.

[1]Hernán Cortés, *Cartas y documentos* (Mexico: Editorial Porrúa, 1969), 191–192.

[2]Ibid., 232.

[3]For more about the beliefs of the ancient Mexicans, see Miguel León-Portilla, *Aztec Thought and Culture: A Study of the Ancient Nahuatl Mind* (Norman: University of Oklahoma Press, 1991), 55.

And sometimes when there was peace with their enemies, they mixed in complete safety, and had carnal relations with men, by which many of them became pregnant and, if they bore a female, they kept it, and if they bore a male, it later was killed.[4]

The myths of the Old and the New Worlds became intertwined. The island of women, beyond the coasts of the South Sea, or Pacific Ocean, of which Gonzalo de Sandoval had heard, and to which years later Hernán Cortés dispatched several expeditions, was given the name of that other isle to the right hand of the Indies. Thus, California made its appearance between legend and reality, receiving at once its magical and lasting destiny as a frontier, a destiny other myths from the Old and New Worlds would confirm.

Nearby, another "discovery" was about to be made and soon linked to the medieval legend of the Seven Cities, founded, so they say, beyond the ocean by Portuguese bishops who had escaped from the hands of the Muslim invaders. The visionary friar Marcos de Niza declared that he saw the Seven Cities during an expedition in 1539 to lands adjacent to California. He said that they were extremely rich in gold and many other marvels. And although the myth of those Seven Cities eventually died out, another endured: Chicomóztoc, the Place of Seven Caves, legendary starting point for the journey of the Aztecs, or Mexicas.

In Search of California

Like a veil torn asunder, the myths invited the search for reality. The insatiable Hernán Cortés, having completed his conquest of Mexico, sent three ships to the Moluccas in 1527; one of these reached its destination. But Cortés also wanted to reach that other island rich in pearls and peopled only by women. Cortés did not know if the place was part of Asia or not. Allowing for the possibility that the island was Cipango (Japan) or perhaps part of Cathay, he ordered Captain Diego Hurtado de Mendoza, upon entrusting an expedition to him in 1532, to be mindful of the other ships he encountered, to see whether they were better and more powerful than his. Also, Hurtado de Mendoza was to discern discreetly whether the dress of those aboard the other ships was adorned with objects of gold, pearls, or precious stones.[5] Thus, two ships led by Hurtado de Mendoza set sail

---

[4]García Ordóñez de Montalvo, *Las sergas del virtuoso caballero Esplandián, hijo de Amadís de Gaula* (Seville, 1510; reprint, Madrid: Biblioteca de Autores Españoles, 1857), 539.

[5]"Instrucción que dio Cortés en 1532 a Diego Hurtado de Mendoza . . . ," in *Colección de documentos inéditos para la historia de España,* ed. Martín Fernández de Navarrete et al. (Madrid: Imprenta de la Viuda de Calero, 1884), 4:167–175.

from Acapulco. That first expedition was lost, but the voyage triggered an ambition that would last for several centuries: to push beyond whatever frontier might hinder the penetration of California.

Cortés arranged a new voyage in 1533. One of the two ships reached the islands today called "Revillagigedo." The other, navigated by Fortún Jiménez, who had incited mutiny on board the flagship, landed in what today is known as Bahía de la Paz. The encounter between the mutineers and the Guaicura Indians of the region was violent. Only two mariners were able to escape in a small boat and return to Puerto de Chiametla in Jalisco. Finally it fell to Cortés himself, having set sail in charge of three ships in April 1535, to take possession on May 3 that same year of what he called the "Land of Santa Cruz." He then drew a very early map of California, which today is preserved in the Archivo de Indias in Seville. In it he sketched the end of a land opposite the coasts of Jalisco and Sinaloa with the correct outline of the Bahía de la Paz, nearby islands, and even the headland that is today called "Mogote." Farther north the map is empty, an uncertain frontier kept open to further penetration.[6]

That which would very soon be known as California, linked to the magic universe of myths, thus was born as a land of frontiers, of scarcely known outlines. From then on, for the fame of its pearls and other riches, California enticed penetrations in a vast part of the New World that was supposed to continue to the northwest until perhaps it joined Asia, or was separated by a strait or passage that linked the Pacific with the Atlantic. In fact, as a land of vague boundaries, California remained an enigma open to worldwide cartographic fantasy until the last quarter of the eighteenth century.

The Uncertain Contours of an Island That Was a Peninsula and Was Thought Once More to Be an Island

The drive to know more about the "island," which by 1540 or before had received the name of California, was at the origin of three more explorations. One was that of Francisco de Ulloa, sent by Cortés, who arrived at the mouth of the Colorado River in 1539 and later went past the island of Cedros in the Pacific. Another, by land and sea, was dispatched one year later by Viceroy Mendoza. Francisco Vázquez de Coronado

---

[6]A reproduction of this and other maps cited on forthcoming pages may be consulted in Miguel León-Portilla, *Cartografía y crónicas de la Antigua California* (Mexico: Universidad Nacional Autónoma de México [hereafter UNAM], 1989).

reached the region of the Seven Cities and advanced beyond New Mexico all the way to Kansas. Captain Hernando de Alarcón repeated Ulloa's voyage and reached the confluence of the Colorado with the Gila. A new map was drawn in which California appeared as a long peninsula beyond which nothing else was known. Viceroy Mendoza, determined to unveil the mystery, ordered Juan Rodríguez Cabrillo to set sail two years later, in 1542. Though he lost his life in the enterprise, thanks to his voyage the outline of California could be drawn to almost the 42d parallel. Famous cartography masters Battista Agnese, Alonso de Santa Cruz, Sebastián Caboto, Giacomo Gastaldi, Pedro Medina, and the great Abraham Ortelius and Gerard Mercator no longer represented the immense country of California as an island but as a great peninsula that continued indefinitely toward the northwest. But while its coastline was known, the interior had been practically ignored, and so California continued to be a frontier, its riches and peoples only a rumor.

By 1565 the galleons that set sail from Manila for Acapulco one after another navigated the length of the California coasts after crossing the Pacific. Through the mists, those on board occasionally saw great forest-covered mountains as well as signs of human presence in the form of clouds of smoke. But California remained an impenetrable frontier. At the beginning of the seventeenth century, a great navigator, Sebastián Vizcaíno, embarked upon an exploratory voyage from Cabo San Lucas past Cape Mendocino. The celebrated cosmographer Enrico Martínez later prepared thirty-six charts. More was being learned about California's contours but nothing about its vast territory.

One of Vizcaíno's fellow travelers, the Carmelite friar Antonio de la Ascensión, greatly undid the results of that voyage. The Carmelite reinstated California's imaginary geography: Through his writings he spread the idea that California was not a peninsula but an enormous island separate from the continent. He also stated that beyond the extreme northern part of the island lay the entrance to the great strait of Anian where the Pacific and Atlantic Oceans merged. Hundreds of maps with California depicted as a big island then were produced by famous cartographers such as Nicholas Sanson d'Abbeville, Jan Jansson, Cornelius Wifliet, and many others. The chimera would last well beyond the beginning of the eighteenth century.

California, "Rim of Christendom"

After much effort by navigators, adventurers, and pearl seekers, the California interior was penetrated at last. The Jesuits, among them the famous Eusebio Francisco Kino and Juan María de Salvatierra, were the ones who, at the end of the seventeenth century, transformed California into what Herbert Bolton called the "rim of Christendom."[7] By the time the Jesuits left California seventy years later, expelled from all territorial possessions of the Spanish king, the rim of Christendom in California had reached Mission Santa María de Los Angeles, close to the 30th parallel. Eusebio Francisco Kino had made more than ten exploratory expeditions to clarify whether California was indeed an island or a peninsula. His maps, admirable examples of modern cartography, gave evidence of the land's peninsular character. Nevertheless, his work was not universally accepted for some time.

A double legacy of grandeur and tragedy was left by the Jesuits: The great and beautiful churches of San Xavier, Loreto, San Ignacio, and Santa Gertrudis give testimony to their labors. The simultaneous dramatic decline of the native Indian population demonstrates what can happen in the encounter between peoples of radically different cultures. Diseases formerly unknown to the Indians, as well as the introduction of what seemed to them to be an extremely strange life-style, destroyed their precarious equilibrium with the environment upon which they had subsisted throughout the millennia. This was the tragic outcome of the desire to push forward, as a frontier, the geographical boundaries of Christianity.

However, the thrust to extend California's frontier was by no means interrupted. Fray Junípero Serra led a group of Franciscans on a new missionary exploration, and, thanks to him, the Christian frontier kept advancing. In less than ten years it moved from San Diego, where a mission was founded in 1769, to the port of San Francisco. The first border then was created in the California interior: The Franciscans were in charge of the northern missions while the Dominicans replaced the Jesuits in the peninsula. Near a place today known as El Descanso, Francisco Palou marked a big boundary stone between those two jurisdictions which from then on became known as the Antigua or Baja California and the Nueva or Alta California. That line—the first internal frontier of California or the Californias—was changed eighty years later. After the Mexican War, to make communication by land possible throughout Mexico, the line was shifted about sixty kilometers to the north. From then on the northern portion became known as Upper California and soon just California, and the southern—first to bear the name—Baja California, or as many Anglos, followed by some Mexicans, would put it, simply and derogatorily "Baja."

---

[7]This is the title of the classic work by Herbert Bolton, *Rim of Christendom: A Biography of Eusebio Francisco Kino, Pacific Coast Pioneer* (New York: Macmillan Co., 1936).

The Presence of the Russians

When the interior of Alta and Baja California finally was beginning to be explored, and missions, ports, and presidios were established, new events shook the Californias. The Spanish ambassador to the Court of Saint Petersburg informed Madrid of unexpected incursions by Russians originating from Siberia. The Jesuit historian Marcos Burriel wrote that "the vast empire of the Russians, or Muscovites, extends all the way to the farthest reaches of Asia . . . and crosses the Southern Sea [that is, the Pacific], until it ends in various places in our America. On one of their voyages, made in 1741, the Russians stepped ashore at 55° and 36' latitude of this coast, that is, in a site that is only a little more than twelve degrees from Cabo Blanco, the last known site in our California. Why, on other trips, would the Russians not be able to go farther south to Cabo Blanco and even Cabo San Lucas?"[8] And with the same irony, provoked by alarm, Burriel also asked if it would suit Our Lord to have Mexico's neighbors be Muscovites, who would catechize the Indians according to Greek Orthodox tradition. Yes, at that time California had a frontier with the Russian Empire!

The concept of frontier—which in the case of California retained the sense of imprecise boundaries between lands and coasts, some partly known and others not at all—began to acquire geopolitical connotations. With the Russian presence in the north and the growing threat of incursions by other powers, it made sense to think that there would be impediments to Hispano-Mexican expansion in what was considered the California region. In fact, the Russian establishments, including some forts, indicated that the neighboring northern territories already were under the dominion of another power.

The Appearance of International Borders

New voyages of exploration along the New World's northwest coast were being conducted, and not only from Mexican ports. They had two principal goals: to clarify remaining geographical enigmas and to establish firmly the interested power's territorial claims. Starting in 1774, exploratory trips in which Spaniards and Mexicans participated side by side were organized from the port of San Blas in Nayarit. Not much later, the English captain James Cook, leaving from the Hawaiian Islands, reached the American coast near latitude 44° 30' in 1778. Next, navigating the

---

[8]This text from Father Burriel is included in Miguel Venegas, *Noticia de la California* (Mexico: Reimpreso por L. Alvarez y Alvarez de la Cadena, 1943), 3:19.

shores in search of the supposed strait that would take him to the Atlantic, he continued north toward Alaska, finally entering the strait that Captain Vitus Behring, in service of Russia, had discovered in 1728. Cook's expedition, which certainly benefited from information supplied by previous Hispano-Mexican explorations, served to fortify England's geopolitical ambitions.

The Pacific Ocean, crossed so many times by galleons from Manila and by other sailors, among them the well-known Francisco de la Bodega y Cuadra, Esteban José Martínez, and Alejandro Malespina, became increasingly subject to the explorations of the Russians and the English as well as the French and also the citizens of a young republic that had adopted the name the United States of America. The Russians had advanced south from Alaska to establish Fort Ross not many miles north of San Francisco. New Spain, the kingdom that would soon become Mexico, was about to establish international borders in California with the empire of the czars. At the same time, in 1786, the Frenchman Jean-François de Galoup la Pérouse explored the California coasts before becoming lost forever in the South Sea islands. But before his shipwreck, he had sent to France testimony, the fruit of his geographic explorations, that kept alive that power's interest in increasing its explorations of the Pacific. Finally, completely unexpected by the Spaniards, Russians, English, and Mexicans, two U.S. ships from Boston rounded the continent at its southern tip and in 1787 entered Port Nootka in Vancouver Island as the most natural thing in the world.

Several violent incidents then occurred, such as the 1789 conflict in Nootka between the English captain James Colnett and the Spanish commander Esteban José Martínez, who had set sail from the port of San Blas in Nayarit. Martínez took the Englishman prisoner and captured his ships, nearly provoking a war between Spain and England.[9] England, which had lost her American colonies along the Atlantic, then focused her attention upon the territories vaguely known as California. The English began to believe that the voyage of the privateer Francis Drake two centuries earlier and his landing near San Francisco, in what he called "New Albion," gave them title to these lands.

As we have seen, ever since 1769 the Californias had a border between the upper portion, under the Franciscan missionaries, and the lower, administered by the Dominicans. At the same time, the Russian establishments continued expanding south beyond the 54th parallel. For their part, the English carried on with explorations under the command of Captain

---

[9]For more about the so-called Nootka incident, see Hubert H. Bancroft, *History of the Northwest Coast*, 2 vols. (San Francisco: A. L. Bancroft and Co., 1884), 1:204–238.

George Vancouver. In addition, they had obtained from Spain the tacit understanding that the territories to the south of the Russian settlements and to the north of the Spanish missions were fair game for exploration and expansion. Thus, over time, the British Dominion of Canada, originally an Atlantic enterprise, came to have coasts on the Pacific. By the early nineteenth century, the United States, for its part, got England to accept a rather imprecise agreement to give it an exit to the ocean through the Oregon Territory. All this was crystalized shortly in various international treaties that affected forever the frontier destiny of the Californias.[10]

California's role as land of frontiers continued. On the eve of the independence of Mexico, at the beginning of 1819, the United States, which had fixed its northern boundary with the Dominion of Canada, made another treaty with Spain. Known by various names, such as the Transcontinental Treaty, or the Adams-Onís Treaty, it recognized the United States' claim to all territories in what could still be considered as Alta California north of the 42d parallel. Thus, the big country of the Californias obtained its first official international border in its extreme north, a border no longer nebulous as it had been with the Russians and the English but well demarcated by virtue of the treaty. The same treaty was ratified in 1832 with newly independent Mexico.

Ironically, when Texas declared itself independent only four years later, the United States tried to alter the treaty, intending to annex Texas and later on the Californias. The issue was decided in 1847 simply according to who was strongest. The U.S. agenda for expansion to the south and southwest, by virtue of Manifest Destiny, was focused principally on the Californias. James Polk, the winning candidate in the 1844 presidential election, had proclaimed his priorities as the complete occupation of the Oregon Territory, up to the borders of Russian settlements, as well as the definitive annexation of Texas and the march toward the Pacific.

Triggered by such ambitions, the war between the United States and Mexico was simply one of conquest, and to Mexico it meant the loss of more than half its territory. During negotiations, U.S. representatives insisted on the transfer of New Mexico and Alta and Baja California. Had Mexico accepted these conditions, the Californias would have become entirely U.S. territory. In other words, their ancient destiny as a frontier would have been over. Born between myth and reality, that destiny would have completely disappeared if the country that in less than one hundred years would become the most powerful on the planet had gained Alta and Baja California. This did not happen. The determining factor was the bold defense carried out by the three Mexican commissioners, Bernardo Couto,

---

[10]For more about this era of New Spain's changing northern frontiers, see León-Portilla, *Cartografía y crónicas*, 171–182.

Miguel Atristain, and Luis Gonzaga Cuevas, who succeeded in retaining the California peninsula for Mexico. Hence, a new and now international boundary separated the Californias. The New, or Alta, California became U.S. territory; the Old, or Baja, California remained Mexican.

The Californias: The Great Challenge of Their Frontier Destiny

For hundreds of years, or at least ever since its magic birth in the indigenous myth of an island peopled by women, and the fabulous tale of that other island to the right hand of the Indies, California (or better, the Californias) kept its frontier destiny. The Mexican cities along the international line, Tijuana, Tecate, Mexicali, and Algodones, form the advance guard along the frontier that boasts, perhaps, the greatest contrasts in the world today.

Unlike the international border between Canada and the United States, or between the countries of Western Europe where communication and border crossings are almost unrestricted, the international boundary between the United States and Mexico constitutes a line that can be crossed legally only by those who show immigration and customs authorities their passports, "*micas*," or other permits. Of course, such restrictions do not apply to people crossing the border from the United States but only to those from Mexico going north. This indicates one very great contrast.

At the dividing line of the Californias, as along the rest of the U.S.-Mexican border, are boundaries that separate not only two countries but also two huge international communities: the Anglo-American and the Ibero-American. Although Mexico and other Ibero-American countries today have completed a new kind of northern expansion by way of the millions of Hispanics who have settled in, above all, the southwest of the United States, particularly in California, it still is true that this border, besides being international, lies between two very different ways of life. On the one side, from San Diego to Alaska, the English language predominates and, only a short time ago, in fact, was declared the official language of Alta California. On the other side, Spanish is spoken from Tijuana to Tierra del Fuego, with Portuguese, a sister language of Spanish, the main language of Brazil. Indigenous languages endure on both sides to varying degrees, although many more people speak them in Ibero-America. While Indian languages have survived in the United States, they are confined to the Indian reservations. In the case of Ibero-America, the national governments have done little or nothing to cultivate and preserve them. In Mexican California not even five hundred people now speak a language native to the region. A striking new experience is that of the many thousands of Mixtec immigrants who, in the last decade, have settled in both Upper and Lower California, thus giving origin to what one could ironically call Mixtec Californias! As we shall see, the theme of linguistic frontiers implies more than one may think.

To note other contrasts: In the United States a technologically advanced civilization keeps developing—with seemingly uncontainable thrust—in which time is money; and efficiency, together with consumerism and comfort, is put ahead of everything. These changes were triggered in Alta California with amazing rapidity when the frenetic search for that Dorado—gold fever—would, for Anglo Americans, disintegrate the frontier. The need to augment the Mexican presence in Baja California was eagerly recommended by Lázaro Cárdenas "to protect it from the expansion coming from the north."[11] The region now supports a new culture, the fruit of the encounter between the descendants of those who created the great Indian civilizations and those who introduced the Spanish life-style with its Mediterranean, Latin, and Christian-Catholic legacy. The human settlements of the two Californias, united for so long, today are very different—radically different, one can say—and not only in planning or architectural features. On one side, opulence is conspicuous; on the other, scarcity of resources, economic crisis, and even, at times, misery. To cross this border is to move between two worlds with sometimes opposing cultures—from the manner of eating and even mealtimes, to the expression of values, beliefs, and hopes.

At the same time that there are great differences, the other reality exists of contiguousness, nearness, and the immediate vicinity, impossible to suppress. It means that what happens on one side sooner or later will influence the other. This is true with natural resources, water, air pollution, and even drainage systems, trade, industry, communication, migration, and social and political structures. To coexist along more than three thousand kilometers with so many differences and yet with the inescapable nearness and its multiple manifestations of interaction presents enormous challenges. At times, antagonism, rejection, hate, and scorn appear.

Recently, the former president of Costa Rica and winner of the Nobel Peace Prize, Oscar Arias Sánchez, wrote an article entitled "El muro de California" (The California wall). After referring to the many problems posed by the enormous differences between the countries of the First and Third Worlds, he focuses upon what has happened in many parts of the world where undocumented immigrants cross or try to cross the borders of rich countries in search of jobs and better living conditions. An example, which in Oscar Arias's opinion may become dramatic, is the case of the California border between the United States and Mexico: "How can one not compare the three-meter-high metal wall being constructed

[11]Lázaro Cárdenas, *Obras* (Mexico: UNAM, 1980), 1:442.

in Southern California with the fateful Berlin Wall? The only human construction on Earth discernable from the moon is the Great Wall of China. In a few years will perhaps this California Wall prove to be the second man-made object that can be seen from space?"[12]

If one wanted to encompass the great challenge by another question, one would have to take note of the future and ask about the possibility of a happier destiny of cohabitation, thanks to better-conceived border relations. The presence of different cultures may be the cause of not only conflicts but also positive exchanges. In this context one may consider the two countries' participation in the Cultural Commission of the Californias.

California, today the Californias, still possesses a frontier destiny. To affirm this statement is to recognize that although challenges persist, there is a renewed and vital force. The challenge of the frontier has been apparent ever since California stopped being a myth and became reality. Today, more than ever, it is interesting to delve into the multiple meanings, not in theory but in reality, of a frontier in geography, economics, and culture. In the case of the U.S.-Mexican border, history is now in some ways being repeated. Less than 150 years ago, many "undocumented" Anglos entered into what was then Mexican territory. They did it sometimes as traders and others merely in search of fortune. Some of them also tried to do things that today's undocumented Mexicans have not even imagined. Among their Anglo "illegal" precursors there were some who had in mind to separate these territories from Mexico, the country of which they were a part. In fact, some of them proclaimed the so-called California Republic, whose flag with a star and a bear stands today close to that of the United States of America, precisely representing one of them.

Will we say that the present-day undocumented Mexicans, who are just "paying a visit," are more dangerous and evil to the United States than their Anglo "colleagues" were to Mexico? The frontier has been and is, among other things, an enticement to expansion. It is also a limitation, a barrier, a wall, and even a ditch that impedes movement. Will there always be a wall in California? Cannot the day perhaps arrive when the door is opened to fair, enriching, and fertile exchanges between Californians of both sides, between Mexicans and Americans—say, with wishful thinking, between all the humans in a continent and a planet originally free of such walls and borders?

[12]Oscar Arias Sánchez, "El muro de California," *Excélsior*, Mexico City, June 2, 1992.

Race and National Destiny

Ramón Eduardo Ruiz

"WE MAKE OUR FRIENDS; WE MAKE OUR ENEMIES," but, to quote a bit of poetic wisdom, "God makes our next-door neighbor." That, perhaps, best sums up how Mexico and the United States, two disparate and unequal nations, came to live next door to each other along a common border two thousand miles long that stretches from San Diego on the Pacific Ocean to Brownsville in southeast Texas. The asymmetrical ties that bind them together embody a complex but at the same time logical relationship, one that reflects the distinctive ethos and history of the two peoples. More unalike and mismatched neighbors cannot be found on the face of the globe. North of the Rio Grande lies a wealthy, industrial, and powerful behemoth, whereas Mexico, which faces it on the other side of the border, is an impoverished Third World country. Although more than a fourth of its population is made up of "people of color," the United States is predominantly a "white man's world," unlike Mexico, peopled by a mestizo folk overwhelmingly of darkish hue. It follows that, from the beginning, differences of race have helped shape the course of affairs between the two nations.

To complicate the picture, in the annals of the United States—to employ a homespun aphorism—racial prejudice is as American as apple pie. Since "the dawn of our history," concedes one North American writer, we have taken "it for granted that members of the Caucasian race" are somehow "miraculously endowed by God or by nature with qualities of mind and of morals" that make them markedly superior "to men of darker skins."[1] Few people familiar with the way of life north of the Rio Grande will dispute that assessment. "Ideas of race superiority," to cite an Afro-American assumption, are a "clear and perceptible thread that runs through the warp and woof of the American fabric," a belief "ingrained . . . with a

---

[1]Edward McNall Burns, *The American Idea of Mission* (New Brunswick, NJ: Rutgers University Press, 1957), 199.

tenacity almost unmatched by that of any other doctrine."[2] At every juncture in American history men of influence and renown have been found in large numbers in the ranks of those who uphold the banner of ethnological bigotry, including, lamentably, some of the most presumably liberal and humane thinkers.[3] True also is the melancholic fact that, outside of South Africa, no country on this earth has endured more racial strife.[4]

Incredibly, the study of diplomatic history, which supposedly examines how people deal with their foreign neighbors, has virtually ignored this dark underbelly of American life. Only a minuscule band of unorthodox scholars acknowledges that the study of U.S. diplomacy, especially for countries of the Third World, cannot be divorced from American race prejudice. Yet, until now, the "history of American imperialism," which victimizes the people of the Third World, has been the prerogative of "diplomatic" scholars, whereas students of politics and society reserve the "race problem" for themselves. Lost in this dichotomy is the linkage between the character of race relations at home and foreign policy abroad.[5]

Not surprisingly, racial prejudice, primarily the superior value ascribed by North Americans to the lightness of one's skin, has influenced their behavior toward others. Indeed, Americans have employed a bifurcated "racial and ethnic foreign policy," one operating "positively toward countries most similar" to them, the "predominantly white," and another, mostly negative in character, "for countries whose inhabitants are predominantly non-white."[6] That, obviously, includes Mexicans, most of whom are, by Yankee standards, "swarthy." To a majority of North Americans, in the pattern of most Western Europeans, success, both the personal and national kinds, has a racial component. That attitude, which often dictates behavior, is one key to the ties between Mexico and its northern neighbor, where whites monopolize the lion's share of financial spoils and control politics.

Racism as History

What we refer to as race prejudice, the cultural malice that not infrequently colors Yankee behavior toward Mexicans, has old roots. In 1855, when Count Joseph Arthur de Gobineau, the most celebrated of the racial bigots in Western thought, completed his *Essay on the Inequality of the*

[2]Rubin F. Weston, *Racism in U.S. Imperialism* (Columbia: University of South Carolina Press, 1972), 36.

[3]Burns, *American Idea of Mission*, 187.

[4]George W. Shepherd, ed., *Racial Influences on American Foreign Policy* (New York: Basic Books, 1970), 97.

[5]Weston, *Racism in U.S. Imperialism*, x.

[6]Shepherd, *Racial Influences*, 80.

Human Races, a work purporting to demonstrate that all significant mile-stones in civilization were the offsprings of what he referred to as Aryan divisions of the Caucasian race, he was summarizing rather than intro-ducing a revolutionary concept. In this polemic, an ideological mishmash, Gobineau included all of the cherished heroes and myths of Western progress: Among his Aryans there were found the customary Greeks and Romans, but also Hindus, ancient Persians, and, of course, the inhabit-ants of western Europe.[7] Americans read and applauded Gobineau's dis-torted pastiche because it embodied so much of what they believed.

The English, the founders of the Thirteen Colonies, had, certainly centuries before Gobineau, planted the seeds of the Anglo-Saxon ideol-ogy of superiority from whence American racism largely comes. Without "understanding why European nations had come to think of themselves in racial as well as political terms," no one, therefore, can explain, to call upon one interpretation, how the United States came to view "its interna-tional role racially." When the Europeans, the English and Spaniards among them, began their conquests of what today is the Third World, they carried with them an assumption of innate superiority over all other peoples, attributed in part to divine endowment. Ultimately, some of their descendants would secularize this conviction, claiming it sprang from nature and not from God. Bear in mind, too, that the conquerors were mostly Christian by faith and Caucasian by genetics. The racism that emerged, henceforth a paramount chord in conquest, sprang step by step out of this "feudal religiosity," as one authority characterized it. The Cru-sades, the Christian onslaught on the Muslim world, is a splendid ex-ample of its consequences. For the crusaders, their enemies were also the foes of God, beyond the pale of "moral" laws. The killing of Muslims was not merely condoned but encouraged, and no act on behalf of the true faith was censurable or dishonorable. In "the gradual transition from reli-gious conceptions to racial conceptions, the gulf between persons calling themselves Christians and the other persons, whom they called heathen, translated smoothly into a chasm between whites" and the dark of skin.[8]

Because of these antecedents, it is not surprising that the history of the United States reveals a startling propensity to embrace a belief in a unique racial destiny that, conversely, helps to explain its interpretation of world power. From the time of the Puritans of the early seventeenth century, the concept of a "chosen people" had permeated American thought; in the "success" of their ancestors, American thinkers believed that they had found empirical evidence for their belief that God's

[7]Burns, *American Idea of Mission*, 200.
[8]Francis Jennings, *The Invasion of America: Indians, Colonialism, and the Cant of Conquest* (Chapel Hill: University of North Carolina Press, 1975), 5.

benevolence was focused on themselves. There is reason to believe, furthermore, that even if no English ideological foundation had existed, Americans would have had to invent a racialist one of their own.

In explaining racial bigotry north of the Rio Grande, other factors, too, must be kept in mind. Contrary to popular opinion, the European conquerors of what is now the United States, like the Spaniards who overran the empires of ancient Mexico, did not discover a wilderness bereft of people. The claim to have populated virgin lands is patently false. The colonization of the United States was, in actuality, a "resettlement, a reoccupation of land made waste" by foreign invaders.[9] Still, up to a few years ago, it was common for Americans to claim that no more than one million aborigines lived north of the Rio Grande.[10] That estimate has been discarded; demographers now calculate that up to fifty million Indians, as the Europeans baptized them, inhabited the "empty" lands between the Pacific and Atlantic Oceans lying north of the Rio Grande. The best guess is about twenty-five million. The earlier estimates simply failed to take into account the horrendous decline in the indigenous population, due particularly to diseases such as small pox, measles, and tuberculosis, that had also decimated the Central Valley of Mexico.[11] Disease alone, however, did not kill off the Indians. European cupidity for land, forests, and water, the native resources, played a major role too. The settlers of North America, like their Spanish counterparts in Mexico, behaved as rapacious conquerors, not merely upon landing on the shores of the Atlantic but, just as true, as they pushed inland, where they found their ambitions blocked by natives who fought to the death to defend their habitats. Thus the ravages of disease simply compounded the ills derived from the European drive to despoil natives of their goods. Only natives essential to European survival were likely to fare better, but not for long.

Killing off natives and robbing them of their property were moral crimes that, says one writer, their "perpetrators could justify only on the ground that the Indians were an inferior people and that the progress of civilization required them to give way to the more richly endowed Caucasians."[12] Thus was born the Indian "problem," as Europeans labeled it. In reality, it had begun with the birth of the colonies, with the charters bequeathed John Cabot and Sir Walter Raleigh, which told them to "respect only lands held by" Christians, ignoring rights of Indians. The Indian thus became the victim of injustices that, to repeat, ran the gauntlet

[9]Ibid., 30.
[10]Ann F. Ramenofsky, *Vectors of Death: The Archaeology of European Contact* (Albuquerque: University of New Mexico Press, 1987), 1.
[11]Ibid., 175.
[12]Burns, *American Idea of Mission*, 189.

from the loss of lands and liberty to death.[13] To justify these crimes against humanity, the sinners invented the image of the Indian as a barbarian or heathen who was, by the logic of the myth, morally and culturally inferior to "civilized" Europeans. The Indian, legend has it, was pushed out to make room for progress, a progress equated with white settlement. Ridding the land of the pernicious Indian was the white man's problem for nearly three centuries. The solution, as it was referred to, "resulted," in the words of one chronicler of the past, "in the development of a race consciousness which made all Europeans forget their differences and unite against a common enemy, the Indian."[14]

The Indian, however, was merely one factor of the racial equation. In 1619, one must not forget, the English colonizers began to import slaves from Africa into the Virginia colony. The English, of course, were not the first to traffic in African slaves in the New World. That dishonor belongs to the Spaniards who, by 1502, had started to employ Africans to plant and harvest sugarcane in their Caribbean colonies. For western Europeans, the legacy of sugar dated from their contact with the Arabs during the Crusades. As early as the seventh century, the Arabs had been cultivating cane in the Levant, from where Normans and Venetians transported the industry to the Mediterranean islands of Crete, Cypress, and Sicily. There black slavery got a toehold. By the fifteenth century, sugarcane and the institution of black slavery had made their bow on the Iberian Peninsula. The nefarious slave trade lasted until the 1860s. From the sixteenth to the seventeenth centuries, an age of shame for humanity, approximately ten million blacks were forcibly transported across the Atlantic by white slavers, among them English colonists and their descendants, the Americans.[15] In the Thirteen Colonies, however, the English did not plant sugarcane; blacks were imported to pick cotton and, to a lesser extent, tobacco. By 1860, on the eve of their so-called emancipation, some four hundred thousand blacks had been forcibly brought to what had become the United States. That slave force reproduced itself many times; at the start of the Civil War, the American republic had over four million blacks, some half a million of them "free" Negroes.[16]

The institution of slavery, which flourished with the invention of the cotton gin, strengthened American racism, not only in the southern states, where the cotton plantation took deep roots, but also in the North. Again, as in the case of the "Red Man," the injustices committed against blacks

---

[13]Weston, *Racism in U.S. Imperialism*, 22.

[14]Ibid., 6.

[15]Robert W. Fogel, *Without Consent or Contract: The Rise and Fall of American Slavery* (New York: W. W. Norton, 1989), 18, 20, 28.

[16]Eugene D. Genovese, *Roll, Jordan, Roll* (New York: Pantheon Books, 1974), 5, 400.

required some kind of moral justification, which according to the whites, was found in the blacks' racial inferiority, attested to by their color and other physical "deformities." The Constitution, embraced by Americans of both North and South, provides a classic example of this opinion. The national charter conferred legal sanction on slavery and, additionally, in the three-fifths argument, stigmatized the Negro as less than a person. Whites were also given the right to import Negro slaves for another twenty years.[17] Later, in the Dred Scott decision, Chief Justice Roger B. Taney of the U.S. Supreme Court ruled that at the time of the adoption of the Constitution its framers had, in labeling blacks inferior beings, conceded them no rights "which the white man was bound to respect."[18] Yet, at the same time, the white male was a hypocrite; although he denied equality to blacks, he did not hesitate, when the opportunity presented itself, to go to bed with black females. Today, reputedly, three out of four "blacks" in the United States have some white ancestry, a vestige left over perhaps from the facile access of whites to slave women during the heyday of the plantation system.[19]

Fate and Destiny

Given these colonial foundations and attitudes that survived the birth of American independence in 1783, it is no wonder that none of the patriot fathers rose much above the common prejudices. George Washington, the father of his country and a slave owner, along with his principal advisors, attempted until the final hour of triumph to keep the battle against Mother England a "white man's war on both sides." Thomas Jefferson's *Notes on the State of Virginia*, written between 1781 and 1785, picture blacks as a race with "a strong and disagreeable odor," much inferior to whites in intelligence, although that did not keep him from having a black mistress. In his experience, he declared, he had never found one black able to utter a thought "above the level of plain narration."[20] Nor did Jefferson confine his unkind opinions to blacks; he held similar views on the inhabitants of lands south of the Rio Grande. He believed it unwise to conquer these regions, not only because they lay far away but also because of the character of their population, "nine-tenths Indian or negroid." The United States should "not be extended beyond the color line of the Rio Grande." James Madison, a contemporary of Jefferson, labeled "obnoxious" the idea of "amalgamating the white and black populations."

---

[17]Weston, *Racism in U.S. Imperialism*, 22.
[18]Burns, *American Idea of Mission*, 189.
[19]Genovese, *Roll, Jordan, Roll*, 414.
[20]Burns, *American Idea of Mission*, 187.

Like Jefferson, he decried the claim that blacks were intellectually the equal of Caucasians.[21]

The racial cant outlasted independence. John C. Calhoun, the southern politico, put all of the "colored races" of humankind under the same tent. Whether "Negroes, Indians or the mixed races of Mexico," it would be "degrading and fatal to American institutions for white men to associate themselves as equals . . . with any people of color."[22] According to Ralph Waldo Emerson, the poet and intellectual, race explained why "the hundred millions of Indians [had] come under the domain of a remote island in the north of Europe."[23] Theodore Parker, the theologian, while opposing the war against Mexico, admitted nevertheless that ultimately "all of the Northern continent would be in the hands of the Anglo-Saxon race." That, he emphasized, did not disturb him because "it would be a blessing to us and to Mexico; a blessing to the world."[24] Even Abraham Lincoln, "the Great Emancipator," asserted that "nature had fixed a gulf between the two races [blacks and whites] which would probably forbid forever their living together in perfect equality." He went on to add that he favored the race to which he belonged "having the superior position."[25]

Out of this racist litany, as well as the ubiquitous American dream of westward expansion, emerged one doctrine, which was to weigh heavily on Mexico. It was baptized Manifest Destiny, hailed by politicos as well as by some intellectuals—Emerson, William Cullen Bryant, and Walt Whitman among them—as a "widener of horizons of opportunity."[26] The drive to expand, as one scholar of this doctrine concluded, "is usually associated with crusading ideologies." For the Arabs it was Islam; the Spaniards found justification for their expansionism in Catholicism; Manifest Destiny was "the equivalent of these ideologies" for the United States.[27]

Born in the 1840s, the doctrine of Manifest Destiny was, nonetheless, hardly novel. Similar affirmations of faith had been heard before. However, its glib catchwords captured succinctly the mood of the nation and overnight received enthusiastic acceptance, as did its author, a lawyer and newspaperman by the name of John L. O'Sullivan who had championed filibustering expeditions to Cuba. For O'Sullivan, who had entry

---

[21]Frederick Merk, *Manifest Destiny and Mission in American History* (New York: Alfred A. Knopf, 1963), 8–9; Burns, *American Idea of Mission*, 188.

[22]Burns, *American Idea of Mission*, 193.

[23]Ibid., 190.

[24]Reginald Horsman, *Race and Manifest Destiny: The Origins of American Racial Anglo-Saxonism* (Cambridge: Harvard University Press, 1981), 180.

[25]Burns, *American Idea of Mission*, 188.

[26]Merk, *Manifest Destiny and Mission*, 40.

[27]Ibid., viii.

to James K. Polk's circle of friends, Manifest Destiny stood for American expansion, if need be to the Pacific Ocean, into territory owned by Mexico. For the more militant of its partisans, Manifest Destiny signified expansion over the North American continent or, in the best of scenarios, over the entire Western Hemisphere. Their propaganda was welcomed with open arms by the press and by a majority of Congress. Oddly, but logically too, Manifest Destiny had less appeal in the South, the home of the cotton slave plantations, divided as it was during the Mexican War over whether the victorious United States should absorb the whole of Mexico. Southern fear of annexing more "colored races" into the United States explains this seeming anomaly.[28]

The Cost to Mexico

This panoply of ideas, prejudices, and dreams of westward expansion bore fruit in Mexico, the dupe of Manifest Destiny. Texas furnished the stage for the drama, "the perfect example," wrote Frederick Merk, "of how Manifest Destiny would work, a pattern to be copied by the remainder of the continent."[29] The Adams-Onís Treaty of 1819, signed by Spain, then still the colonial master, and the United States, had affixed the boundary between them at the Sabine River. After its independence, Mexico inherited that boundary line. All the same, the United States almost immediately made attempts to modify it, trying to encroach on Texas and gazing longingly at California.

Until the end of the eighteenth century, these territories remained largely unsettled, with the possible exception of New Mexico. Washington's acquisition of Louisiana from France in 1803, leaving Spain to face the unruly Americans, drove Madrid to establish presidios in Texas, trying, in that manner, to fortify the province and to attract settlers from other parts of New Spain. Few of these colonizing schemes bore fruit; one that did bequeathed Moses Austin, a former Spanish subject, a concession to settle three hundred American families in Texas, who were permitted to bring their slaves with them but could not sell them, whereas their children were born free. The settlers had to be Catholics and swear allegiance to Spain. Taking advantage of the political turmoil in Mexico after independence, which made impossible enforcement of these provisions, the American colonists, whose numbers had multiplied, openly ignored the religious requirement and flaunted the slavery restrictions. Before long, American settlers outnumbered the Mexicans in Texas; of its nearly twenty-five thousand inhabitants in 1825, fewer than thirty-

[28]Ibid., 24, 39.
[29]Ibid., 46.

five hundred were Mexicans. Of the American colonies, only two, Austin's and another, were legal; the rest were trespassers. Most colonists were militant Protestants, blissfully ignorant of the Spanish language; disdainful of Mexicans, their laws, and customs; and, additionally, fiercely loyal to the United States. After Mexico abolished slavery in 1829 and then banned further immigration from the United States, the colonists declared their independence in 1835.

While this drama transpired, Joel R. Poinsett, Washington's minister, who never failed to meddle in Mexican politics, was telling Mexican authorities that his country was ready to buy Texas. Mexico had eventually to ask for his recall; however, his successor, Anthony Butler, a crony of President Andrew Jackson and a land speculator in Texas, again told Mexican officials of his country's wish to acquire Texas and, more alarming, to move its boundary west of the Nueces River, thus placing it squarely in New Mexico. In Texas, meanwhile, the American colonists began to recruit allies in New Orleans and New York, promising to reward their services with fertile lands in Texas. While this transpired, officials in Washington feigned innocence, ignoring Mexican demands that they enforce their own neutrality laws that barred citizens of the United States from participating in foreign wars. When the Texas colonists took up arms, Mexico dispatched an army to defend its territory. To its chagrin, the Texans, at the battle of San Jacinto, defeated it. Mexico vowed to fight on but let matters stand.

Expansionists in the United States, the spokesmen for Manifest Destiny, broke the truce. The wish to annex Texas but, of far greater importance, to take California, led to war between Mexico and the United States. As the election of 1844 documents, Manifest Destiny had popular support. After all, as Walt Whitman proclaimed, what did "miserable, inefficient Mexico—with her superstition, her burlesque upon freedom, her actual tyranny by the few over the many—what has she to do with the great mission of peopling the New World with a noble race?"[30] Promising to annex Texas and, by implication, acquire California, Polk, a southern expansionist, easily won the presidency. His election, Mexicans knew, meant war. Not to be outdone, John Tyler, a slaveholder from Virginia and the departing president, convinced Congress to annex Texas on February 27, 1845; the Texans quickly conferred their stamp of approval.

When, in protest, Mexico City recalled its minister, Polk ordered an American army to march across the Sabine; invade Texas; move south of the Rio Nueces, Mexico's northern border; and camp on the shore of the Rio Grande. With "flagrant contempt for international law," wrote Justo

[30]Ramón Eduardo Ruiz, ed., *The Mexican War: Was It Manifest Destiny?* (New York: Holt, Rinehart and Winston, 1963), 8.

Sierra, a Mexican historian, an American army "invaded the territory of a nation" at peace with its neighbor. Expecting hostilities, Polk sat down at his desk to write a declaration of war. After a skirmish at Matamoros, a hamlet on the Rio Grande, where Mexican soldiers killed or wounded sixteen Americans, Polk went before Congress to deliver his message of war. To the draft he had prepared earlier, he added merely one phrase: "American blood," he swore, "had been shed on American soil." After less than a year of fighting, an American army captured Mexico City. By the Treaty of Guadalupe of 1848, Mexico surrendered to the United States all lands from California to New Mexico, almost half of its territory.

No nation in modern times has ever lost as much of its territory to a conqueror. Yet, because victory came so easily for the United States, one question always comes up. Given the chauvinism of the times and expansionist sentiment, why did Washington not annex all of Mexico? The answer, not unimportantly, has much to say about the nature of Manifest Destiny and the character of American racism. Clearly, the answer is complex. One cannot ignore the fear of a sectional conflict between North and South in the United States, then looming on the horizon; the annexation of all of Mexico would have greatly exacerbated it. Also, much of Mexico's lands were believed unfit for slavery, the gist of the sectional issue, and thus not coveted by expansionist southerners. And there was the possibility that total annexation might lead to a costly guerrilla conflict with Mexicans. In trying to explain why Mexico survived the military fiasco of 1847, all of these reasons must be kept in mind.

Nonetheless, there is another, perhaps more valid, explanation. Cultural and racial arrogance, intimate bedfellows, lie at the root of American restraint. Although Polk's justification for war dwelt on Mexico's violations of "solemn treaties," expansionists proffered a more truthful version. To quote Whitman, one of the most vociferous, his country had a right to these Mexican lands by "a law superior to parchments and diplomatic rules"—the law of beneficent territorial utilization. As others of this inclination put it, says Merk, the claim of the United States rested on "the well-founded and legitimate rights of industry and intelligence."[31]

This argument, in the euphemism of that time, referred to the fact that at least two-thirds of Mexico's population, according to the expansionists, was "colored." Half were Indians, and most of the others mixed bloods, mestizos and mulattos. Only a fraction of its population was "white." According to the *New York Evening Post*, the Mexicans were Indians, "Indians as Cortez conquered three hundred years ago, only rendered a little more mischievous by a bastard civilization." To "incorporate Mexico," pontificated Calhoun, "would be the very first instance of

[31]Merk, *Manifest Destiny and Mission*, 153.

incorporating an Indian race; for more than half of Mexicans are Indians
. . . I protest against such a union as that. Ours, Sir, is the Government of
a white race."[32] To cite the *Illinois State Register*, Mexico's people were
"but little above the negro."[33] As Merk states, "The tendency was to fuse
attitudes towards Mexicans and free Negroes and the ethics of enslavement of a race into one conglomerate of emotion."[34] Citizenship could
not be conferred on half castes and Indians. No matter how voracious the
land hunger, explains Albert Weinberg, "the prospect of amalgamation
with assumedly inferior peoples spiked the appetite and caused the ambition to continental dominion to be postponed to a distant future."[35] Clearly,
regeneration, a hallmark of Manifest Destiny, had limits: Expansionists
preferred to acquire lands unencumbered by "colored races." American
race prejudice, ironically, had saved Mexico from disappearing from the
face of the globe.

That same racist attitude, quite clearly, kept Yucatán, a province whose
criollo (white) oligarchy could not wait for Washington to annex it in the
aftermath of the war, in the Mexican republic. Whites in the United States
considered the Maya Indians, three out of four inhabitants of the peninsula, to be "indolent, apathetic, stupid and sunk in superstition." Both in
the North and in the South, Democrats, who controlled Congress, feared
that racial problems would arise if Yucatán were joined to the United
States. The "annexation of such a land," in short, invited "problems and
little else."[36]

The Old and the New

For some scholars, Manifest Destiny represents the pinnacle of American racial jingoism. True, no conquest of territory of the Mexican magni-
tude occurs again. The acquisition of the Mesilla in 1854, although partly
brought about by veiled threats of renewed American military hostilities,
was, as the history books state, the Gadsden Purchase. That notwithstanding, during the so-called rebirth of Manifest Destiny (the "new") in the
years from 1898 to 1915, additional territories in the Pacific Ocean and
Caribbean fell into the lap of U.S. expansionists, all but Hawaii the booty
taken from Spain in the War of 1898. The United States claimed the Philippines, Puerto Rico, and the Pacific Islands for its empire and, disguised

[32]Ibid., 157.
[33]Albert K. Weinberg, *Manifest Destiny* (Chicago: Quadrangle Books, 1963),
157.
[34]Merk, *Manifest Destiny and Mission*, 157.
[35]Weinberg, *Manifest Destiny*, 160.
[36]Frederick Merk, *The Monroe Doctrine and American Expansionism* (New
York: Alfred A. Knopf, 1966), 198.

as a protectorate, Cuba. The people who dwelt in these tropical territories were, by culture and race, thought to be inferior to whites. On this basis they were denied, in the case of the Philippines, self-government; in both Cuba and Puerto Rico, the right of suffrage was restricted, on the conviction, to quote Adolph Myer, a congressman from Louisiana, that "inferior races" could not be trusted "with the ballot."[37] Hence, the racism that had relegated Negroes to second-class status in the United States was applied to the conquered people in the American empire. These acquisitions, as one author refers to them, were "America's Negro empire."[38]

Clearly, the spirit of Manifest Destiny, whether "old" or "new," had weathered the years. Racism was especially alive and well among Republicans, some of whom, in their party platform of 1896, made known their displeasure at the idea of inviting the mixed races of Mexico into "the temple of freedom." Earlier, the ideologues of the Republican party had pledged their faith in the "Manifest Destiny" of their country; as the "great nations," they announced, rapidly absorbed "all the waste places of the earth," the United States "must not fall out of the line of march."[39]

Racism, furthermore, fed on the ups and downs of the American economy. The late nineteenth century was a time of recurring depressions, particularly those of 1873 and 1893, when jobs were hard to find and the chimeric "safety valve" of fertile, free western lands was coming to an end. Fear of competing for jobs with immigrants stoked the fires of racism among workers and kept it alive among frightened middle-class intellectuals who hid their racism behind euphemistic phrases that, among other bogeys, warned their countrymen against becoming "the dumping ground for known criminals and professional paupers . . . and [against the] alien ownership of the land."[40]

In the second half of the nineteenth century, to exacerbate matters, social Darwinism captured the fancy of Americans, feeding anew the fires of racism. However, Darwinism, to underline, was not the source of the dogmatic racism of the late nineteenth century. It was merely "a new instrument," claims one observer, "in the hands of the theorists of race."[41] Still, Darwinism went on to become the "dominant rationale of American imperialism." Calling on the subtitle of the *Origin of Species*, which spoke of *The Preservation of the Favored Races in the Struggle for Life*, American imperialists found more justification for their subjugation "of

[37]Weston, *Racism in U.S. Imperialism*, 12.

[38]Ibid., 7.

[39]Julius W. Pratt, *Expansionists of 1898* (Gloucester, MA: P. Smith, 1959), 2.

[40]Richard Hofstadter, *Social Darwinism in American Thought* (New York: G. Braziller, 1959), 186; Merk, *Manifest Destiny and Mission*, 237.

[41]Hofstadter, *Social Darwinism*, 172.

weaker races." Darwin, however, had written about pigeons. Few anti-imperialists, moreover, sallied forth to question the belief of their adversaries in white supremacy.

Almost all American intellectuals and writers of note, not surprisingly, were both social Darwinists and imperialists. To catalogue their names is to compile a list of famous Americans. One was John Fiske, the historian, who asserted that the "work [of] the English race . . . is destined to go on until every land on the earth's surface . . . not already the seat of an ancient civilization shall become English in [the] . . . blood of its people."[42] According to Josiah Strong, whose book *Our Country: Its Possible Future and Its Present Crisis* (1885) sold 175,000 copies, "God was training" Americans "for the final competition of races—the struggle for existence. . . . If I read not amiss, this powerful race will move down upon Mexico and beyond," testimony to the "survival of the fittest."[43] Carl Schurz, just off the boat from Germany, opposed annexing Cuba because its people resembled Mexicans. John W. Burgess, a historian who taught Theodore Roosevelt at Columbia University, preached that it was the "white man's mission . . . to hold the reins of political power in his hands for the civilization of the world and the welfare of mankind."[44] To cite Julius W. Pratt, "Modern imperialism could ask for no more sweeping justification."[45] It was no accident, therefore, that Roosevelt, whose *Winning of the West* concluded that a racial war to the finish was inevitable with the Indian, should justify his seizure of Panama from the Republic of Colombia by proclaiming that backward nations must not stand in the way of the march of civilization.[46] William Jennings Bryan, his Democratic rival, found time to scold Roosevelt for inviting Booker T. Washington, the Negro leader, to dine at the White House.[47] David Starr Jordan, president of Stanford University, divided the people of the world into superior and inferior races, relegating Mexicans to the bottom, describing them as "ignorant, superstitious . . . with no conception of industry or thrift."[48] Meanwhile, Woodrow Wilson, fated to plague Mexico, was writing in 1901 that democracy was to be found only in countries "begotten of the English race," alleging that to bestow Anglo-Saxon codes on Third World peoples would be a "curse . . . not a blessing" because they were in the "childhood of their political growth."[49]

---

[42]Pratt, *Expansionists of 1898*, 4.
[43]Burns, *American Idea of Mission*, 208; Hofstadter, *Social Darwinism*, 178.
[44]Weston, *Racism in U.S. Imperialism*, 16.
[45]Pratt, *Expansionists of 1898*, 10.
[46]Weston, *Racism in U.S. Imperialism*, 16.
[47]Burns, *American Idea of Mission*, 188.
[48]Ibid., 48.
[49]Weston, *Racism in U.S. Imperialism*, 19.

Paradoxes

History, an old saying goes, tends to repeat itself. There are no sharp breaks with the past, merely transitions. That truth helps explain American attitudes and policies toward Mexico during much of the twentieth century. Nations, it is alleged, have only interests, which may be quite true. But, it must not be forgotten, those interests are defined by human beings, and they carry with them a cultural as well as a racial baggage that, in large measure, is part and parcel of the complex whole. Clearly, economic and political interests shape the behavior of a nation's leaders, but cultural factors also influence it. And racial attitudes as well as racist behavior are an integral part of culture as well as of economics. When analyzing the foreign policies of the United States, for instance, cultural arrogance, of which the attitude of racial superiority is a vital part, cannot be dismissed. During World War II a combination of racial bigotry and greed led to the internment of Japanese Americans but not citizens of German or Italian descent. Shall we dismiss, asks one writer, "as wholly implausible the notion that the United States would not have dropped on Germany the atom bomb it did drop on Japan?" The reasons for international conflict are multiple; but when you add the racial factor to the inebriant brew of "national, class, religious, ethnic and tribal lines of cleavage," they bring their "own accretion of greater glandular involvement and emotional violence to all of the other elements of conflict."[50]

Since the beginning of the nineteenth century, the world has undergone profound changes. One of them is striking: the separation into Northern and Southern Hemispheres, sign of the growing gulf between "have nations" and "have-not nations." With the exception of modern Japan, all of the rich are white; regardless of what apologists may say, this is no mere accident of history. Much of this appalling picture is by design. Twentieth-century relationships between Mexico and its neighbor to the north fit into that pattern.

After a rocky start, affairs between the United States and *porfiristas*, more "white of skin" than dark and, moreover, willing to play ball with American investors, were friendly. That the *porfiristas* exploited the "brown man of Mexico" ruffled no feathers in Washington or on Wall Street. During the militant phase of the Revolution of 1910, when radical reformers, eager to aid forgotten campesinos, threatened the status quo, Washington turned hostile. When the threat subsided in 1923, the diplomatic calm returned. The Mexican oil expropriation of 1938, a decision brought on partly by the intransigence of American oil magnates who were convinced that Mexicans did not have either the will or the know-

---

[50]Shepherd, *Racial Influences*, x.

how to manage the industry, again led to stormy seas. The return to conservative politics friendly to American business interests restored good relations, though the brown man of Mexico was again low man on the totem pole.

Despite these twists and turns in the diplomacy of the United States, certain aspects of its peculiar association with Mexico remained constant. The immigration restrictions enacted by Congress in the early 1920s punished Mexicans. Amid the hard times of the Great Depression of the 1930s, Washington officials deported one-half million Mexicans, many of them born in the United States. Earlier, over the protests of Mexican authorities, Texas Rangers had lynched Mexicans along the border; in 1915, during the days of the Plan de San Diego, racial antagonism led to "violence, vigilante tactics and arbitrary action by the Texas Rangers." According to a report by an American Secret Service agent, more than three hundred Mexicans were killed, "many in cold blood," in the vicinity of Brownsville, Texas.[51] Until after World War II, the segregation of Mexican children in public schools, balconies for Mexicans in theaters, and special days set aside for Mexicans to use public swimming pools were not unknown in the southwestern states. Then, as now, most Mexicans lived in barrios, a form of ghetto. When prohibition became the law of their country, American "investors" built saloons, gambling casinos, and whorehouses in Mexican border towns, which were patronized by Yankee tourists who journeyed south to do what they could not do in their own communities.

Currently, the growing invasion of the United States by poor Mexicans, most of them dark of skin, who flock north seeking jobs, increasingly alarms white Americans in the Southwest. Along the border of Tijuana, the Mexican city south of San Diego, some Americans have organized border watches, as they say, to stem the flow of "illegals." Other American residents, unwilling to live next door to the shanties of the "undocumented," as Mexicans refer to them, call on the police to rid their communities of the "undesirables." On the rim of Tijuana, American soldiers, at the request of immigration officials, erected an iron barricade to discourage Mexicans from entering the United States.

Simultaneously, another international scene plays out. If they cannot go to Europe, American tourists flock to Mexico; catering to them is one of Mexico's most lucrative industries. From Tijuana to Matamoros, border towns have boomed because of American visitors who yearly spend millions of dollars on Mexican artifacts of every kind. On the U.S. side, Cinco de Mayo festivals are popular with merchants and Chicano students, whose ancestors left Mexico years ago, and "ethnic" restaurants,

---

[51]Colin MacLachlan, *Anarchism and the Mexican Revolution* (Berkeley: University of California Press, 1991), 57.

patronized by hungry gringos, serve up "Mexican food" in every town and city of the Southwest. Conceived in this fashion, relations between Mexico and the United States, obviously, go far beyond the narrow, traditional bounds of diplomacy, trade agreements, or investments. When racial and cultural differences are brought into play, the stage is much larger. As this happens, the common prejudices of Americans surface; one of them, to emphasize once more, is racial, the disdain for and fear of people of dark skins, among them Mexicans. No understanding of U.S.-Mexican relations, whether historical or contemporary, is possible without taking it into account.

Racism and *Mestizaje*

Moisés González Navarro

RACISM HAS BEEN AN IMPORTANT FACTOR in the history of Mexico and the United States as, indeed, it has constituted a significant aspect of the experience of all the nations of the world. From their respective beginnings as independent nations, Mexico and the United States sought to increase their "desirable" populations, to colonize vast unsettled lands with "strong stock," and to use to their own advantage the strengths resident in the other's "human resources."

Competition to achieve their respective self-interests was exacerbated by the markedly different language, culture, and religion of their peoples. Much of the conflict was either rooted in, or expressed in terms of, the official concepts of racism (one race's perceived superiority over others and its contempt toward the supposedly inferior ones) in the United States and of *mestizaje* (the promotion of racial mixture) in Mexico.

The Era of Instability, 1821–1860

In opposition to the hierarchical social structure of the Mexican colonial period, racial equality was proclaimed by Miguel Hidalgo (November 29 and December 6, 1810); José María Morelos (October 13, 1811); the Constitution of Apatzingan (1813); and the Spanish *cortes* (February 9, 1811, March 18 and November 9, 1812, and April 29, 1821); and it was confirmed by the Plan de Iguala of February 24, 1821. After independence, the Supreme Constituent Congress of the Mexican Empire ordered that in all public and private documents there should be no classification of citizens by racial origin. Because colonial laws had degraded Indians by treating them as minors on the grounds that they needed protection, which served only to further diminish them, independent Mexico's institutions were to be based on equality.[1]

---

[1]Moisés González Navarro, "Instituciones indígenas, en el México independiente," in *La política indigenista en México: Métodos y resultados*, 2d ed.,

In mid-December 1821, Agustín de Iturbide boasted of Mexico's great wealth and urged Mexicans to welcome foreigners with open arms.[2] On December 29th of that year, the empire's Foreign Relations Committee divided foreign relations into several categories. Relations with those who "by nature" belonged to the first group included the "savage Indian nations." Whether pacific or warlike, these were not seen as a threat, given the obvious superiority of the imperial troops in discipline, arms, and cavalry. In any event, the most feared were the Comanches because of their skillful use of spear and rifle, even though they lacked strategy and discipline. The committee considered it necessary to continue the practice of giving them gifts to prevent the United States either from encouraging them to engage in hostile actions against the empire or from using them to introduce contraband into provinces as vast, fertile, and sparsely populated as New Mexico. Since 1810 the Mexicans had not been able to prevent the Apache, Lipan, and Comanche tribes from carrying out their raids; the Indians had therefore managed to capture horses from the militia and livestock from haciendas and towns, many of which they pillaged to the point that settlers had to "live within gunshot distance and to walk in single file, even when on their way to chop wood."[3]

The Anglo Americans, the second group categorized in foreign relations, sought to occupy the Espíritu Santo Bay, San Bernardo, Orcoquizac, and other ports within Mexican territory. The committee believed (or perhaps it wanted to believe) that the United States desired only to establish commercial ties, because the two dominant powers of the north—Mexico and the United States—were united in their desire to preserve their independence and freedom vis-à-vis a hostile Europe. However, there was danger in Texas because its fertile soil, benign climate, mineral wealth, and other natural products made the province a "paradise" coveted by both Europe and the United States. Increasing its population would be its best defense; the Spanish Crown had attempted to do this without success. Settlers might come from New Orleans, or Texas could be populated with the many poor people living in the empire, by soldiers and officers of the Mexican army, and by members of the Spanish expeditionary forces who wished to remain in Mexico after independence. The committee feared that when the empire least expected it, hordes of people could enter Mexico from the United States, like the Goths and Ostrogoths

---

ed. Alfonso Caso et al. (Mexico: Instituto Nacional Indigenista, 1973), 209–212, 221–223.

[2]Dieter George Berninger, *La inmigración en México, 1821–1857* (Mexico: Secretaría de Educación Pública, 1974), 27.

[3]Mexico, Secretaría de Relaciones Exteriores, *La diplomacia mexicana*, 3 vols. (Mexico: Tipografía Artística, 1910), 1:85–87, 103.

who left the banks of the Danube and the Thames to lay waste to the Roman Empire. The committee preferred as settlers the Irish (Catholic, hardworking, and enemies of the English) and German Catholics such as those who earlier had successfully colonized the Sierra Morena in Spain.

Russia, the third foreign relations category, as of 1728 had taken possession of Cabo Mendocino up to Puerto Bodega, very close to San Francisco; sixty-five years later, when the Russians established themselves in Nootka, the Spanish government became aware of these activities. According to a Franciscan missionary who had recently arrived from California, Mexico faced losing not only that province but Sonora and the two Pimerías as well.[4] Meanwhile, the committee recommended that both Californias be colonized by Chinese, by Mexicans (providing them with land on the same terms that had been offered to the settlers of Texas), and by those condemned to more than two years' imprisonment, especially those sentenced to death. Finally, "foreign relations as a matter of policy" centered on Spain, the last category. The empire owed the latter "its being, its language, its religion, its educational system, and its civil and political structure, even though Spain had not done either what it could or should have done [for Mexico]."[5]

The imperial envoy, José Manuel Zozaya, presented his credentials in the United States on October 12, 1822, while Mexico still believed that the North American navy would come to its aid in case of war against Spain. Nevertheless, within just two and a half months Zozaya became convinced that their designs on Texas would eventually make Americans enemies of Mexico. He noted that their arrogance caused them to regard Mexico as inferior and their hubris to believe that Washington would become the capital of all the Americas. "In time they will become our sworn enemies," said Zozaya, but he reassured his government that from a military standpoint the Americans were no threat outside their own territory. The chargé d'affaires who succeeded him, José A. Torrens, was nonetheless concerned about the fate of Texas, where three thousand North Americans already lived along with barely two hundred Mexican soldiers who were incapable of expelling them, much less of patrolling a long and ill-defined border.[6]

---

[4]In the eighteenth century, "Pimerías" referred to the two parts of the territory inhabited by the Pima Indians in what is now Arizona, Sonora, and western Chihuahua.

[5]Juan Francisco de Azcárate y Lezama, *Un programa de política internacional*, Archivo Histórico Diplomático Mexicano, no. 37 (Mexico: Publicaciones de la Secretaría de Relaciones Exteriores, 1932), 5–72.

[6]Mexico, Secretaría de Relaciones Exteriores, *La diplomacia mexicana*, 1:85–87, 103.

The situation in Texas continued to concern Mexican officials in the years that followed. A member of the boundary commission headed by General Manuel Mier y Terán noted in 1828 that of the two hundred inhabitants of Béjar only ten were Mexican—and of the "lowest class"—predicting that this colony would be the spark igniting the fire that would leave Mexico without Texas.[7] Although the statement was an exaggeration, the commission member had observed a reality: the growing imbalance between foreign settlers and native Texans.

Populating Texas proved complicated, however, because of the problems of slavery and race. Many of the settlers were black slaves brought into Texas against the law in various ways. In 1833 the Mexican consul Francisco Pizarro Martínez rejected as immigrants even those blacks who had been freed, on the grounds that they were actually slaves in disguise and, especially, because "people of color" were immoral and lazy. For those reasons, Consul Pizarro Martínez also opposed the entrance of blacks from Liberia and Jamaica and, in general, from the Spanish and English Antilles despite the geographical proximity that lowered transportation costs.

Disagreement about slavery, although significant, was not the only point of contention between Mexicans and Americans. Father Muldoon pointed out that Americans and Mexicans in Texas were as different as oil and water. Americans looked down on Mexicans as an "ignorant, fanatic, and arrogant race," and they did not worry about being hated by them because one Anglo Texan was thought to be worth four Mexicans. Mexicans retaliated by calling North Americans "heretics, scoundrels, and fugitives from justice." Nevertheless, Juan N. Almonte acknowledged in his 1834 report on Texas that the early immigrants who came from the south of the United States had customs that were rather strange but not immoral.[8] The Texas War of Independence increased their contempt for each other. According to Anglo Texans, Mexican soldiers could not compare to the "handsome, strong, and courageous Texans," to which Mexi-

---

[7]Mexico, Comisión de Limites, *Diario de viaje de la comisión de límites: Que puso el gobierno de la República, bajo la dirección del Exmo. Sr. general de división D. Manuel Mier y Terán, lo escribieron por su orden los individuos de la misma comisión, D. Luis Verlandier y D. Rafael Chovel* (Mexico: Juan R. Navarro, 1850), 117–119.

[8]Carlos Bosch García, comp., *Documentos de la relación de México con los Estados Unidos*, vols. 2–4 (Mexico: Universidad Nacional Autónoma de México, Instituto de Investigaciones Históricas, 1983), 2:330–332. Celia Gutiérrez Ibarra, *Cómo México perdió Texas: Análisis y transcripción del informe secreto (1834) de Juan Nepomuceno Almonte* (Mexico: Instituto Nacional de Antropología e Historia, 1987), 39–40, 45–49.

cans replied by calling them the *"god dammes."*[9] The Anglo-Texan rebels attributed their eventual victory over Mexico to race: Mexico was weak because it was a country of Indians, except for the few whites who controlled the land and the bureaucracy and commanded the army.[10]

Ten years later, after the United States had invaded Mexico, some North American diplomats opposed Mexico's total annexation to prevent the American race from being infected by the virus of Spanish administrative corruption.[11] Unfortunately, some in Mexico also accepted the negative stereotypes of their country. Early in 1848, there were liberals who, under cover of the pseudonym "various Mexicans," accounted for their nation's defeat in somewhat similar terms: They divided the seven million Mexicans into four million Indians and the rest of "mixed" race. Of the former, three-fourths did not even know that Mexico had become independent; they were enslaved by haciendas and dominated by the clergy through payment of parish taxes and tithes. Only three hundred thousand of the remaining whites and mestizos belonged to the economically productive class. In short, just as U.S. Chief Negotiator Nicholas P. Trist had recently observed, Mexico was not really a nation.[12] Apparently, this reality led the conservative Lucas Alamán to write to his patron, the duke of Montelone, about his fears that, with the departure of the American army, Mexico's greatly outnumbered whites would fall victim to a caste war.[13] Although the American army routed the Indian invaders of the hacienda administered by Alamán, the Mexican government asked the United States for three or four thousand soldiers to quell the Maya uprising in Yucatán—a proposal that the U.S. government considered impractical.[14]

The North American victory of 1847 meant, among other things, that the United States came into possession of California, where a few years earlier the first American immigrants had declared that they could easily defeat the Mexican soldiers, who consisted of starving, lazy mestizos. In a similar vein, American travelers wrote that, with a few exceptions, there

[9]Bosch García, *Documentos*, 2:529; José Enrique de la Peña, "Reseña y diario de la campaña de Texas," in *La rebelión de Texas; Manuscrito inédito de 1836, por un oficial de Santa Anna. Edición, estudio y notas de J. Sánchez Garza* (Mexico: Impresora Mexicana, 1955), 35.

[10]Bosch García, *Documentos*, 3:346–349.

[11]Ibid., 4:800–807.

[12]Vito Alessio Robles, *Coahuila y Texas desde la consumación de la independencia hasta el tratado de paz de Guadalupe Hidalgo*, 2 vols. (Mexico: Talleres Gráficos de la Nación, 1945–1946), 2:404–407.

[13]Lucas Alamán, *Documentos diversos*, 4 vols. (Mexico: Editorial Jus, 1945–1947), 4:257.

[14]Bosch García, *Documentos*, 4:964–965.

were no people in the United States as miserable and morally contempt-ible as the "hybrid race" of New Mexico.[15]

When California's gold rush began in 1849, a number of bosses in Sonora and Sinaloa encouraged their workers to emigrate. The new Cali-fornians, however, proved hostile to Mexicans. California banned Mexi-can immigrants and Californios (Californians of Mexican ancestry) from mining. Moreover, despite the protests of Mexico's Foreign Minister Fernando Ramírez, many Mexicans were forced to leave California.[16] The policy was justified by a racist explanation: English-speaking Califor-nians asserted that in their cruelty Mexicans could be compared only to the "thugs" of India; on Sundays the Mexican "vampires" got drunk and lost all the gold they had mined during the week, but because this was their idea of enjoying themselves, there was no need to feel sorry for them. The Mexicans were like savage Indians and could never meet Ameri-can standards of civilization. Such characterizations masked reality, how-ever; Mexicans were resented because they were better miners.[17] Even though they were American citizens, Californios faced severe discrimi-nation. One of them proposed in Monterey that all should be accepted as white except those of "inferior race." Because many Californios were dark skinned, being defined as "white" was extremely important to them. Yet dividing the former Mexicans of California into "whites" and "infe-rior races" constituted a violation of the Treaty of Guadalupe, implying the continuation of war with Mexico.

The new rulers perceived distinctions even among the so-called infe-rior races. One Anglo legislator accepted the civilized, but not the sav-age, Indians; another rejected blacks as mere "laboring machines," or human motors, as workers of all races would be characterized years later by the positivists. Another legislator equated Africans with natives of the Sandwich Islands and with Chileans, Peruvians, and "Mexico's lower classes." Still another opposed both black and Mexican workers because their labor demeaned that of the whites.[18] Anglos rejected Californios because they were descendants of Spaniards and because the latter had

[15]David Weber, ed., *Foreigners in Their Native Land: Historical Roots of the Mexican Americans* (Albuquerque: University of New Mexico Press, 1973), 71.

[16]Moisés González Navarro, *Anatomía del poder en México* (Mexico: El Colegio de México, 1983), 74–76.

[17]Leonard Pitt, *The Decline of the Californios: A Social History of the Spanish-Speaking Californians, 1846–1890* (Berkeley: University of California Press, 1966), 52–53.

[18]Robert F. Heizer and Alan J. Almquist, *The Other Californians: Prejudice and Discrimination under Spain, Mexico, and the United States to 1920* (Berke-ley: University of California Press, 1971), 99–101, 107, 110–111, 143–144.

Moorish blood, "ergo, Mexicans were at least Hottentots."[19] Discrimination was not limited to verbal insults. On July 15, 80 "brave" Mormon veterans of the War of 1847 arrested 110 "greasers," accusing them of murder and theft. In 1849–1850, many men from Sonora were beaten, expelled, or hanged. Anglo hostility against Mexicans was made worse by the presence of Sonoran women in bars, but their attraction for the Anglo Californians was purely sexual; in that period, an Anglo would seldom marry a Spanish-American woman because he would thereby lose status.[20] Resentment of the Sonorans' mining skills, sexual rivalry, and alcohol provoked many fights in which—as might be expected—Sonorans were the losers, especially because Anglos thought no more of killing them than they would of killing rabbits.[21]

Anglos in California subjugated Mexicans in various ways. On April 13, 1850, they imposed a monthly tax of twenty dollars on foreign miners, resulting in the immediate return of five hundred Sonorans to Mexico. Californios, however, claimed protection under the Treaty of Guadalupe.[22] In California's Calaveras County, Mexicans were even more fiercely persecuted. Their properties were taken away, their houses were set on fire, some were murdered, and the majority were driven out. Joaquín Murrieta, who was regarded by Anglos as the archetypical Mexican villain, responded to these attacks by terrorizing Calaveras County from the winter of 1852 to the summer of 1853.[23] North Americans of Mexican descent continued to be discriminated against and for more than a century were accused of being the product of a mixture of Spaniards, Indians, and blacks—that is, hybrids.[24]

Long after the war, North Americans continued their designs on Mexico. Secretary of State John Forsyth proposed turning the southern republic into a protectorate by promoting American immigration and constructing railroads. In this way, the United States could enjoy the advantages of annexation without its responsibilities, which would include the burden of Mexico's ignorant and hybrid population.[25] What was not achieved by peaceful means, Henry A. Crabb tried to accomplish through violence. On March 26, 1858, he notified the prefect of Altar of his

    [19]Richard H. Morefield, "The Mexican Adaptation in American California, 1846–1875" (Ph.D. diss., University of California, Berkeley, 1955), 23.
    [20]Pitt, *Decline of the Californios*, 54–72.
    [21]Morefield, "Mexican Adaptation," 75, 82, 88–90.
    [22]Ibid., 8, 15, 45.
    [23]González Navarro, *Anatomía del poder*, 77.
    [24]Weber, *Foreigners in Their Native Land*, 17, 53, 72.
    [25]Paul V. Murray, *Tres norteamericanos y su participación en el desarrollo del Tratado McLane-Ocampo, 1850–1860* (Guadalajara: Imprenta "Gráfica," 1946), 6.

intention to settle in Sonora under the laws of colonization and at the invitation of prominent citizens of that state who were actually Americans living near Sonora. Four days later, the authorities of Ures, Sonora, rejected his expedition with shouts of "Long live Mexico, and death to filibusters!" This took Crabb by surprise for, in light of Mexico's "industrial maxims," he had expected to be received "with open arms." The Mexicans cut off Crabb's head and kept it in an earthenware pot of vinegar for several days. This savage and barbarous act put an end to further filibuster expeditions.[26]

Conflicts between Americans and Mexicans (from both sides) were frequent and ranged from the mild to the extreme. For example, in the spring of 1856 a North American objected to being hanged by a Mexican because he was a "greaser." During the week of July 19 to 26 of the same year, Anglos living in Los Angeles took up arms in fear of a "Mexican revolution."[27] Most of the Anglos in California were convinced that Mexico should be Americanized. But because they were so superior to the Sonorans in "bravery, natural intelligence, valor, size, and strength," the question was how this might be accomplished. As American institutions were not suited to foreign countries, taking over Sonora would give rise to agrarian problems and to additional difficulties with Indians and slaves. There was no lack of newspaper polemics on the supposed cruelty of Californios, which was blamed on their descendance from the "Spanish race." The Californios retorted by pointing to the impunity enjoyed by those who persecuted Spanish Americans and by asking which of the two races was more vile and degenerate.[28] In Texas, Juan Nepomuceno Cortina, "the red bandit of the Río Grande," began his warlike activities on July 13, 1859, when a sheriff arrested one of his servants. On September 28, with shouts of "Long live Mexico, and death to gringos!" Cortina and his followers liberated the prisoners. Some historians have considered him a "social revolutionary" because he offered a redemptive program to Mexicans resident in Texas. By the middle of 1860, he had vanished into the San Carlos mountains of Tamaulipas.[29]

[26]Luis G. Zorrilla, *Historia de las relaciones entre México y los Estados Unidos de América, 1800–1958*, 2 vols. (Mexico: Editorial Porrúa, 1965), 1:373; Frederick C. Turner, *The Dynamic of Mexican Nationalism* (Chapel Hill: University of North Carolina Press, 1968), 43; Sergio Calderón Valdes, comp., *Historia general de Sonora*, 3 vols. (Hermosillo: Gobierno del Estado de Sonora, 1985), 3:146–149.

[27]Pitt, *Decline of the Californios*, 26–27, 37–38, 161–162, 189.

[28]Ibid., 205–209.

[29]Wayne Moquim with Charles Van Doren, eds., *A Documentary History of the Mexican Americans* (New York: Praeger Publishers, 1971), 230–233; Toribio Esquivel Obregón, *Apuntes para la historia del derecho en México: Relaciones Internacionales, 1821–1860*, 4 vols. (Mexico: Antigua Librería Robredo de José

Racial divisions also occurred in Mexico. Debate over Chinese and blacks came to the fore in Maximilian's Council on Colonization during its discussion of a petition to introduce one hundred thousand settlers consisting of Africans, "Indo-Asians," and Chinese. Baron de Sauvage supported the petition because the Chinese were "the most submissive, docile, and loyal to their masters," and Africans were humble, robust, and fit for work in the tropics. Mexican members of the council were opposed. They preferred immigrants who would improve their country's "dark-skinned racial mixture," and they did not share the belief in the morality of Africans and Chinese. The council president alleged that Asians offered no economic advantage because of their inaptitude for rural labor and that in the cities they would not only ruin the local artisans but also demoralize them with their "abominable vices." He also rejected Africans because, inevitably, they would slacken from working hard and become lazy and, above all, because of their "ugly" racial characteristics. Only white immigrants would solve the colonization problem.[30] Ironically, in the north, not a few Americans wanted to cleanse the United States of the "foul stain" of the Mexican race.[31]

The Age of Consolidation, 1860–1910

In Mexico, although some referred to Indians as parasites and savages, others were favorably impressed by their facial features.[32] *Mestizaje*, which was considered the way to raise the Indians from their subjugation, was criticized by some because it would create a race of bastards (an epithet commonly used for Mexicans in the United States). This argument was refuted by those who believed that well-educated Indians would not inherit their parents' vices.[33] Meanwhile, Juan Cortina, oblivious to these anthropological speculations, increased his popularity among the "Mexican-Texans," who were obliged to travel with an American passport in the midst of a "civil war between races." During elections, the *mantecosos* (greasers) rapidly turned into American citizens, as did Cortina

---

Porrúa e Hijos, 1948), 4:596–597; Weber, *Foreigners in Their Native Land*, 32, 207; Zorrilla, *Historia de las relaciones entre México y las Estados Unidos*, 1:403.

[30]Niceto de Zamacois, *Historia de Méjico desde sus tiempos más remotos hasta nuestros días*, 18 vols. (Barcelona: Parres y Compañía, 1878), 18:957–964.

[31]Gastón García Cantú, *Las invasiones norteamericanas en México* (Mexico: Ediciones Era, 1971), 208.

[32]Daniel Cosío Villegas, *Historia moderna de México: La república restaurada vida social* (Mexico: Editorial Hermes, 1956), 80, 152, 165, 222, 247, 268, 311–312.

[33]Ibid.

himself, who frequently changed his nationality according to which side of the river he was on. What cannot be denied is that during the Tuxtepec revolt of 1876, whereas some in the United States accused Cortina of being a turncoat, Porfirio Díaz, the leader of the insurgents, named Cortina supporters to official posts in Matamoros—a region where many Texans thought nothing of killing Mexicans and where many Mexicans took pride in killing Texans.[34]

Although the presence of North Americans on the border frequently raised Mexican fears of a new dismemberment of national territory, especially after the capital was linked to the United States by rail, these fears were not shared in official circles, where it was believed that the United States would oppose annexing territory inhabited by Mexican mestizos, Cuban mulattos, and Dominican blacks who, to make matters worse, were Catholic.[35] The Mexican diplomat Matías Romero engaged in a lengthy polemic with the Catholic newspaper *El Tiempo* from May to September 1889, arguing that no American political party favored the conquest of Mexico because of the danger of acquiring territories inhabited by people of a different race, language, and religion and with different customs. Don Matías used the paradoxical argument that the best way to prevent annexation was to open Mexico to the United States by conceding to it every reasonable advantage. Annexation would thus become unnecessary and even dangerous. This had been the purpose of the policy of alienating unoccupied public lands and of the very "liberal" railroad and mining concessions granted to foreigners. *El Tiempo*, in any event, wanted Mexico to be colonized by Latins, and Romero tried to placate it by explaining that North American Protestants would object to the incorporation of Mexican Catholics, who would reinforce their American coreligionists.[36]

In some Mexican and American circles, religion played a rather important role in relations between the two countries. Father Agustín de la Rosa, for example, never traveled on streetcars or trains because they were North American.[37] In the plan he presented in January 1887, Heraclio Bernal partly agreed with the priest from Guadalajara when he demanded that preference be given to Mexicans in making railroad concessions, and

[34]Mexico, Comisión Pesquisidora de la Frontera del Norte, *Informe de la Comisión Pesquisidora de la Frontera del Norte al Ejecutivo de la Unión sobre depredaciones de los indios y otros males que sufre la frontera mexicana* (Mexico: Imprenta de Díaz de León y White, 1874), 149–150, 162–163.

[35]Zorrilla, *Historia de las relaciones entre México y los Estados Unidos*, 2:29.

[36]Matías Romero, *Estudio sobre la anexión de México a los Estados Unidos* (Mexico: Imprenta del Gobierno, 1890), 6–7, 11, 14, 17–19, 22, 25–26, 29, 31, 33–34, 39, 45, 48, 60–62, 64, 72, 80, 95, 97, 104–105.

[37]J. Ignacio Dávila Garibi, "El Padre Rositas," *Memorias de la Academia Mexicana de la Historia* 12, no. 2 (April–July 1953): 113.

Cajeme (chief of the Yaqui rebels) spurned the proposal of a North American to build a railroad, because "we Mexicans do not need to have foreigners come here to take us by the hand to make the sign of the cross."[38]

Nonetheless, according to the railroad promoter William S. Rosecrans—whose views were later supported by Presidents Manuel González and Porfirio Díaz—peaceful conquest had prevailed over the opposition of President Sebastian Lerdo de Tejada. Pacific intentions, however, did not prevent Rosecrans from blaming Mexico's meager development on its population's being five-eighths Indian.[39] Another railroad promoter, Edward L. Plumb, asked that the United States occupy Baja California to prevent the region from falling into the hands of an inferior and heterogeneous population, which would give rise to endless difficulties for his country; but he generously offered to let Mexicans retain their religion. This was the same Plumb who, inspired by Manifest Destiny, in 1855 had proposed to the State Department that the United States make a clean sweep of Mexico to create a single race, speaking one language, with the same form of government and close commercial ties.[40]

Ulysses Grant, however, in the spring of 1880 announced that his country was mainly interested in trade with Mexico and that there was no possibility of its annexing Mexican territory, even if the Mexican people were to so desire. The Civil War general rejected annexation because Mexican Indians were illiterate and lacked ambition, and it would take them many years before they could participate in the "American spirit"— that is, capitalism—even though Mexicans worked for practically nothing.[41] According to Alexander Robey Sheperd, a wealthy mine owner in Batopilas, Chihuahua, one of his major problems with the Indians was their ignorance, a difficulty that apparently he overcame by paying them regular wages. In 1896 he predicted that with its cheap labor and silver coinage Mexico would become the richest country in the world.[42]

More important because of their number than the American capitalists were the Mormon colonies, which were almost universally detested by Mexicans for being "Yankee and Mormon." Although some in Sonora

[38]Fausto Antonio Marín, *La rebelión de la Sierra (vida de Heraclio Bernal)* (Mexico: Edición América, 1950), 137–139; Fortunato Hernández, *Las razas indígenas de Sonora y la guerra del Yaqui* (Mexico: Talleres de la Casa Editorial "J. de Elizalde," 1902), 147.

[39]David M. Pletcher, *Rails, Mines, and Progress: Seven American Promoters in Mexico, 1867–1911* (Port Washington, NY: Cornell University Press, 1958), 46.

[40]Ibid., 73–80, 92–105.

[41]Ibid., 152–153, 158–159, 163, 172, 179–181.

[42]Ibid., 184, 190–191, 195, 200–207, 211, 214, 217–218.

perceived Mormons as a threat to Mexico's social institutions, the Chihuahua government recognized the progress they achieved through hard work—and not by working secret mines at night, as many envious Mexicans preferred to believe. Mexicans did not like the Mormons, "perhaps because of their religion or because of questions of race."[43]

When it became known in 1889 that two prosperous Texas blacks planned to establish a colony with a thousand black families, the journalist E. M. de los Ríos did not base his opposition on the traditional difference between aristocrats and plebeians but on the fact that the white race was the most civilized. According to the journalist, even the educated among the African, Mongolian, and native American races had remained in inferior positions, and in Australia the real men were the ants. *El Tiempo* objected to the colonization because the blacks who were contemplating it were not vigorous inhabitants of Africa, "but corrupt, effeminate, and degenerate inhabitants of the South" of the United States. Acknowledging that by natural law men are born equal, the Catholic newspaper nevertheless argued that education and work created differences that no one could erase and, above all, that blacks were "so ugly!" The blacks who came to Tlahualilo in 1895 sparked new and even more determined opposition, which another Catholic newspaper justified on the grounds that they were of a "race ethnologically inferior to ours," mixed with *zambos* (a mixture of Indians and Africans) of a physical and moral culture infinitely worse than the "pure race of our Indians, who are themselves already debased enough." Finally, irrespective of impurities and inferiorities, the colony of blacks, which was founded in Durango in April 1895, was devastated by a smallpox epidemic. A North American official who came to investigate whether the colonists had died of starvation found that only sixty blacks were left: The epidemic had killed another sixty, seventy-eight had returned to the United States, and the whereabouts of twenty-five were unknown.[44]

Mexicans also were ambivalent about Indian immigration. In the late nineteenth century and early in the twentieth, there was a rumor that Indians would be immigrating from the United States. Some Mexicans welcomed them because the Indians belonged to the same race as primitive Mexicans, but without the latter's vices. On the other hand, a Catholic newspaper objected to them because they might represent a danger if they were to settle near the U.S. border.[45]

---

[43]Moisés González Navarro, *El Porfiriato: La vida social* (Mexico: Editorial Hermes, 1957), 170–180.

[44]*El Imparcial*, November 15, 1900; *El Tiempo*, October 16, 1895; *Semana Mercantil*, October 21, 1895.

[45]*El Tiempo*, October 15, 1891; Mexico, Secretaría de Estado, *Memoria presentada al congreso de la Unión por el Secretario de Estado y del Despacho*

In February 1889 an important strike took place in the English mine La Trinidad, in Sonora; the dispute arose because the mining company paid with vouchers that could be exchanged only in the company store. The strike began with a racial confrontation when several Mexicans vented their resentment with shouts of "Death to the *gringos cabrones* [bastards]!" Yelling insults escalated to throwing rocks, until the foreigners fired into the air and were rescued by the police. The mining company asked London for support, and the English government complained to the Mexican about the frequent strikes. President Díaz ordered the governor of Sonora, Ramón Corral, to protect the English "within the law." The latter proudly replied that the strike had already ended and that its leaders were in jail, for he protected all companies regardless of their nationality. He refused, however, to accede to the mining company's demand that the leaders of the strike be drafted into the army, claiming that it was inadequate punishment for the crime. He also indicated that labor peace would be restored if the company were to pay in cash instead of chits, and he asked the firm to resolve the problems of the strike through the judicial process. Perhaps Corral did not agree to all the company's requests because he knew that the strikers enjoyed the sympathy of the entire population.[46]

Labor conflict also erupted in American-owned companies in Mexico. In 1902 approximately one thousand North Americans lived in Cananea, Sonora, the site of the Cananea Copper Company. The following year, the company's school, directed by an American woman, admitted only the children of American employees; in 1906 it had one hundred students. The school claimed that it did not discriminate because it was open to Mexicans if places were available (which they almost never were); in any event, it discriminated economically because the school fees amounted to three dollars a month.[47] The discrimination against Mexicans was made evident when, in the famous Cananea strike of 1906, local workers struck over the fact that Americans were paid more than Mexicans. Actually, the owner, William C. Greene, had already earned a bad reputation in his own country by withholding part of his workers' wages for hospital services that were not provided. In any event, North American workers in Cananea believed themselves to be superior to Mexicans, whom they considered indolent and stupid.

---

de Fomento, Colonización e Industria de la República Mexicana, Olegario Molina, enero 1905–junio 1907 (Mexico: Imprenta y Fototipia de la Secretaría de Fomento, 1909), 179.

[46]Ramón Eduardo Ruiz, *The People of Sonora and Yankee Capitalists* (Tucson: University of Arizona Press, 1988), 109–112.

[47]Ibid., 86–88.

On January 16, 1906, a group of Mexican workers founded a secret society known as the Unión Liberal Humanidad (Liberal Humanity Union), which became associated with the Mexican Liberal Party, a group in political opposition to the Díaz regime. Esteban Baca Calderón of the union objected to the "blond, blue-eyed" men who were paid more than Mexicans and who occupied management positions.[48] Governor Rafael Izabal held the Unión Liberal Humanidad responsible for the distribution of handbills that described as an unparalleled abomination the fact that "on Mexican soil" a Mexican should be worth less than a Yanqui, a black, or a Chinese. The *rurales* (rural police) killed several strikers and wounded many more. Almost worse than the incident was the appearance of Governor Izabal at the scene accompanied by armed North American soldiers and civilian volunteers, and still worse was his bizarre justification of the wage differentials on the grounds that North American brothels charged five pesos and Mexican brothels charged only three. Naturally, Izabal was not held responsible for his actions by the national government, and the official press explained that Americans were paid more because of their higher productivity. On the other hand, on June 3, 1906, the U.S. Western Federation of Labor congratulated the Mexican strikers and encouraged them to continue their struggle; a short time later, it was learned that three hundred Americans secretly supported the Cananea strike.[49]

There also was friction between Mexican and North American workers, not just between the Mexicans and U.S. mining entrepreneurs, especially on the railroads after construction had begun on a large scale in the 1880s. In August 1906 a strike in Torreón, Coahuila, brought about the dismissal of a number of Mexican and American stokers. And in mid-1906 two hundred railroad workers went on strike because Hungarians were paid higher wages. The Mexican boilermakers' union asked the president in that year to intervene to prevent more unjustified dismissals of nationals. Porfirio Díaz replied that because industrial competence included elements of biological selection, Mexicans could not be paid the same as foreigners because of the Mexicans' physiological deficiencies, hereditary defects, racial failings, and inexperience in industrial work; only the last reason, inexperience, may have had some validity. At the beginning of 1906, the workers of the Monterrey Casa Redonda Railroad went on strike, complaining about despotic treatment by an American inspector. Similarly, the stokers of the Monterrey Central Railroad struck because an American was given a position that corresponded to that of a Mexican; in this instance, President Díaz ordered some American em-

---

[48]González Navarro, *El Porfiriato*, 316.
[49]Pletcher, *Rails, Mines, and Progress*, 250.

ployees to be fired, possibly to reduce tension between Mexicans and Americans.[50]

Mexicans employed on the Southern Pacific Railroad went on strike amid shouts of "Death to gringos!" on July 1, 1906, because their wages were reduced.[51] In 1908, *El Imparcial* supported an order to make Spanish the exclusive official language of the railroads so that natives could demonstrate their superiority over outsiders. In 1909, American dispatchers resigned because, under terms of the railroad merger, they were obliged to train Mexicans to take the place of foreigners. They also were supposed to share their 150 pesos per month with the Mexican apprentices during the latter's two-year preparation for taking the required examination. When North American workers successfully negotiated payment by kilometer, a majority of the North Americans, Canadians, and English, as well as a few Mexicans, approved this agreement, which lasted two years. In brief, American capitalists rationalized the low wages they paid to Mexican workers in a number of ways: The Mexicans' productivity was lower than that of Americans. Thanks to Mexico's mild climate, there was no need to give the natives a wage increase that they would use to get drunk and then not show up for work. Finally, because the Indians knew only how to drink and to gamble, they could not be trusted to own land.[52] The Porfirian aristocracy and intellectuals agreed with this assessment.

Since the early years of the Porfiriato, a one-hundred- to two-hundred-kilometer strip of land stretching from Piedras Negras to Matamoros had been occupied by a Mexican community whose men were strong, combative, and frugal as well as expert horsemen and marksmen. Those men had still to put down roots on either side of the border. On the American side, the enormous expanse of Texas was sparsely populated. Settlers of Mexican origin were not prosperous enough to have an influence commensurate with their belief that they had once owned that land. The remaining population consisted of recent immigrants from Germany, England, Ireland, Scotland, Poland, and France.[53] Such was the situation when the "salt war" broke out in 1877. After an initial victory, the Mexicans of El Paso were defeated by the Texas Rangers, a victory that meant intensified violence against Mexicans on both sides of the border.

In 1889, Mexicans were deported from McCullock County; the following year, as a result of the lynching of a Mexican in a mining town in Presidio County, both sides suffered dead and wounded. The Anglos

[50]González Navarro, *El Porfiriato*, 304–307.

[51]Ibid., 308–309.

[52]Ruiz, *People of Sonora and Yankee Capitalists*, 13, 23.

[53]Daniel Cosío Villegas, *Historia moderna de México: El Porfiriato. Vida política exterior, segunda parte* (Mexico: Editorial Hermes, 1963), 35.

accused the Mexicans of being mutinous, and the Mexicans called the Anglos racists.[54] According to Victor S. Clark of the U.S. Department of Commerce and Labor, with the exception of a few miners in Sonora and Chihuahua, Mexican immigrants were Indian (in physical appearance, temperament, character, and mentality) with a slight "infusion" of white blood.[55] However, they were very different from the American Indians in their language and religion. Some American companies preferred to hire Mexicans precisely because, thanks to their nomadic nature, they could work anywhere. Perhaps because Mexicans on the American side of the border considered themselves to be superior to those on the other side, they declared that in the event of war between Mexico and the United States, they would fight for their country of birth.[56]

On November 10, 1910, Antonio Rodríguez of Jalisco was burned alive in Rock Spring, accused of having murdered an American woman— naturally, a white woman. The Mexican press reacted violently. *El País* protested that because that sort of punishment was reserved for blacks in its sickening contempt, the killing equated "the sons of Negritude with the scion of Cuauhtémoc, a race not inferior to the porkmen of Chicago, the knights of the hogs." *El Diario del Hogar* observed that if North Americans wished, they could exterminate the blacks, but warned: "Don't pick a quarrel with Cuauhtémoc's race because you are but a vile worm and your venomous lancet will not touch the Spartans of Latin America." If Mexico did not receive satisfaction, the paper declared, Mexicans should not return to the United States, a nation of "blond barbarians." In Mexico City, stones were thrown at the *Mexican Herald* newspaper office and other American businesses and houses, and an American flag was set on fire. In Guadalajara, hometown of the victim, mobs went on a three-day rampage of destruction of homes and stores belonging to Americans, and there was a boycott of American music. At the request of U.S. Ambassador Henry Lane Wilson, three newspapers were shut down in an effort to control the disturbances.[57]

---

[54]Zorrilla, *Historia de las relaciones entre México a los Estados Unidos*, 2:56–57.

[55]Victor S. Clark, "Mexican Labor in the United States," *Bulletin of Bureau of Labor*, no. 78 (September 1909): 467, 469–471, 473, 475, 477–478, 483, 485– 489, 491–492, 494–497, 500, 505, 507–509, 513, 515–516, 521–522.

[56]Moquim, *Documentary History of the Mexican Americans*, 230–233.

[57]Cosío Villegas, *Vida política exterior, segunda parte*, 414–421; Servando Ortoll, "Turbas antiyanquis en Guadalajara en vísperas de la Revolución de Díaz," *Boletín del Archivo Histórico de Jalisco* segunda época, 1, no. 2 (May–August 1983): 7, 12; Gabriel Antonio Menéndez, *Doheny el cruel: Episodios de la sangrienta lucha por el petroleo mexicano* (Mexico: Bolsa Mexicana del Libro, 1958), 218.

The Revolutionary Era, 1911–1940

A much more serious event was the uprising of the Mexican Liberal Party in a fragile alliance with filibusters who attempted to take over Baja California in January 1911. The comedian and politician Dick Ferris was determined to obtain Baja California by purchase or by force. The writer Jack London supported this movement in its early stages; later he withdrew because he was first and foremost a white man and only then a socialist. The filibusters had grave difficulties because of their different languages and nationalities.[58] President Díaz informed the Mexican Congress that the Mexican Liberal Party's army was made up of American filibusters whose fantastic plan was to found a socialist republic. The Liberal Party replied that their ranks did indeed include men who were not of the Mexican race, but who were brothers in their ideals. The Porfirian traitors, it alleged, had forced hundreds of Mexicans to emigrate to the United States by making them "slaves in their own land." In turn, the Mexican consul in Los Angeles, writing under a pseudonym, responded to Ricardo Flores Magón, one of the leaders of the Liberal Party, that, as a Mexican patriot and a *cholo*,[59] he should stop believing in "socialism and other *pendejadas* [asinine ideas] that lead nowhere . . . and that, above all, he should not send any more gringos to Mexico." Although in Tijuana the number of Mexicans in the "expeditionary" army fell to only 10 percent, the Mexican Liberal Party justified the army's composition on the grounds that its foreign members were ideological brothers and that, furthermore, Francisco Madero's revolutionary army included many Americans. Meanwhile, Ferris went on insisting that he would make Baja California a land of white men.[60] Of course, the peninsula did not become either white or socialist, and it did not fall into American hands.

In their youth, a number of prominent Mexicans living on the border with the United States fiercely defended their pride in being Mexican. For example, at the turn of the century, Nemesio García Naranjo, in spite of being white with blue eyes, wealthy, and well dressed, protested the contempt with which Anglos treated poor, brown-skinned Mexican children. At the beginning of this century, José Vasconcelos in Texas had a similar experience to García Naranjo's, as did Abelardo Rodríguez in

[58]D. Wayne Gunn, *Escritores norteamericanos y británicos en México* (Mexico: Fondo de Cultura Económica, 1977), 66; Lowell L. Blaisdell, *The Desert Revolution: Baja California, 1911* (Madison: University of Wisconsin Press, 1962), 39–47, 57, 63, 74.

[59]At the time, the word *cholo* was a pejorative term that referred to lower-class mestizos from the south; Flores Magón was from Oaxaca.

[60]Blaisdell, *Desert Revolution*, 122, 129–130, 133, 139, 149–150, 156, 173, 176, 185–186.

Arizona.[61] On crossing the border at Laredo in 1917, the lawyer Genaro Fernández MacGregor saw a customs officer slap a Mexican laborer, who slunk away in fear. The incident angered him because he perceived it to be a "symbol of the attitude of both races."[62] Not a symbol, but a reality was the murder of 1,477 foreigners during the revolutionary years 1910–1919, of whom 136 were North Americans, including both civilians and military men. The majority—58.4 percent of the total—were murdered in Chihuahua, Tamaulipas, and Sonora. Nonetheless, according to the Mexican consul in El Paso, Texas, American police killed 391 Mexicans in the period from 1911 to 1919.[63] In the opinion of Frederick Turner, the number of North Americans murdered in Mexico during that period was lower than the number of Mexicans lynched in the United States during the five years from 1915 to 1920. Shouts of "Maten a los gringos!" (kill the gringos) and "Kill the greasers!" echoed in both countries.[64]

The U.S. occupation of the port of Veracruz in 1914 provoked a wave of anti-Americanism. For example, the Plan de San Diego, Texas, of January 6, 1915—believed to have been written by the radical John K. Turner—declared that all blacks in the United States would be free on February 20, 1915; that Texas, New Mexico, Arizona, Colorado, and Upper California would be returned to Mexico; that the Indians of Arizona would recover all their lands; and that blacks would be helped to establish an independent republic. In the end, except for an attack on two small towns in Texas in June 1916, this movement was without consequence. Nevertheless, American authorities accused Venustiano Carranza of having ordered the murder of General Emiliano Navarrete to prevent him from revealing Carranza's ties with the authors of this plan.[65]

The Protestant minister Guy Inman boasted that, thanks to his preaching in Coahuila, many young people despised the Latin races for their weakness, their unwillingness to save money, and their lack of respect for

[61]Colección Porfirio Díaz, Mexico, Universidad Iberoamericana, 1:48, 51.
[62]Ibid., 1:58.
[63]Lawrence A. Cardoso, *Mexican Emigration to the United States, 1897–1931: Socio-Economic Patterns* (Tucson: University of Arizona Press, 1980), 62; Moquim, *Documentary History of the Mexican Americans*, 191.
[64]Turner, *Dynamic of Mexican Nationalism*, 212.
[65]Clarence Clemens Clendenen, *The United States and Pancho Villa: A Study in Unconventional Diplomacy* (Ithaca, NY: Cornell University Press, 1961), 235; U.S. Congress, Senate, Committee on Foreign Relations, *Senate Document, Investigation of Mexican Affairs, Preliminary Report and Hearing of the Committee of Foreign Relations, United States Senate pursuant to S. Res. 106 directing the Committee of Foreign Relations to investigate the matter of outrages on citizens of United States in Mexico.* 66th Cong., 2d sess., December 1, 1919–June 5, 1920 (Washington, DC: Government Printing Office, 1920), 9:1201–1224, 1271–1306, 2688.

women—all characteristics attributed to the Mexicans.[66] Unlike Inman, who was a spokesman for peaceful conquest, Senator Albert Fall of New Mexico gathered together a large group of believers in the Big Stick policy. These men vented their spleen on Mexico during 1919 and 1920, but not on Porfirio Díaz because he was only one-sixteenth Indian, not one-quarter, and he was a throwback to a type of conquistador. On the other hand, Fall characterized the Yaqui Indians as the most treacherous people on earth; someone else added that the Indians were savages who believed they had been robbed and were fighting to recover their properties. Another businessman expressed the opinion that Mexicans in the south were more valuable than those in the north, because the latter had inherited the vices of the Indians, with none of their virtues. Two years later, the U.S. secretary of state described the Mexican race as semicivilized.[67] When young George Patton took part in General John Pershing's punitive expedition against Pancho Villa, he found Mexicans to be "half-savage and completely ignorant."[68]

Visitors to the United States such as Carlos González Peña returned the favor. In 1918 he wrote that American road workers were vulgar, dirty, and unpleasant; that they stank of rancid butter and putrid tobacco; and that Mexican *pelados* (penniless nobodies) did not suffer by comparison.[69] One of the risks of such hasty judgments is that the races are easily confused. Salvador Novo, for example, was surprised, even annoyed, when in El Paso, Texas, he heard people who were "obviously Mexican" pretending to speak Spanish with difficulty;[70] they were probably *pochos* (a negative term for Americanized Mexican Americans). The lawyer Genaro Fernández MacGregor, on the other hand, recalled that in 1931 he and his wife were not taken to be foreigners; in Washington even their accents did not make them seem different, because there were so many naturalized Americans in the capital.[71]

[66]Samuel Guy Inman, *Intervention in Mexico* (New York: G. H. Doran, 1919), 53, 78–79, 96, 135, 140, 146–152, 169–171, 177–181, 188–192, 212–213, 223–227.

[67]Senate, Committee on Foreign Relations, *Investigation of Mexican Affairs*, 9:6–7, 27–28, 1406, 1744; 10:2075, 2204–2209, 2218, 2222, 2226, 2403, 2650–2657, 2661–2667, 3343–3345, 3369–3372, 3373; Robert Freeman Smith, "Estados Unidos y las reformas de la Revolución Mexicana, 1915–1928," *Historia Mexicana* 19, no. 2 (October–December, 1969): 211.

[68]Friedrich Katz, *La guerra secreta en México*, 2 vols. (Mexico: Ediciones Era, 1982), 1:353.

[69]Felipe Teixidor, *Viajeros mexicanos (Siglos XIX y XX)* (Mexico: Ediciones Letras de México, 1939), 237, 242.

[70]Ibid., 280–282.

[71]Genaro Fernández MacGregor, *El río de mi sangre: Memorias* (Mexico: Fondo de Cultura Económica, 1969), 345.

In 1929, Manuel Gamio conducted a broad survey of Mexicans in the United States. He employed racial and religious criteria, although he did not define the former because the number of whites was very small and because he could not find a reliable source for that particular figure. His study demonstrates that among Anglos there was widespread contempt for Mexicans, whom some considered to be childlike or crazy, just as Justo Sierra had noted fifty years earlier.[72] Mexican immigrants, like most Mexicans in Mexico, looked down on blacks and Chinese as inferiors. Many complained that neither *pochos*, nor *bolillos* (a slang term for whites), nor the American Federation of Labor (AFL) liked them— apparently out of a mixture of racial prejudice and fear of competition. There is recorded the case of an illiterate wife who extolled the virtues of her spouse because, even though he is "Indian, he is a very good person and a real man." A light-skinned cobbler from Jalisco objected strenuously to a sign in San Francisco that prohibited the entrance of blacks, Mexicans, and unleashed dogs into swimming areas. Notwithstanding his protests to the Mexican consul, the sign stayed up for a long time. This prohibition was also widespread in Los Angeles.

An even more serious example of discrimination occurred on a train traveling from Kansas City to Topeka. Several American passengers screamed at Mexicans riding on the train that they did not want to travel with colored people. When some of the Mexicans vented their anger by shouting at the waiters who refused to serve them, the cowboys shot the Mexicans' hats full of holes. The color white opened many doors, and a person having fair skin and light eyes was considered to be Spanish or Italian. In one case, a Mexican with those physical characteristics and similarly mistaken for a Greek, an Italian, or a Spaniard jokingly replied that he was a Yaqui Indian. In California a Mexican arguing with an Anglo contended that he and his countrymen were legally white, even though they were people of color, because they had no black blood. In Arizona and New Mexico there was less racial discrimination. When a fair-skinned Mexican woman was asked if she was Spanish, she replied that in Mexico there were women with blonde hair and light complexions just as there were in any country of the world. Some American women of Mexican descent preferred Mexicans from Mexico because they were not as vulgar as *pochos*. In contrast, there was the native of Cananea who had emigrated to the United States when he was seven years old. He and his

[72]Manuel Gamio, *Mexican Immigration to the United States: A Study of Human Migration and Adjustment* (Chicago: University of Chicago Press, 1930), xiv–xv; Manuel Gamio, *El inmigrante mexicano: La historia de su vida. Notas preliminares de Gilberto Loyo sobre la inmigración de los mexicanos a los Estados Unidos de 1900 a 1967* (Mexico: Universidad Nacional Autónoma de México, 1969), 87, 94–102.

children were dark-skinned and did not speak English, and they decided to keep their Mexican nationality because their American nationality was of no use to them.[73]

To better understand the importance of race in the United States, it is worth recalling that in the 1920s eugenics, a science whose purpose was to demonstrate the genetic inferiority of blacks and Mexicans, gained respectability.[74] Furthermore, Protestant missionaries opposed the immigration of Mexicans because their Catholicism stood in the way of their becoming Americanized. Some Texans attributed the propensity of Mexicans to return to their homeland to a "homing pigeon" genetic condition; others, without getting involved in anthropological questions, rejected Mexicans because they were not Nordic. A 1924 U.S. law banned entrance to individuals having more than 50 percent Indian blood; but because many Mexicans were pure Indian although culturally mestizo, the law declared that Mexicans were "white" in order to avoid confusion. This measure irritated the AFL because Mexican workers brought down wages. Some AFL members who were openly racist compared Mexican workers to crawling bugs such as the boll weevils of the South.

This racism arose from a 1916 theory that America's greatness, based on its immigrants from northern and western Europe, was threatened by Mexican "bastards," the best example of an inferior race produced by the mixture of bad Indian and good Spanish blood. Some nativists in the United States went to the extreme of maintaining that Mexicans were "born Communists," and there were genetics specialists who predicted that the American Southwest would lose in the twentieth century what it had won in the nineteenth as a result of those contemptible Mexican animals who wanted only to eat, sleep, and fornicate. John C. Box, a Democratic representative from Texas, tried for two years to halt Mexican immigration with the support of labor unions, small farmers, social workers, experts in eugenics, and public welfare agencies. They were defeated by special interest groups that needed cheap labor, despite the fact that enemies of Mexican immigration had contracted with the novelist Kenneth Roberts to "demonstrate" the racial inferiority of Mexicans and to criticize their high cost to the public welfare system.[75]

---

[73]Gamio, *El inmigrante mexicano*, 113–130, 135–151, 153–173, 177–185, 186–201, 203–204, 210–218, 219–228, 230–251, 256–267.

[74]Juan Gómez-Quiñones and David Maciel, *Al norte del Río Bravo: Pasado lejano, 1600–1930* (Mexico: Siglo Veintiuno, 1981), 174.

[75]Mexico, Secretaría de Relaciones Exteriores, *Memoria* (1928–1929), 1566–1567; Cardoso, *Mexican Emigration to the United States*, 111–143; Moquim, *Documentary History of the Mexican Americans*, 251–253; Gómez-Quiñones and Maciel, *Al norte del Río Bravo*, 31–33.

In the years of the Great Depression, racism intensified. The archbishop of San Francisco, who was chairman of California's Commission
on Immigration and Settlement, added yet another reason to those already
mentioned: Mexicans did not assimilate to the United States.[76] Despite
the 1929 crisis, the director of the Department of Agriculture of the Los
Angeles Chamber of Commerce insisted that Mexicans should remain,
whereas the Chamber's manager objected to them as long as there were
unemployed white workers, not because of their skin color but because it
was "a question of citizenship and of law."[77] In response to deportation
measures, voluntary repatriation reached its peak in 1931, a year that coincided with a nationalist campaign in Mexico in favor of "our race, our
economy, and our culture." Meanwhile, the League of United Latin American Citizens won its case before the U.S. Supreme Court, alleging that
Mexicans belonged to the white race and that, therefore, it was illegal to
segregate them in schools for racial reasons.[78]

Throughout the 1930s racial problems contributed to a number of
strikes. In one of the bloodiest, which took place in mid-1933, the authorities of Kern County, California, maintained that their opposition to
the strikers was justified because their obligation was to protect the farmers, the county's best people, and not the Mexicans, who were only "trash.
. . . We herd them like pigs."[79] In 1942 it was reported in Los Angeles
that, for genetic reasons, young men of Mexican descent fought with dag-
gers. Matters worsened the following year, when sailors, soldiers, and
civilians rampaged through Los Angeles for a week attacking "pachucos";
in this they were encouraged by the Hearst newspapers. The fascist countries noted that the Los Angeles police agreed with Hitler's doctrines of
racial superiority. To counter negative publicity, at Nelson Rockefeller's
request the press stopped associating North Americans of Mexican origin
with crime. When the Mexican ambassador in Washington asked the State
Department for a formal investigation of this problem, President
Roosevelt's wife, Eleanor, condemned the racial character of these riots
which, in any event, continued in San Diego, Chicago, and other American cities.[80]

---

[76]Gamio, *Mexican Immigration to the United States*, 118.

[77]Camile Guerin-González, "Repatriación de familias inmigrantes mexicanas
durante la gran depresión," *Historia Mexicana* 35, no. 2 (October–December
1985): 245–272.

[78]Mexico, Secretaría de Relaciones Exteriores, *Memoria* (1931–1932), 328.

[79]Mexico, Departamento del Trabajo, *Memoria* (1933–1934), 197–199;
Mexico, Secretaría de Relaciones Exteriores, *Memoria* (1932–1933), 230–236;
Carey McWilliams, *North from Mexico: The Spanish-Speaking People of the
United States* (New York: Greenwood Press, 1968), 191, 194.

[80]McWilliams, *North from Mexico*, 257–261, 266.

Mexican authorities became very sensitive to U.S. racial discrimination. For example, in 1915 the Ayuntamiento (city council) of Mazatlán banned foreign movies depicting Mexicans as villains. Above all, the Mexican government tried to convince the North American people that, from an ethnological standpoint, Mexicans belonged to the white race and that they therefore had the same rights as Caucasian North Americans. Nevertheless, as late as 1943 the archbishop of San Antonio protested that Mexicans were not allowed to enter some churches.[81] Braceros (Mexican contract workers) resented being treated worse than Japanese laborers.[82] Although there was less racism in California than in Texas, in 1960 the Los Angeles chief of police blamed the "great problem" of the Latinos on the fact that many of them had recently emigrated from "savage tribes living deep in the mountains of Mexico. I do not believe," he declared, "that genes can be ignored when studying people's behavior patterns."[83] Hollywood had agreed with that assessment for many years. In a 1934 movie, *Bordertown*, Paul Muni had played a Chicano rejected by a young society woman because he was a savage who should go back to his tribe in the slums of Los Angeles.[84]

North Americans of Mexican origin held the First Mexicanist Congress in Laredo, Texas, September 14–22, 1911. They were still outraged over the recent lynching of León Cárdenas Martínez and the burning alive of Antonio Rodríguez, neither of which had been punished. Their purpose was to defend themselves against the bad children of Uncle Sam who thought they were superior to Mexicans thanks to the magical word "white."[85] In 1916 the *New Republic* published an optimistic article on how little racial prejudice there was in Texas, where brown-skinned schoolchildren were better than Anglos in writing, drawing, and music; as good in mathematics; and behind only in English.[86] Of course, as has been noted, discrimination continued, as did the ambivalence of North Americans of Mexican origin regarding Mexico, a country they admired for its beauty but where they could never be anything but *pelados*, no matter how hard

---

[81]Mexico, Secretaría de Relaciones Exteriores, *Memoria* (1942–1943), ii, 27–34; *El Pueblo*, April 12, 1915; McWilliams, *North from Mexico*, 272.

[82]*Novedades*, August 22, 1944; Mexico, Secretaría de Economía, *Memoria* (1947–1948), 401–402.

[83]Mexico, Secretaría de Relaciones Exteriores, *Memoria* (1948–1949), 214; *Excelsior*, September 29, 1949; *El Nacional*, June 17, 1952.

[84]Emilio García Riera, *México visto por el cine extranjero* (Mexico: Ediciones Era: Universidad de Guadalajara, Centro de Investigaciones y Enseñanzas Cinematográficas, 1987), 13, 20, 56, 63, 82, 98, 115, 139, 179, 188, 210–211, 215–216, 221, 233–234, 239, 257.

[85]Weber, *Foreigners in Their Native Land*, 145–146, 250.

[86]Moquim, *Documentary History of the Mexican Americans*, 261–262.

they worked.[87] Still, when asked if they were "Spaniards," they replied that they were proud to be Mexicans; and in California, ditties circulated about disgusting Mexican scoundrels who turned their backs on Mexico.[88] This attitude gave rise to the myth of "La Raza" (the race), which includes both North Americans of Mexican origin and Mexicans south of the border. The former called themselves "Mexican Americans," and not a few boasted of being dark skinned like "the dark Virgin of Guadalupe." Others were opposed to this reverse racism, especially when the word "Chicano" began to define the quasi nationality of a subculture. In any event, in 1970 some Mexican Americans decided to substitute the term "pueblo" (people) for "La Raza" because the issue was not ethnic but cultural; basically, they rejected the notion of the "melting pot" in order to reaffirm their own cultural identity.[89]

Mexican immigration law grew increasingly restrictive, especially after 1921 and even more so with the depression of 1929. Its objective was to prevent the entrance of blacks, British Indians, Syrians, Lebanese, Armenians, Palestinians, Arabs, Turks, and Chinese because of "scientific" proof that admixture of their blood would "debase" the race.[90] The population law published on August 29, 1936, proposed to promote *mestizaje*, assimilate foreigners, protect nationals, and educate the indigenous population—in general, "to protect, preserve, and improve the species." For this purpose, it introduced the novelty of different quotas for immigrants depending on their ability to assimilate racially and culturally. The Population Law of 1938 accepted without limitation nationals of the American countries and of Spain, as long as they declared that they had no racial prejudices and were willing to form a Mexican mestizo family. In 1939–1940 the law added the Portuguese; in 1941–1944, all Europeans; and, finally, in 1947 it included the Philippines among the countries of unrestricted immigration.[91] As the new law published ten years later clearly stated, Mexican immigration policy was not discriminatory, but selective.[92]

[87]Ibid., 281.

[88]Gamio, *Mexican Immigration to the United States*, 52, 55, 90, 107, 117, 129–131, 143–145, 198, 201, 211–214.

[89]Gómez-Quiñones and Maciel, *Al norte del Río Bravo*, 197.

[90]Mexico, Secretaría de Relaciones Exteriores, *Memoria* (1925–1926), 158; (1926–1927), 512–513.

[91]*Constitución Política Mexicana con reformas y adiciones . . .* (Mexico: Ediciones Andrade, 1945), 423–460; Mexico, Secretaría de Gobernación, *Memoria* (1939–1940), 221–225.

[92]Mexico, Cámara de Diputados, *Diario de debates* (January 7, 1946), 3–5.

The Myths of *Mestizaje* and Assimilation

The United States and Mexico continue in conflict over the racial differences of their own as well as each other's citizens. Nearly two hundred years after the establishment of the Mexican nation, intergovernmental conflicts are increasingly evident with respect to the northward movement of the Mexican population, the southern movement of U.S. capital, cultural differences, and the treatment of the citizens of each country by the other. The pivotal points of difference are openly expressed by North Americans who compete for jobs, Mexicans who continue to lament the nineteenth-century loss of territory to the United States and fear further intervention, Americans who predict a Mexican reconquest of the U.S. Southwest by sheer force of immigration, and Mexicans who hold their northern-bound countrymen and -women in contempt. Individuals and communities on both sides of the border are divided by the thriving principles of racism.

North America's Shifting Frontier (1713–1853)

North America in 1713 according to the Treaty of Utrecht

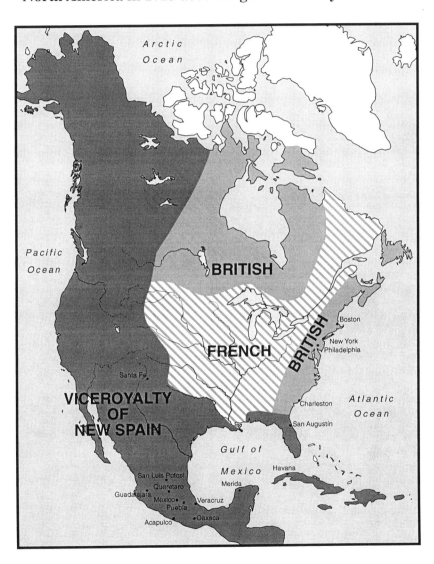

North America in 1763 according to the Treaty of Paris

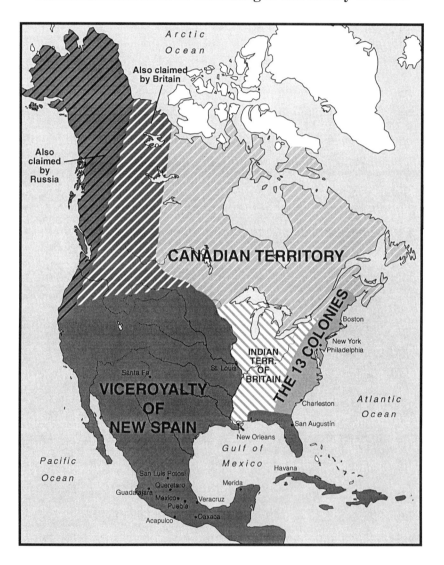

North America, 1803

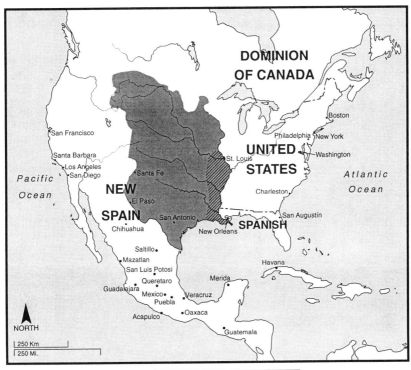

Louisiana Purchase, 1803 according to United States

Louisiana Purchase, 1803 according to Spain

North America according to the Adams-Onís Treaty, 1819

U.S.-Mexican Boundary according to the 1832 Treaty

Texas, 1836

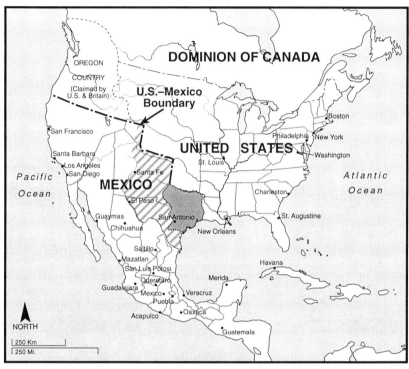

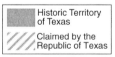

Historic Territory
of Texas

Claimed by the
Republic of Texas

U.S. Invasion of Mexico, 1846–1848

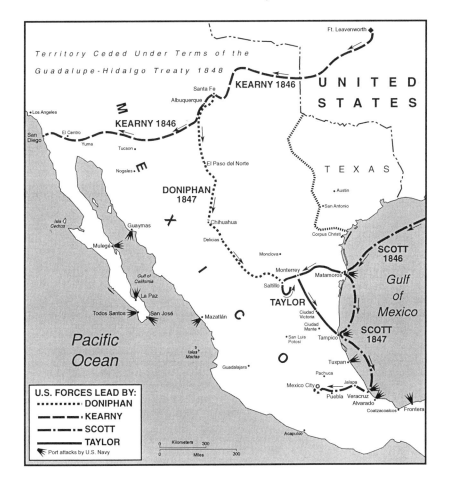

North America, 1853

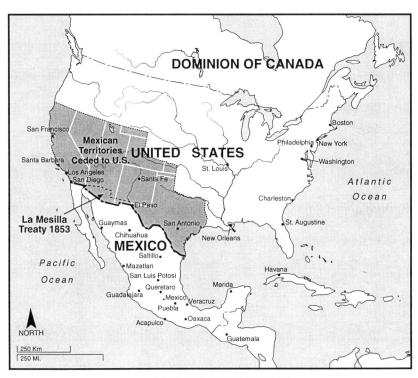

Mexican Cultural Identity in a U.S. City: The Roots of Collective Action in Los Angeles

José Manuel Valenzuela Arce

THE UNITED STATES IS HOME to more than twenty-two million "Hispanics," a vague concept that refers mainly, because of their large numbers, to persons of Mexican origin concentrated in Texas (4.5 million) and California (8 million, with 3.5 million living in the Los Angeles area). Their reality is circumscribed by a number of factors: worldwide ethnic conflicts and xenophobia, the deterioration of the industrial and the expansion of the service sectors, and the political and economic decline of organized labor in the United States.

These structural changes in U.S. society have affected the manner in which the Mexican-origin population has participated in the work force. Immigration policy, such as the Immigration Reform and Control Act (IRCA), also has had an impact. The conditions of many undocumented Hispanics living in the United States changed significantly when they were amnestied; it became possible for them to move about and interact, not only with family members as in the past, but also in the public arena.

IRCA, however, resulted in restrictions for a large number of Mexican-origin workers who were not amnestied and who became the object of increased abuse and discrimination. Many employers took advantage of the situation to pay less than the minimum wage to undocumented workers, who frequently received only ten dollars per day. Joel Ochoa, communications director of the California Immigrant Workers Association (CIWA),[1] cites cases of workers in the garment industry who

---

[1]Interview with Joel Ochoa, communications director of the California Immigrant Workers Association in Los Angeles. CIWA is an AFL-CIO program established with union funds in 1987, after the amnesty law was approved during the Reagan administration. Its objective is to provide social services to its members and facilitate the processing of papers of those individuals in need of regularization.

were paid less than one hundred dollars for a forty- or fifty-hour work week, in addition to many other illegalities that took advantage of the situation of undocumented workers.

These considerations provide the context for an analysis of conflicts involving people of Mexican origin in the United States, particularly in California. Because cultural identities shape collective action, this chapter will examine movements that illustrate a significant ethnicization of social conflicts. It will analyze four manifestations of social action taken by people of Mexican origin: the Mothers of East Los Angeles, the Placita Olvera, the Hotel and Restaurant Workers' Union, and *cholismo*. These are movements that have different rationales, participants, and social contexts but that are connected by the fundamental way in which they protest against the social subordination of people of Mexican origin in the United States. They play a leading role in the construction and reconstruction of the processes of cultural identification on the border between the United States and Mexico, and they help create a spirit of collective social action in the Mexican-origin population in the city of Los Angeles.

Collective Action: The Mothers of East Los Angeles

The Mexican and Chicano barrios of Los Angeles are excellent representations of the socialization and cultural transmission through which Mexican culture has been created and recreated in the United States. The barrios have been the locus for one of the most important collectives involving people of Mexican origin in recent years: a social movement known as the Mothers of East Los Angeles.[2]

Organized by the Catholic church of Santa Isabel and named by Father John Moretta, the Mothers of East Los Angeles began on May 24, 1985. Its original objective was to oppose government plans to construct a state prison in the community. In a television interview, the governor of California argued that he could not understand why the residents of East Los Angeles did not want the prison, considering the fact that its inmates were their own people. The outraged members of the Committee of Mothers of East Los Angeles began a campaign to collect signatures against the prison and to organize protest marches. For more than a year, Monday after Monday, they marched, carrying lighted candles. The movement gained momentum with thirty-six other organizations offering support and as many as thirty-five hundred people joining the marches.

---

[2]In addition to published sources, this section is based on interviews with Juana Beatriz Gutiérrez and Lucy Ramos, leaders of the Mothers of East Los Angeles, and with Father John Moretta of Santa Isabel Church in East Los Angeles.

The Mothers of East Los Angeles movement aroused deep sympathy and popular support in the area, which was inhabited principally by people of Mexican origin. Juana Beatriz Gutiérrez, director of the group, reflected on the community's previous silence in the face of the freeway construction of the 1950s, when many members of the community who were evicted from their residences were incapable of organizing a response: "I believe that our people were sleeping, we did not dare [to act]."[3]

However, the Mothers of East Los Angeles movement went beyond the context of the prison location to incorporate cultural aspects strongly rooted in the daily life of the Mexican-origin population in the United States. The barrio of East Los Angeles is not only a space for the social interaction on which common interests are built, but it implicitly maintains a vigorous cultural production and reproduction where the *nosotros* (we) embraces people who share a language, worldview, life-style, and social status. At the same time, residents perceive that in the United States these identifying characteristics are associated with living conditions that are inferior to those of the Anglo population. Juana Beatriz Gutiérrez comments in this regard that "the majority are people who work, who support themselves, and who do not depend on welfare. What is obvious is that the government pays no attention to this part of the city. Here there are no parks and schools like the ones built in Beverly Hills and the Valley."[4]

In this context, the community opposed construction of an oil pipeline—the same one that already had been rejected by the citizens of Malibu. The pipeline went from Santa Barbara to Carson, and the East Los Angeles community's objections were based on a simple but fundamental position: "If it goes through your yard, it can go through mine; if it cannot go through your yard, don't put it through mine." In April 1987 the Mothers of East Los Angeles led a fight against an attempt to install an incinerator—one that would burn hospital toxic waste—in the area; the community considered it to be a health hazard.

The Mothers of East Los Angeles movement began as an independent organization seeking direct action through use of public arenas, the news media, and legal resources; it has been a major participant in reactive struggles against policies directly affecting the East Los Angeles community. In these confrontations, its demands have met with inertia—members of the Hispanic population living in the area were not considered to be interlocutors in the determination of policies and decisions. In this sense, the movement has challenged a widespread normative practice in the United States.

[3]Josefina Vidal, *La Opinión*, July 27, 1987.
[4]Ibid.

In addition to specific demands related to protection of the population, this movement is aimed at redefining the conditions of interlocution between the Hispanic community and the state and local governments. It is an active way to confront authority and redefine those who should take part in making decisions that concern the community. Furthermore, this movement is political to the extent that it proposes to upset the boundaries set by a system of institutions from which the Hispanic population has been excluded.

Inasmuch as its adversaries have been government representatives, the Mothers of East Los Angeles movement has centered its arguments in a minority-politics style. In such politics, class elements are absorbed into a broader but equally important concept, the *nosotros*, which is the setting of interaction and interrecognition where the identifying traits that become important are primarily associated with ethnic affiliation. An additional, important element in the ideological configuration of the Mothers of East Los Angeles movement has been the participation of the Church, which, as in other community movements, has played a central promotional and organizational role.[5]

The Mothers of East Los Angeles established a bridge that served to mediate between the different levels of social action because community members participate in the movement for a specific objective that directly concerns and affects them in their everyday life and that constructs a double image of the *otros* (others), who assume different faces: on the one hand, the distant authorities and government officials who have the power to make decisions that have a significant impact on the residents of East Los Angeles, and on the other, specific Hispanic government officials who actively participate in the community.[6] In this way, both the macro and micro dimensions of the action are involved because a problem that is rooted in the quotidian setting of the community can be resolved only in the larger dimension of decision making in the state of California. The Hispanic population considers its own action to be an element of mediation between both levels to the extent that it has been publicized through the media and has received attention through the community's connections with assembly members and political personalities.

Even though the East Los Angeles community succeeded in holding up the specific projects mentioned here, the conflict has not yet ended.

---

[5]Although it is evident that religious organizations played an important role, in some cases a leadership role, in the social movements of the Mexican-origin population, it is not currently possible to evaluate their true significance or specific characteristics because that was not one of the objectives of this research. Nevertheless, a careful evaluation of the role of religious organizations in the social movements of U.S. minorities is of major importance.

[6]Gloria Molina and Lucille Royball, for example.

Although the movement has demonstrated its ability to delay the prison and incinerator projects, it is still too early to present a final image of the achievements of the Mothers of East Los Angeles. Nevertheless, the movement has been a cohesive element in the collective action taken by the Mexican-origin population in Los Angeles, as well as in the collectivization of experiences through which large groups of this community found ways to organize themselves and to participate in political life.

The cultural identity of the Mexican-origin population is a crucial cohesive element in social action. The Mothers of East Los Angeles movement cannot be analyzed on the basis of a merely instrumental logic, as presented in the resource-oriented action paradigm. The identity-oriented model better explains this movement's action, bounded as it is by the demarcation of adversaries in which ethnicity plays the distinguishing characteristic.

Collective Memory: The Placita Olvera

Human beings give meaning to life through their acts, their dreams, their utopias, and their projects: These are what weave together the many possible histories that are connected in human interaction.[7] What dominant cultures record, proscribe, and forget is accompanied by memories that live on and are interwoven with popular visions through which the "common people" interpret their reality and participate in constructing a meaning for life. They are interpretations that merge, join together, influence each other, and deny and confront one another. From disputes among these different ways of constructing social and symbolic meaning are derived various positions, differing opinions, and conflicts.

Alessandro Portelli refers to Walter Benjamin's approach, which differentiates between a lived and a remembered act, in which the former is limited to a *life experience* and may even be forgotten, whereas the latter expresses the process of anamnesis in which past is incorporated into present and is limitless to the extent that it embraces what happens before and after the event.[8] Thus, memory recovers past acts and events not as what has happened but as processes that project into the present. Therefore, this recovery means considering the way in which acts are processed, transformed, and interpreted by memory. It is a historical invention that is based on reality, but that involves the interest and desires of those who give it meaning.[9] History also represents a battlefield on which the

---

[7]In addition to published sources, this section is based on an interview with Viviana de Bonzo, leader of the Placita Olvera movement.

[8]Alessandro Portelli, "¿Historia oral? Historia y memoria: La muerte de Luigi Trastulli," in *Historia y Fuente Oral* 1 (1989): 29.

[9]Ibid.

various social groups and actors try to influence its meaning; they seek to be reflected in it and to organize it in accordance with their own plans and desires.

Olvera Street represents the struggle to determine the direction taken by history to mount a symbolic memory confrontation. It is a movement that goes beyond the interests of the individual merchants and residents of the street; the Placita Olvera represents one of the symbolic referents of *mexicanidad* (Mexican identity) in Los Angeles. It is a small area that concentrates Mexican tastes, food, handicrafts, music, and feelings in the very heart of the city. It is a place that acts as memory of origin; nonetheless, it also represents a disputed area in the face of attempts to erase that past and abolish memories. Olvera Street is the symbolic space where subordinate cultures face the *strategy of the imaginary*, which is the dominant vision of those who, holding power, impose their meaning on history.

This is the point where the active dimension of collective memory is located, and it is stressed as a historical fact relevant not to the event but to the memory.[10] Thus, as Regine Robin suggests, by understanding collective memory as that which expresses control of social ownership of the past,[11] one may understand the self-construction of identity to be a *commemorative novel*, a process by which an individual, a group, or a society thinks of its past by modifying it, displacing it, deforming it, and by inventing memories, glorious past forbears, affiliations, and genealogies.[12]

In addition to merchants and community members, the struggle to preserve the Mexican identity of Olvera Street was strongly supported by a group of well-known Chicano intellectuals and artists,[13] including Rodolfo Acuña, Juan Gómez-Quiñones, Luis Valdéz, and Diego Vigil, who organized themselves into a Mexican Conservationist Committee to fight against the dilution of Mexican culture and for preservation of its features from diffusion by multicultural arguments. The committee stressed the Mexican origin of the plaza and pointed out that, even though Chinese and Italian buildings were found there, the people who lived in the area were Mexican. As Acuña said, "People, not buildings, make history"; and Auxiliadora Sánchez summed it up in her statement: "We grew up here and we have lived here all our lives. . . . Many of the buildings were

---

[10]Ibid.

[11]Regine Robin, "Literatura y biografía," *Historia y Fuente Oral* 1 (1989): 69.

[12]Ibid.

[13]On June 22, 1990, nearly three thousand persons marched in demonstrations in defense of Olvera Street, among them Edward James Olmos, Luis Valdez, and Vicky Carr.

owned by people of other races, but their clients and we who live here are all Mexicans."[14]

Olvera Street was named in 1877 for Agustín Olvera, the first magistrate of Los Angeles County, who in 1850 built his adobe house there, joining those built earlier by Francisco Avila and Pio Pico, deputy of San Diego and the last Mexican governor of Alta California. The plaza area was known as Sonora until 1925, and it has been inhabited by Mexicans since 1781, when a dozen people from the area of Sonora and Sinaloa founded the town of Los Angeles. At the end of the 1920s Christine Sterling proposed that Olvera Street be preserved as a symbolic expression of Los Angeles's Mexican heritage. Thus, in April 1930 the street was designated as a place to celebrate Mexican culture, where *posadas* (Christmas festivities) would be held and the patriotic Mexican anniversaries of May 5 and September 16 would be commemorated.

In 1984, when Olvera Street was declared a historical monument, it came under the administration of the State Department of Parks and Recreation. The Los Angeles City Council contracted with The Old Los Angeles Company to rehabilitate and manage what was identified as the Pico-Garnier area (the Pico Building, the Merced Theater, the Masonic Temple, and the Garnier Building). Unfortunately, neither the state, county, nor city gave it adequate support, and in addition the project was interrupted in 1986 due to changes in federal tax laws that prevented The Old Los Angeles Company from making use of a number of tax exemptions that were part of the original contract. The controversy grew more heated when on March 22, 1990, the Los Angeles Board of Scholars[15] declared that the redevelopment plan proposed for the Placita Olvera by the Association of Olvera Street Merchants gave too much emphasis to the Mexican role in that area.[16]

The proposal for making Olvera square multicultural argues that the Mexican role there has been overemphasized. On the other hand, those, like Alfonso Ríos-Bustamante, who have committed themselves to defending the little square as a Mexican cultural center reply that not only has the Mexican presence not been overemphasized, but that it also has not been sufficiently represented. They have questioned also the motives of the state government in stressing the multicultural features of the supposed founders, without taking into account the real native settlers (primarily Indians and Mexicans).

[14]*Unión Hispana*, May 4, 1990.

[15]A private group of historians who were against the redevelopment plan for the Placita Olvera because their historic interpretation differed from that of the Association of Olvera Street Merchants.

[16]Roberto Rodríguez, "Group Fights for Presence on Olvera St.," *Hispanic Link Weekly Report* 8, no. 22 (June 1990).

The Placita redevelopment project was subjected to a study to determine its economic feasibility. In response to the demands of a community fighting to preserve the plaza as a cultural center, an "expert" hired by the state of California decided that there was nothing historical to preserve.[17] In June the City Commission on Parks and Recreation approved a plan to permit private urban development companies to participate in restoring the Placita, and it also offered merchants the possibility of collaborating in the project as partners, through capital investment.[18] For its part, the Association of Olvera Street Merchants declared the street to be an element in defending and upholding cultural memory. Thus, the Placita Olvera became the symbol of a struggle to reclaim the Mexican past in the face of the proposal to give more importance to "other cultures," and symbolically it is a dispute over integration of the past as a referent for organizing the present.[19]

[17]People were divided over the Olvera Street issue, but the Mexican population was certain that the plaza belonged to them. Nevertheless, the principal leaders of the Mexican-origin population assumed different positions. Gloria Molina backed the defenders of Olvera Street, whereas Richard Alatorre approved the plan presented by the City Commission on Parks and Recreation. Molina, for example, declared: "We need to rapidly develop a major plan in order to take the lead in preserving the birthplace of Los Angeles." *Noticias del Mundo*, June 12, 1990.

[18]*La Opinión*, June 19, 1990. The redevelopment plan approved on June 11, 1990, consisted of a $30-million project; the city of Los Angeles would contribute $16 million and the rest would come in equal parts from the redevelopment company and local businesses.

[19]Juan Gómez-Quiñones stated: "The office of the park curator has not served to educate the public, mainly because of incompetence. Instead, it has served as the vehicle for a pernicious idiosyncrasy and as the organizer of pressure groups to oppose the Mexican community. In both instances, the curator has shown little professionalism and given proof of anti-Mexicanism." In addition, he asserted:

> Moreover, the need for commercial development and to improve the structures at a cost of 30 million dollars is given as the reason for granting multimillion-dollar investors a major role. But public funds in the amount of sixteen million dollars are now available for earthquake improvements. Also, the businessmen are to raise 15 million in order to retain their businesses. Thus, the real estate developers will use public funds, demand money from the merchants and also keep 50 percent of the property. There is no compelling reason to make any real estate investor dominant. Nor is there any adequate explanation why the Pueblo complex should be divided among different authorities. The Pueblo is public property, from north to south, from east to west.

Juan Gómez-Quiñones, "Momento decisivo: El pueblo vs. inversores inmobiliarios," *La Opinion*, June 24, 1990.

The movement on Olvera Street began as a protest intended to defend the specific interests of the merchants on the square. But the movement's ideological boundaries—as defined by its symbolism, its forms of organization, and its means of action—thrust it into the political arena, where it openly confronted an institutional vision that endeavors to diminish the Mexican-origin population's cultural influence. Thus, the most important feature of the struggle is the symbolic connotation of Olvera Street as a founding referent, as a cultural marker of *mexicanidad*, or as someone observed, as the heart of that *mexicanidad*.

The battle of Olvera Street expresses the struggle for the cultural identity of the Mexican-origin population in the United States in the desire for referents that are not just nostalgic or affective figures, but elements setting the order and norms of action that, in their evolution, contend for their participation in the social construction of space. For this reason, the defense of Olvera Street summoned forth not only the merchants but also the people of the community and Chicano activists who, in theoretical or emotional ways, perceived that stripping Olvera Street from the Mexican community signified taking away something that belonged to them, symbolically attacking them, and breaking a visible link in their historical memory.

The Olvera Street movement, like that of the Mothers of East Los Angeles, offers no guarantee that its objectives have been attained. Nevertheless, the immediate results have been successful: The plan to transform the little square into a multicultural center has been stopped.[20] One of the most significant consequences of the movement to defend Olvera Street was that it gave rise to public discussion and unified various Chicano groups and political personalities who lent support and committed themselves to the defense of the plaza. They regarded the struggle as a search for forms of redefinition of the social participation of minority groups.

The movements to which we have referred here are unique in that they included widespread community participation and the support of various Chicano organizations. This phenomenon could be related to the double process of differentiated access to jobs and of barrio segregation, but it also employs different forms of social interaction where collectivization is associated not so much with a class—which is also present—as with an ethnic identification.

[20]On June 2, 1992, the citizens of the city of Los Angeles voted not to open for bidding the businesses of the Placita Olvera. They granted the merchants of the area the right to negotiate long-term contracts, although the length of those agreements was not determined.

Collective Bargaining: The Hotel and Restaurant Workers' Union[21]

During the last twenty years there have been widespread and drastic changes in job structure in the United States.[22] In the 1960s the city of Los Angeles was an important industrial center, with 30 percent of its work force employed in manufacturing—a considerably higher percentage than in the rest of the country. However, the situation changed dramatically in the 1969 to 1988 period. The service sector expanded while manufacturing diminished.[23] Services became the most important employment base and industries producing durable goods like steel and automobiles lost their relative significance. Within manufacturing, industries were divided into two groups: those using very high and those using very low technologies.[24] As a result of these changes, the work force in the city of Los Angeles has undergone a process of deindustrialization, Hispanization, and feminization. The economic recession has reinforced some of these features, especially as regards the supply of labor and number of hours worked, the payment of wages below the legal minimum, and unsafe and exploitative working conditions, typically issues around which labor unions are organized.[25]

Paradoxically, the restructuring of labor unions in Los Angeles depends on incorporating and organizing the mainly Chicano and other Hispanic labor population, which sometimes faces discrimination and stereotyping connected to old prejudices directed mainly against immi-

[21]This section is informed by an interview with María Elena Durazo, secretary general of the Hotel and Restaurant Workers' Union.

[22]Morales and Ong indicate that it is not an exaggeration to consider the United States (and in that country, Los Angeles) as the primary generator of growth in the world economy. To illustrate: "During the decade of the seventies the work force in the United States grew by 25 percent (from 82.8 million to 105 million people), one of the most rapid growth rates in the world." Rebecca Morales and Paul Ong, "Immigrant Women in Los Angeles," *Economic and Industrial Democracy* 12, no. 1 (February 1991): 65–81.

[23]The earlier tendency occurred even though in absolute terms manufacturing jobs grew only from 880,000 to 904,000; nevertheless, Los Angeles has not experienced the high levels of deindustrialization that other areas, such as Chicago, have experienced; during this period, Chicago lost 324,000 manufacturing jobs, and New York lost 406,000. Ibid. However, this situation has changed during recent years.

[24]Morales and Ong demonstrate this process for the city of Los Angeles, citing as the high-tech industries aerospace, communications, and electronics: among labor-intensive industries, textiles, clothing, and furniture grew at a time when these industries were declining in other parts of the United States.

[25]Throughout the different areas of Los Angeles, one may observe workers forming lines early in the morning along certain corners in hopes of their being hired by someone.

grant workers, who are considered to be responsible for unemployment and lower wages or are openly accused of being scabs. Labor unions must abandon their old attitudes of indifference to active participation by Hispanic workers and their prejudices that sought pretexts to keep them out, including the recurrent one of language. Demographic changes, particularly those that are increasing the representation of Hispanics in the work force, require that Hispanic workers' demands, needs, and political culture be taken into account by labor unions. In fact, recent experience includes union movements made up mainly of Hispanic workers. Some, notably the hotel and restaurant workers, have been successful.

More than fifty years ago, hotel and restaurant workers of Los Angeles began to unionize with the support of labor organizers from the San Francisco area. Waiters, cooks, chambermaids, and bellhops launched a number of independent movements in spite of laws restricting strikes, work stoppages, and demonstrations. Workers who organized faced repression and even, at times, prison. The different groups that until then had operated separately joined together in 1975 into a single labor union under a contract that covered approximately twenty-two thousand workers.

In subsequent years, two major transformations affected the union. First, Hispanic workers, even though they had always participated, increased their membership dramatically. And second, the hotels and restaurants became parts of huge national and international chains and corporations. The latter development, especially, presented new challenges to labor leaders who proved incapable of responding satisfactorily to the new reality.

In Los Angeles the leaders of Local 11 of the Hotel and Restaurant Workers' Union began to abandon their earlier policy of working with the community and with other unions to resolve labor problems. As a result, the union's strength and membership declined, and by the end of the 1980s it had less than thirteen thousand members. Old racist attitudes continued to thrive among union officials. Although 70 percent of the members were Hispanic, the officials rejected workers' demands that agreements reached by the union should be translated into Spanish and that bilingual meetings should be held. Furthermore, neither the union's organizers nor the office staff spoke Spanish, and its newspaper appeared only in English, demonstrating the leadership's lack of interest in increasing participation by the Hispanic workers who accounted for the majority of its membership. The dispute was taken to court, eventually reaching the California Supreme Court. The lawsuit "cost the Hotel and Restaurant Union hundreds of thousands of dollars," according to the testimony of María Elena Durazo, president of Local 11. The union lost the lawsuit to the workers; ironically, the union's members paid the expenses of a trial in which their own representatives presented anti-Hispanic racist arguments.

A struggle over control of the union local began. In public acts and in the news media there emerged a confrontation between two visions of the Hispanic population.[26] One reflected the views of the racist union leadership, then dominated by Anglo males; the other, led by a Hispanic woman, represented a group sensitive to labor and social discrimination. The old union leaders were opposed not only by union members but also by members of the Los Angeles Hispanic community. (The movement was supported by Gloria Molina, for example, at that time a member of the Los Angeles City Council.) The conflict ended when the secretary of the Los Angeles local left the city and vanished, forcing the union's national headquarters to take charge of the situation. In April 1989 the union's national officials held elections in which María Elena Durazo won a significant victory with almost 85 percent of the vote. Thus, she became the first Hispanic woman to head a sizeable union local in California—one that represents most of the hotels in the Los Angeles area, including East Los Angeles and more than 140 restaurants.

At present, Local 11 of the Hotel and Restaurant Workers' Union has 180 delegates, 25 percent of them women and 90 percent Hispanic. The office staff, organizers, and representatives are Hispanic and almost all of them speak Spanish. Furthermore, most contracts are translated into Spanish, the organization's newspaper and meetings are bilingual, and its benefits include legal assistance in immigration matters. The local was the first in the United States in which the organization of undocumented workers and protests against the raids practiced by the Immigration and Naturalization Service were proposed.

A core demand of this organization has been recognition of seniority, which is important because the economic recession has had an effect on the number of hours per week worked by hotel and restaurant employees, with certain advantages enjoyed by those with the greatest seniority. The local also has protested against the racist and sexist attitudes of many hotels and restaurants, which restrict Hispanic men to work as waiters and kitchen helpers, while relegating Hispanic women to work as chambermaids.[27]

[26]The conflict included a legal struggle because union officials refused to give the opposition group its membership lists.

[27]The union has been involved in the following conflicts: (1) eleven female employees of the Hyatt Hotel chain, among them María Elena Durazo, were arrested on October 17, 1989, while demanding working conditions and benefits similar to those already received by other workers in the state and nation. The company, which has about 1,300 workers, the majority (79 percent) Hispanic,

The Hotel and Restaurant Workers' Union movement is of special interest because of the way in which collective action was structured. It hinged not so much on economic demands—even though the people working in this branch of the industry received very low wages—but on the discrimination practiced against them by their own union representatives. The traditional union structure circumscribed the manner in which change could be organized from within. Thus the movement incorporated various external organizations and political figures, chiefly organizations with large Hispanic membership but also organizations that engage in community work.

Like the participants in the movements of the Mothers of East Los Angeles and for the defense of Olvera Street, the Hispanic hotel and restaurant workers resorted to public action and to large-scale use of the media to expose the discrimination against the Hispanic population in the workplace. The movement was successful insofar as it overcame the entrenched opposition to Hispanic participation in the leadership and benefits of union activities. It offers a clear example of the future for many of the labor organizations in Los Angeles. A major demand will be action against segregation through language. While demands for higher wages and better working conditions have been central to union activities in this sector, the active Hispanic presence in the union has given a strong Hispanic cultural accent to its actions and demands.

Collective Identity: *Los Cholos*[28]

One of the characteristics of the 1950s in the United States was a sharp rise in the birthrate. During that period, population increased by twenty-eight million, and over 40 percent of the postwar population was

---

required them to work ten-hour days, without overtime pay, and it was unwilling to grant paid holidays, such as Martin Luther King Day. (2) In June 1988 more than 3,000 workers marched, demanding a new contract for employees in the hotels of Los Angeles and Beverly Hills. They were supported by the American Federation of State, County, and Municipal Employees (AFSCME), the public employees' union, which has 1,150,000 members. (3) On January 24 the Bel Air Company refused to pay the back wages that had been negotiated in the contract, causing a work stoppage. (4) Finally, there was a boycott of Canter's, the largest fast-food restaurant in Los Angeles, because it had refused to pay health and retirement benefits, was unwilling to raise salaries, and had initiated a racist campaign of intimidation. The restaurant had changed working hours and fired those workers who arrived late, declaring: "Go back to Mexico; we don't want you here." Also, it had accused workers of having AIDS; and, as an act of intimidation, it stuck pins in voodoo dolls that represented immigrant workers.

[28]This section is based on interviews with *cholos* from different barrios of East Los Angeles, persons involved with youth programs, and mothers of *cholos*.

less than twenty years old. Not only did this situation accelerate the process of urbanization, but it also created conditions for various forms of collective expression by the young people of the United States. Nonetheless, above and beyond the "counterculture" attitudes that prevailed among the young, it became important in the barrios inhabited by Mexicans and Chicanos to maintain an identity defined mainly through ethnic loyalties.

The pachuco of the 1940s and 1950s began to be replaced by a new and widespread expression among Mexican-origin urban youth in the barrios of Los Angeles:[29] *cholismo*. The term was an old concept that took on a new meaning,[30] primarily through informal networks of young people who shared similar experiences (tastes, cultural referents, economic disadvantages, feelings of impotence, resocializing processes, discrimination due to ethnic origin, the redefinition of traditional forms of family organization, the drug use that "emerges" in all social sectors, dependence on violence to determine boundaries of power, and segregated barrios) that served to nurture cultural practices and symbolic referents.

Cholismo highlights, above all, the use of symbolic elements as a way to delineate the cultural profile of what is Mexican, as a flamboyant form of recovering and reinventing the past, and as a reserve of resistance for the Chicano movement. Elements such as murals, drawings, and tattoos were used by the movement to exhibit its loyalties and to demarcate its allegiances. Predominant among the *cholos* (those who practice *cholismo*) have been religious images of the Virgin Mary and Jesus Christ, symbols of the homeland represented by the Mexican Indian and Mexican flag, nostalgic hometown tales, and daily experiences of a life marked by violence, drugs, lust, and death. Living "homies" (hometown boys or "homeboys") have their deeds and might recorded in their *placasos* (nicknames), but the memory of those killed in interbarrio battles is perpetuated in murals or graffiti. In a multicultural city like Los Angeles, the importance of visual discourse is fundamental. If, as Carlos Monsiváis has pointed out, mural painting in postrevolutionary Mexico was a simple didactic way to transmit ideological messages to a generally illiterate population, in Los Angeles visual discourse plays a primordial role. It is fitting that Los Angeles should be considered the "city of murals," which is the way the multiethnic discourse of the city is made explicit.

[29]According to the 1930 U.S. census, more than half of Mexican-origin families lived in urban areas. Richard Griswold del Castillo, *La familia: Chicano Families in the Urban Southwest, 1848 to the Present* (Notre Dame, IN: University of Notre Dame Press, 1984).

[30]On the origins of *cholismo*, see José Manuel Valenzuela Arce, *¡A la brava ése! Cholos, punks, chavos banda* (Mexico: El Colegio de la Frontera Norte, 1988).

In the United States, where the constituent symbols of national identity are those of power and violence and there is admiration for the military, it is natural that many young people should express themselves by
joining the armed forces. This was the case of *cholismo* through the *vatos*
(boys) who went to war. These young men went to distant lands to defend
their country and *democracy* as a means of constructing a glorious return
that would enable them to open doors to upward mobility and to win greater
social acceptance.

Cholos are homogeneous because of their poverty, their background,
and their generational affinities, and also because of their collective identity based on the culture they share as Mexicans. Some of the elements
repeatedly found in *cholismo* are broken homes, lack of family understanding, and loneliness. Their families are subject to profound transformations that create feelings of cultural shame: parents and children
speaking different languages and conflicts arising from the processes of
resocialization and of shaping a cultural meaning to give order to life.
These conditions make it difficult to define family standards of behavior,
because they involve different meanings for roles and relationships. The
failure of primary socialization processes faced with the reorganization
of family relations, the limitations and shortcomings of the educational
system as regards the needs of the Hispanic population—particularly the
Chicano and Mexican—and the absence of positive identity referents to
reinforce self-esteem combine to determine the fatalistic vision observed
in *cholos*. This vision is manifested in many self-destructive ways, especially in interbarrio killings and drug use.

In the barrio, *cholos* find the fundamental element of resocialization
within which they channel their emotional needs, feelings of belonging,
and power. The majority cultural settings do not offer them options in
which they might see themselves reflected. Starting out with numerous
negative reinforcements, *cholos* have discovered that they are not Anglo,
that they are discriminated against, and that the culture of the United States
is not their culture; neither, however, do they identify with their parents'
culture. Their hybrid condition denotes an inferior status, established on
the basis of limitations deeply rooted in tradition, language, skin color,
and socioeconomic level. Much of the response to the barrio youth organizations has consisted of police activities and educational programs. The
barrios, however, reflect the serious problems existing in U.S. society,
especially among all young, poor minorities. There are played out the
cultural conflicts and biases of the primary and secondary socialization
processes, as well as the differentiated forms of the integration of ethnic
groups within institutional processes.

A particular distinction of the *cholos* is their "shocking" dress. What
is their purpose in wearing such strange and garish clothes? It does not

represent the extravagance of the punks or the domesticated rebellion of the New Wave; rather, it signifies taking daily symbols out of context, decodifying them, accentuating their features, integrating them as elements of identity demarcation, using them to denote nonconformity and to stir up suspicion of those peculiar identities assumed by the poor. Let us look at the symbolic components of *cholismo*.

With old songs, romantic ballads and rock music of the 1950s and 1960s, and ambivalent nicknames that stand for both power and defenselessness, the *cholo* takes risks with an image of stoicism, a show of courage, and the security offered him by his barrio; but he lacks social standing and economic resources, and he has no defense against police extortion and roundups. His means of expression are as limited as his status; his language is impoverished, and he uses more gestures than words. Life is hazardous, unpredictable, and the number 13 is therefore an echo of uncertainty. His range of interaction is small and narrow, and for this reason his loyalties are limited to his barrio, to his family: "My barrio is my *cantón* (home), it's my 'homeboy' (meaning friend), because all my *compas* (short for *compañeros*, or buddies) are there."

In clothing, the *cholos* express these images: *güainitas* or *tecatitas*, which are sandal-like shoes made of cloth, used in work that requires long hours of standing; Levi's or dickies, which are the men's work pants (also used by *cholas* [young women]) that come in khaki, blue, gray, and green colors and are the brand imposed by the rhythm of the industry; Pendleton shirts, which are flannel work shirts worn in cold weather; *paliacates* (large kerchiefs) for the head, which are an atavistic tradition originating in the countryside and which have been widely used by construction workers to wipe off sweat; *mallas*, which are a kind of hair net and make clear the tertiary nature of the Mexican work force in the United States, where they are used as a hygienic measure; sleeveless cotton tank tops, which are used as undershirts in cold weather or as work shirts in hot weather; *güainitas* and the thick rubber bands that are used in some stages of industrial production and usually wrapped around workers' hands.

These "strange" garments were taken from the workplace to become part of the *cholo*'s eccentric wardrobe outside his job. They are visible signs of his employment, daily objects that, when transferred to other settings, seem threatening and designed to attract criticism. The apprehension they arouse is not due to the objects as such, but to the use made of them as elements of a group identity and the way in which the dominant groups and society as a whole perceive them.

Cholos also decodify fundamental symbols of the cultural profile of Mexicans, such as the Virgin of Guadalupe, angels, Christ, symbols of the homeland, images of the Mexican woman, and habitual aspects of the barrio and familiar routines that in group consumption become distant and exotic signs. The compulsive use of these symbols denotes the available landmark of identity, the founding myths that are magnified so that they will not fade away and that are altered so that they may be better represented.

The sign of belonging to an ethnic group is worn on the epidermis, and profound identities take on a theatrical air, a presence that is a challenge and a statement. Therefore, symbols are boldly displayed on the wardrobe; they are declarations of loyalty that adhere to the skin, that are stamped on walls, their walls. There is room for everything on these walls, even for the deceased, who are integrated into the life of the barrio in anecdotes, memories, and graffiti. They are signs of belonging, the available ways to say *yo* (I), *nosotros* (we), my *jefa* (boss, extended to mean mother), my *novia* (girlfriend), my *carnales* (buddies; literally, blood brothers), my *torcida* (imprisoned person), my *compa fileready* (friend who was knifed) or *cuiteado* (shot), my barrio, my *jale* (job), my *raza* (group), my relationships, my everyday life. In addition, there are imaginary affiliations, derived from the generic setting, that indicate my homeland, my city, my past, and my founding myths.

The lowrider is associated with the *cholo*, who objectifies his distances in his car equipped with hydraulic shock absorbers and sometimes even painted with murals. Driving around in his *ranfla* (*cholo*-style car), the lowrider fulfills *cholo* fantasies. His car's bodywork is an altar to his identity. *Cholos* select "oldies," old cars that, like their social status, are low; those who make them higher are imitating the gringo. Although his symbols are conventional, with the exception of graffiti and some of his language, the code to their meaning must be searched for within the *cholo*'s quotidian setting, his life experiences, his interpersonal networks.

Gangs are observed to have heteroclite motivations and behavior, as well as various forms of organizing a meaning for life that are inscribed in the groups' cultural constitution, their histories, and their socioeconomic conditions.[31] *Cholos* act according to codes of honor and pride that define them. The *cholo* and *chola* live in a constant process of proving themselves; it begins with rites of initiation into the barrio where the young man or woman almost always must confront several barrio members.

[31]Black youth gangs organized themselves according to a materialist logic. Chinese gangs, whose members have higher levels of education and organization, do not act within a barrio or corner context and do not require symbolic elements to identify them as part of a group. White gangs, however, focus on racial elements; they do not claim a barrio or territory, but a race. Their action is more symbolic. They exist to assert and propose, while the Mexican gangs exist to remonstrate. Interview with Harold Westner, coordinator of Programa de Asistencia Estudiantil de Los Angeles.

Furthermore, life in the barrio requires meeting many demands, including in some cases obedience to veteran members and knowing how to respond to affronts against one's turf, one's graffiti, and any other gang member.

The identity acquired by belonging to the barrio incorporates a bravery continually subject to tests that become vitally important and that have entered an uncontrollable dimension in which honor is not tested against itself, or even against members of other barrios, or society as a whole, but against death. Death is not consigned to the future or to probability, but exists as a daily certainty; this is one of the most profoundly distinctive characteristics delimiting the expression of *cholismo*.

Without generic referents and indifferent to the options offered by institutional proposals, *cholos* live in the present and maintain a fatalistic vision within their quotidian setting. They do not cross the boundaries of their generic setting except in terms of an implicit delimitation that reproduces the ethnic differentiation found in U.S. society. This vision is expressed in the words of one of the *cholos*: "*Raza con raza*, we are killing each other." The barrio also redefines social roles. Although not an area of greater equality, the codes of the barrio embrace both men and women. *Cholas* take part in almost the same activities as men, and they occupy similar positions in daily routine.

Within the transborder quotidian setting, *cholos* appear to be readopting a symbolism that flourished as a means of cultural resistance during the Chicano movement and that spilled over into the barrios. The Chicanos returned to founding myths as a resource to bolster a proscribed identity. They made use of symbolic referents to direct their action. These symbols were incorporated into the barrios, where the *cholos* took them up as elements demarcating identities and group differences.

Intense interaction in the transborder quotidian setting made it possible for *cholismo* to expand on both sides of the border. The generic setting contributed to the recovery of symbolic elements anchored in a common origin: the Virgin of Guadalupe, homeland symbols, the image of the Mexican Indian, the *charra* (Mexican cowgirl), the mother. In its religious symbolism the barrio mimics the global community. Nevertheless, symbols also are constructed from the quotidian setting—violence, the barrio, death, madness. The decodifying of symbolic products in terms of their specific ownership and use gives meaning and directionality to the action of groups. Therefore, the *cholo's* expression has been formed from the use of everyday objects.[32]

---

[32]It is pertinent to note that *cholismo* arises from objective conditions of life as experienced by these young people and that it is this common experience that

Cultural Identity as the Basis for Collective Movements

This chapter has examined different experiences of social action in which the Mexican-origin population of Los Angeles has played a leading role. This is a population that, like other minority groups, suffers from many disadvantages in society as a result of sociocultural inequality. In addition, the Mexican-origin population disputes with the dominant culture in the U.S. symbols in which identities and variabilities are constructed. That struggle affects the country's image, which is historically organized in terms of a dominant culture that is highly racist and discriminatory. Therefore, the movements analyzed in this work, regardless of their specific motivations, appear in a setting of symbolic demarcations where ethnicity, even more than class affiliation, is the central factor in forming a collective.

Los Angeles exhibits a significant social polarization, characterized by a process of economic reorganization, deteriorating living conditions, and increasing inequality in income distribution, as well as a substantial number of immigrants, young people, and women who enter the labor market in disadvantageous conditions. The major features of this situation are a trend toward deindustrialization; the growing importance of the service sector; the Hispanization of a labor force that works in disadvantageous and often discriminatory conditions, especially the undocumented workers; and the feminization of the labor force, in which women are the ones who face conditions of greatest exploitation and lowest earnings. One of the basic features observed not only in Los Angeles but all over the United States is the presence of a sociocultural division of opportunities that is expressed at the occupational, social, political, and cultural levels.

Traditional collective positions are weakened in the face of a neoliberal discourse that proclaims individualism and education as the univocal way to social advancement but that closes its eyes to inequality, poverty, and racism. Some workers seem to internalize this discourse, attributing their poverty to the fact that "we have no education." By accepting this argument, they abandon the goal of achieving dignity in their work as well as demands for a wage enabling them to live decently. Thus, the apparent alternative would be to get more education rather than to be treated with respect and to recover lost work opportunities and benefits. Furthermore, in U.S. society there is a marked gender distinction that is reflected in women being paid less than men in all ethnic groups. This situation especially affects Hispanic and black women, who are found at

---

permits them to construct symbols of identity. See Valenzuela Arce, *¡A la brava ése!*

the lowest levels of the work structure, confirming the prevalence of an important division of opportunities based on ethnic and gender variables.

Formal organizations such as the Hotel and Restaurant Workers' Union, community movements such as the Mothers of East Los Angeles and the defenders of the Placita Olvera, and, at the informal level, *cholismo* share cultural identity referents that constitute fundamental elements for shaping the social action of the Mexican-origin population in the United States. Cultural identities make it possible to identify the group and its differentiation from the *otros* (others), who share neither the characteristics nor the objectives of the collective identity.

Cultural Relations between
the United States and Mexico

Carlos Monsiváis

THE CULTURAL RELATIONSHIP between the United States and Mexico is an inexhaustible and all-pervasive subject that is, in fact, one of the three or four major themes of contemporary Mexico. How is it possible to describe the cultural network linking two countries that share a border of almost three thousand kilometers? What is the history of the impact of one culture on the other, of the resistances, the compromises, the assimilations? Cultural relations influence everything, and they have been operating continuously and tenaciously for two centuries. This essay arbitrarily uses the 1950s as the starting point for trends that actually began much earlier; but one has to start somewhere.

The Routes of Pilgrimage: From Chalma to Disneyland

During the four successive administrations of Presidents Adolfo Ruiz Cortines (1952–1958), Adolfo López Mateos (1958–1964), Gustavo Díaz Ordaz (1964–1970), and Luis Echeverría Alvarez (1970–1976), Mexico's Americanization steadily advanced in the midst of emotional outbursts of nationalist and Third World sentiment and an officially voiced nostalgia. In August 1961 the Latin American governments meeting in Uruguay (Cuba was absent) signed the Charter of Punta del Este, which was part of the Alliance for Progress strategy promoted by the government of John F. Kennedy. In its opening lines, the charter states: "We, the American Republics, hereby proclaim our decision to unite in a common effort to bring our people accelerated economic progress and broader social justice within the framework of personal dignity and political liberty."[1]

[1]The Charter of Punta del Este, in Lincoln Gordon, *A New Deal for Latin America: The Alliance for Progress* (Cambridge: Harvard University Press, 1963), 118.

In 1962, John and Jacqueline Kennedy arrived in Mexico City. Their Catholicism, the aura of ecstatic publicity that surrounded them, and the historic reconciliation promoted by the Mexican government achieved what no one had expected: The visit was a huge success.

In the ringing words of an obscure primary-school teacher, who subsequently drowned in an attempt to cross the Río Bravo, the "first generation of North Americans born in Mexico" had emerged. This "denationalization" was reinforced by a discredited state ideology, the bureaucratization of civic education, the exhaustion of traditions now rendered "ineffective," the ceremonial use of patriotism against North American protectionism, and ideological onslaughts from the right wing. Many Mexicans increasingly held a private idea of what was *national* and harbored their concept of *madre patria* (motherland) in their most intimately held mythologies.

At the same time, the logic of social development required closer attention to the North American model. What in the 1950s had been admired from a distance now took on urgency. To "denationalize" was to acquire psychological solvency and social fluidity and to constantly compare Mexico unfavorably to the United States. The latter's racism and rampant exploitation of natural resources were overlooked, and there were those who accepted, as the only true version, the Hollywood image of Mexicans. It was no longer necessary to propagate the Black Legend of "primitives." The stupor of a middle class that had become Americanized—that is, "modernized" through a process of reverential imitation—cut down on the need for control mechanisms. And among Mexico's upper classes it became fashionable to speak of belonging to two countries, one by birth and the other by virtue of life-style and the ability to rapidly accommodate the mind-set of the "man of his time."

Still, broadly based fear of being infected by "alien cultures" only exacerbated feelings of weakness and vexation. Its geographic proximity to the triumphs of international capitalism meant that Mexico was not only further doomed but at the same time offered a great opportunity—a process that was accompanied by controversies, dire prophecies, and well-intentioned nationalism. And if Americanization took a while to reach its zenith, there were several reasons for this: Mexico's cultural and social diversity; the weight of its anti-Yanqui traditions; the vigor of a nationalism that throughout a long period of Mexico's history was the preferred way to explain the link between the daily life of the Mexican people and the impositions of the state; the series of "theoretical" commentaries on the background of their sexual attitudes; the rage and pacification of Mexico's labor movements; the festive spirit of the Mexican people and their ability to internalize repression.

President Díaz Ordaz embraced the most dogmatic version of nationalism when he mourned the end of Mexico's isolation: "In our provincialism we had been proud and naively confident that, at a time of youthful unrest the world over, Mexico would remain an untouched island." He went on to say: "Mexico does not accept solutions that go against the essence of its being!"[2] But who was authorized to speak on behalf of Mexico, and what *was* the essence of its being? In 1968 official nationalism denounced as unpatriotic the student movement clamoring for a nationalism that would not be manipulative and would respect human rights, and that would be open to the forces of internationalization; for, in spite of everything, as Octavio Paz writes in the *Labyrinth of Solitude*, "We are, for the first time in our history, contemporaries of other men."[3]

For most Mexicans, in their closed society, to be internationalized could only mean to be Americanized. Therefore, when President Echeverría Alvarez attempted, by decree, to spearhead a "resurrected" nationalism, he was derided and rejected by the elite. Traditional attire had turned into costumes, and folkloric dances had come to depend more on the inventive skills of Hollywood and Broadway modistes and choreographers than on Aztlán and Chichen-Itzá. In another (or in the same) order of things, there was propagation and internalization of concepts taken from American sociology and sociological journalism. *The Hidden Persuaders* dealt with those who work in advertising;[4] *The Organization Man* was about the employees of large corporations;[5] *The Lonely Crowd* described the changes that occur when going from the essentially autonomous "inner-directed" individual to the "other-directed" victim of the conspiracy of examples;[6] *The Affluent Society* referred to the creation of artificial and gratuitous needs;[7] and the most widely known concept was certainly the one contained in *The Status Seekers*, a term that suddenly acquired dignity.[8]

---

[2]Fourth Presidential Report on the State of the Nation, September 1, 1968.

[3]Octavio Paz, *The Labyrinth of Solitude: Life and Thought in Mexico* (New York: Grove Press, 1962).

[4]Vance Oakley Packard, *The Hidden Persuaders* (New York: D. McKay Co., 1957).

[5]William H. Whyte, *The Organization Man* (New York: Simon and Schuster, 1956).

[6]David Riesman, *The Lonely Crowd: A Study of the Changing American Character* (New Haven, CT: Yale University Press, 1950).

[7]John Kenneth Galbraith, *The Affluent Society* (Boston: Houghton Mifflin, 1958).

[8]Vance Oakley Packard, *The Status Seekers: An Exploration of Class Behavior in America and the Hidden Barriers That Affect You, Your Community, Your Future* (New York: D. McKay Co., 1959).

The glorification of status dictated changes in domicile, choices in appearance, the selection of restaurants and vacation spots, and the pursuit of a suntan and the "right" brand names. Above all, status was defined by the automobile, which went from being a necessity to a declaration of wealth, a mobile announcement of the exact social position of its owner, a straightforward autobiography. In middle-class families, status was a visit to Disneyland; families traveled so that their children might get used to a "quality fantasy."

Their parties are elegant, and oh boy, what banquets!
But I wouldn't want to be there.
All they talk about are famous men,
and no one ever mentions Elvis Presley.[9]

For Mexico's middle-class youth, rock music opened the door to contemporary feelings. One after another, from Bill Haley and Little Richard to the Beatles and the Rolling Stones, rock stars became, in the eternalized instant of being heard, New Age prophets. Of course, Mexico's relationship with other cultures was not dependent solely on rock music; it took various forms thanks to movies, literature, theater, and dance. But because of the "youth ideology," it was most deeply rooted in a music in which young Mexicans could express themselves and feel themselves part of a global fraternity.

Previously, relations with North American culture were left to the cultural vanguard. Thanks to the translations of Salvador Novo in the 1920s, the Mexican public, whose attention had been focused on French poets, began to take an interest in the poetry of American writers. In subsequent years, authors such as Ernest Hemingway, William Faulkner, John Dos Pasos, F. Scott Fitzgerald, and John Steinbeck were widely read. In the 1960s the French theory of the "director-author" brought about a rediscovery of American movies. No longer seen as just "gringo" products, they were reappraised in light of such great directors as D. W. Griffith, John Ford, Fritz Lang, George Cukor, Nicolas Ray, Raoul Walsh, Val Lewton, and Buster Keaton. Then the "thrillers" of Dashiell Hammett, Raymond Chandler, and Chester Himes began to influence the Mexican novel. But nothing approached rock in seducing the Mexican mentality.

In the emergence of middle-class youth culture, rock provided, at last, instant access to the "age." Early on, it was the energy of rock that satisfied their musical demands: Chuck Berry, Little Richard, and most blatantly Elvis Presley introduced other kinds of behavior and a frenetic vitality. And when Elvis Presley's *King Creole* was shown in Mexico in 1958, the authorities came to associate rock with "contemporary vibes"

[9]Rock song of the 1960s.

and with violence. At its first screening, rioting broke out, with the young audience dancing in the aisles; the police were called in; the film was banned; and rock was seen as a threat to public order.

Less shocking for its critics were the Spanish-language versions, whose "frenzied rhythms" they found to be acceptable. And, as always happens, youthful behavior gradually began to change with the arrival of the Beatles and the Rolling Stones.

Fidel, Fidel, ¿Qué tiene Fidel
Que los americanos no pueden con el?[10]

The 1959 victory of Fidel Castro's guerrilla army showed Latin Americans another way to become international—through the steady advance of a revolutionary mentality. (In 1965, Che Guevara would propose the "creation of one, two, three, many Vietnams in Latin America.") According to the implied theory, to be revolutionary was by definition to be contemporary because there could be nothing more modern than the defense of social justice. Spurred by the Cuban Revolution, there was a renewal of anti-imperialism and the hope (ephemeral) that violence could be transformed into humanism. In the 1960s spirit of Latin American solidarity, crowds paraded in Lima, Buenos Aires, Bogotá, and Mexico shouting "Cuba yes, Yanquis no!" The good news was that a tiny country, only ninety kilometers off the coast of the empire, was capable of standing up and finding its identity in defending the exploited.

Furthermore, the Cuban Revolution restored as a goal what was assumed to be nonexistent—a truly Latin American culture. Such varied phenomena as the area's literary "boom," songs of social protest, a rediscovered history of radicalism, and above all, what had been considered impossible—a diversity of cultural options—gave credibility to the notion of a Latin American culture. Sectarianism intensified, the Cuban Revolution made extraordinary progress in health and education, and this new reading of the Latin American process revived and updated the perspectives of the Popular Front years. So there really did exist colonization and ethnocide, the looting of raw materials, North American support for oppressive regimes, and the need to redefine the meaning of "civilization" and "barbarism." But the subsequent inertia of Castro's strongman rule degraded or nullified the influence of the Cuban Revolution, which, after its initial openness, now locked itself into political dogma. Such dogmatism led, for example, to *Calibán* (1971), the exiled Cuban writer Roberto Fernández Retamar's essay, which arbitrarily divided intellectual and artistic creation between supporters of Ariel representing the

---

[10]"Fidel, Fidel, What's Fidel got/That the Americans can't handle him?"

imperialism and pronorth sentiment described by José Enrique Rodó,[11] as opposed to those who believed in Calibán, the truly independent spirit falsely presented as a monster;[12] and to *How to Read Donald Duck* (1972) by Armand Mattelmart and Ariel Dorfman, an extremely solemn study of the industry of culture and of popular culture. After repeating the obvious—that is, use of the comics as a vehicle for capitalist ideology—Dorfman and Mattelmart proceeded to form a treatise from their rather slight subject matter:

> We have more than demonstrated that the world of Disney is a world that seeks to be without material concerns, where production in all forms has disappeared—industrial, sexual, daily work, historical—and where antagonisms are never the social ones of conflict between good and evil, between the more and less fortunate, between the stupid and intelligent. Therefore, the material basis for every action taken in the concrete world of our daily life does not exist for Disney characters. Purged of the secondary sector—industrial production that is the origin of contemporary society and the foundation of the power of the bourgeoisie and of imperialism—the only infrastructure available to Disney that permits him to give body to his fantasy and shape to his ideas, and that automatically represents the economic life of his characters, is the *tertiary* sector—the one that emerges to serve industry and is totally dependent on it.[13]

Very much influenced by the Cuban Revolution, Marxist critics of that period wrote about the enslaved masses, conquered for capitalism by the subliminal messages of the comics, especially those of Superman and the symbol of plutocracy, Donald's rich Uncle McDuck. These conquered masses were so supine that they worshipped commercial sports as though they were the *patria* herself, and in their wooly fervor, they saw television as the pulpit of the new Grand Inquisitor, whose center was North American imperialism and whose influence reached everywhere. What actually happened was perhaps more crucial but much less apocalyptic. By insisting on the power of cultural "penetration," an expression that presupposes the cultural virginity of Latin America, a reverse process of consecrating the area's culture united the opponents of the commercial offensive. The theory of "successful manipulation," the deification of technology through supposedly vital channels, was incorrect, to say the least. It was more a case of the popular classes acknowledging their lack of options and creating alternatives as best they could.

[11]José Enrique Rodó, *Ariel* (Boston: Houghton Mifflin, 1922).
[12]Roberto Fernández Retamar, *Calibán: Apuntes sobre la cultura en nuestra América* (Mexico: Editorial Diogenes, 1971).
[13]Ariel Dorfman and Armand Mattelmart, *Para leer al Pato Donald*, 2d ed. (Buenos Aires: Siglo Veintiuno Argentina, 1972), 152–153.

Anti-imperialism was not confined to just sectarian interpretations. The train of events from the 1950s to 1970s—the Korean War, the execution of Ethel and Julius Rosenberg who were accused of atomic espionage, the daily consequences of the cold war, mistreatment of undocumented workers, racial violence in the Deep South, the criminal cynicism of the Central Intelligence Agency (CIA), the invasion of Santo Domingo, and above all, the Bay of Pigs invasion and the Vietnam War—sharply reminded Latin Americans of the content of imperialism. In fiery response to all of this, there were demonstrations, which were broken up by police action, and individual protests. For example, on November 4, 1965, the poets Carlos Pellicer and José Carlos Becerra were arrested in front of the U.S. embassy in Mexico City for distributing printed copies of a letter to U.S. Ambassador Fulton Freeman, which read:

> No, Mr. Ambassador, things are changing. Now we are ready for anything. Do you understand? North American interventionism, everywhere and at all levels, has brought down on you a magnificent avalanche of hatred and scorn. Do you honestly believe that your young men go to war in a spirit of heroism or patriotic enthusiasm? Don't you have enough of a problem—as inhuman as it is absurd—with your black men born in the United States?
>
> Believe me, Mr. Ambassador, when I say that I, like many Indo-Americans, will take the utmost advantage of the fear and stupidity of the government you represent.
>
> Carlos Pellicer

Pellicer's action was considered barely newsworthy. There was absolute control of the media. In 1967, with the death of Che Guevara in Bolivia, there was a revival of the Pan-American ideals of Simón Bolívar among students, academics, and writers. In his "Lineas por el Che Guevara," Carlos Pellicer cried out:

> His recent death calls to us all,
> it is the flame that ignites the fire anew,
> it is the joyful participation we need,
> so that we do not die of our dreams.[14]

Anti-imperialism, which was central to popular thought and feeling in Latin America, historically depended on categorical experiences—invasions, despoilment of territory, the imposition of dictators, systematic economic plunder—and on the universally accepted version of the

---

[14]Carlos Pellicer, "Lineas por el Che Guevara," *Cuadernos Americanos* 157 (March–April 1968): 105.

North American as the *Other*, the aggressor, the invader, the depredator, even the heretic. Well into the 1980s this continued to be the image of the *Other*: racism, police brutality, military and economic offensives, the imposition of a "unipolar world." But "empire" was a concept that could be assimilated in many different ways, and, given the enormous number of Hispanics in the United States, for millions of Latin Americans the *Other* ceased to be an absolute and partially became something that could be "expropriated" to varying degrees, not because the American way of life was so idealized, but rather because, through the distorted lens of their situation, many immigrants thought they saw a horizon of great opportunities that would open up to them.

The changes in attitude were dramatic. In 1965 tens of thousands of Latin Americans took to the streets to protest the U.S. invasion of Santo Domingo. In 1989, even though only a few groups in Latin America—all businessmen—approved the invasion of Panama, there was minimal protest against so arrogant an act, which, in the wake of bombarding the civilian population, left thousands dead. This lethargy had various origins: the feeling of worldwide impotence, which was heightened and confirmed by the Persian Gulf War; the poverty or lack of alternatives in countries where the vast majority of their populations had no economic future and where there was no such thing as a genuine democracy; the high degree of dependency on foreign investment; and the broadening scope of Americanization.

The Counterculture in Mexico: Those Who Left Voluntarily and Those Who Were Never Included

Between 1965 and the end of the Vietnam War, the growing counterculture in the United States claimed to offer and represent an alternative to the "American Way of Life" with its sweeping conformity, its malls, its suburban conglomerations, and its strict hierarchies. In defiance of the "Silent Majority," the counterculture flaunted its predilections: its search for altered states of mind and spirit; its passionate study of expressions of Oriental culture; its Free Speech Movement, with the use of "fuckyou" as a catharsis summing up the violence and "free form" of social relations; its resistance to government and academic authoritarianism; its recreation of utopias through communal living; its rejection of all aspects of conventional behavior; and its rock culture, which was a total and absolute vision of "consciousness expansion," characterized by that great generational conformity—the use of marijuana, amphetamines, LSD, peyote, and mushrooms.

Initially, U.S. intervention in Vietnam was the overriding concern of the counterculture. "Hell, no! We won't go!" Rather than commit murder in My Lai or die facedown in mud, it was better to drop out of the "system," burn draft cards, demonstrate in front of the Pentagon, and insist on the value of human life and all life on this planet.

Young Mexicans who adopted the counterculture—but not with that name—were not driven by an event of the tragic dimensions of Vietnam. At first they were little groups that listened to rock with mystical fervor, scoffed at family conventions, observed Partido Revolucionario Institucional (PRI) politics with indifference or contempt, and were irritated by the traditional versions of Mexico and its horizon of possibilities. They did not believe in "progress," they hated the careers planned for them by their families or expected of them by society, and they were not impressed by the modern trappings of material possessions. In their world of the *onda* (literally, the wave, but meaning the counterculture), they celebrated sensual pleasures and made fun of the values sacred to their parents and grandparents. They sought a return to nature that would rebuke the consumer society, and, without much theoretical consistency, they declared an end to nationalism. Mexico's counterculture was interested less in theories than in defiant or rebellious attitudes such as the destruction of numerous moral taboos and the repertory of apocalyptic and antiapocalyptic prophesies taken from the Beatles, the Rolling Stones, The Who, Bob Dylan, Jimi Hendrix, Janis Joplin, Led Zeppelin, Jefferson Airplane, and the Grateful Dead: "The answer, my friend, is blowin' in the wind,"[15] as well as "Freedom's just another word for nothing left to lose."[16]

In 1968 the student movement, the Tlaltelolco massacre, and irrefutable evidence of the nature of Mexico's government speeded up change and expanded the presence of the counterculture. For political, sexual, and emotional reasons, thousands of university students, mostly middle class, found in the Americanization proposed by the counterculture a way of rejecting the government and traditional moral and cultural values. Why should they accept a conservative mentality bound to the nineteenth century? How could they believe that the president was literally the "father" of the Mexican people? How could they not detest the idea of repeating, without variation, the lives of their parents and grandparents? In its initial stage, this counterculture could display an impressive catalog of partial achievement and self-destructive obsessions that included:

• Rock, something more than a kind of music, which aroused emotions that would have been inconceivable just a few years earlier and that were accompanied by new physical and oneiric sensations. It also

[15]Bob Dylan, "Blowin' in the Wind."
[16]Kris Kristofferson-George Foster, "Me 'n' Bobby McGee."

introduced urban lyrics expressed in such devastating phrases as "I can't get no satisfaction, but I'll try,"[17] and "Father Mackenzie, writing the words of a sermon that no one will hear."[18]

• Drugs (marijuana, acid, mushrooms), the cult of induced ecstasy, sensual excesses, derangement of the senses to foster the illusion of adventure, experiments to achieve other spiritual goals. "All your dreams are on their way, see how they shine," wrote Paul Simon in "Bridge over Troubled Water."

• Esoterism, the certainty of realities that could be experienced only by unorthodox means. This implied a rejection of doctrines assimilated more through inertia than conviction—that is, Christianity, Marxism, Freudianism.

• A new consciousness of the body, intensified by music, drugs, and the idea of breaking down moral and mental barriers. This brought with it more frequent and indiscriminate sexual activity that was less guilt ridden, although still imbued with machismo.

• Ecotopia, the utopia of a return to nature, alternative medicines, macrobiotic foods. Here was the start of the ecological movement.

• Communes, an attempt to dissolve individuality, to lead a shared life of self-sufficiency.

At its peak—from 1968 to 1972 or 1973—the Mexican counterculture flaunted its life-style and spurned society's opprobrium. From the capital to Huautla, up to San Francisco and back to the villages around Mexico City, hirsute hippies wearing huaraches and carrying backpacks gathered to discuss philosophy and the litany of their disdain for the establishment. They were the object of governmental repressive measures that were applauded by bishops and businessmen alike. They were arrested and had their hair chopped off; their occasional rock concerts were broken up by the police, who either found or planted marijuana on them. And in 1971, in Avándaro in the state of Mexico, a rock festival set off an explosion of obscenities, a shameless exhibition of wanton behavior, and a wave of enthusiastic self-congratulation—"The Avándaro Nation doesn't trust anyone over thirty and believes in anything that intensifies your senses and heightens your perceptions." For three days they celebrated with an exuberance appropriate to the occasion; crowded together, drinking beer, passing around joints of marijuana, the working-class *chavos* (guys) ratified the inevitable: their conversion to the ideal of "youth" produced by the culture industry. They expropriated the *alivia* (turn-on) from the *onda groovy* (groovy wave); they abandoned a nationalism of family and government they did not believe in; they rejected the established so-

[17]Mick Jagger-Keith Richards, "Satisfaction."
[18]John Lennon-Paul McCartney, "Eleanor Rigby."

ciety that excluded them; and they moved to a psychological sphere where they could experience their senses to the utmost and where they could postpone adult responsibilities or dismiss them as an absurd burden. And music drove their exuberance. Every good rock song was a "hymn to joy" played at full blast during a blissful high.

At Avándaro, classist and nationalist ideas began to lose their grip on young people. Repression, the exorcism campaign carried out in articles and homilies, the banning of rock concerts, and the "call to reason" suggested that the Avándaro alternative would be ephemeral. Actually, in a short time, lack of resources, despair over dead-end activities, and the brazen life style of the *nacos* (parvenus)—the old *raza de bronce* (the "race of bronze," as the masses were called)—destroyed the dreams of the Avándaro Nation. But many *chavos* were determined to continue in their search for their own space, and they transcended imitation by finding in rock music psychological benefits hitherto unknown to them. They may not have read Carlos Castañeda and Aldous Huxley, or memorized Jack Kerouac and Allen Ginsberg, or studied shamanism, or experienced Europe through the jazz records mentioned in Julio Cortázar's *Hopscotch*,[19] or pored over the details of the *The Tibetan Book of the Dead*,[20] or passionately investigated the many levels of meaning in "Sergeant Pepper's Lonely Hearts Club Band," or recited the titles of all of Elvis Presley's records since Sun Records. But they were many, and they knew that unless they were modern they were nothing in their own eyes. So they looked over the resources available to them: rock music, tribal life, movies and television, drugs, and the brutal naturalness of sex. And they repeated their challenge: "If you won't let us be modern any other way, this is the way we'll be."

Middle-class youth fled the counterculture only to be replaced by the *nacos*. The latter did not share the former's yearning for Huxley's "doors of perception"; they did not attribute metaphysical powers of exaltation to drugs (they enjoyed marijuana in exactly the same way that they enjoyed alcohol); they did not delve into the messages of rock; they did not compose poetry to the "dark side of the moon." Nonetheless, thanks to the euphoria of rock music with its attendant stimulants, they did find a place for themselves where they were not rejected. They represented the new México *profundo*, who gathered together in groups, hated the police, made trouble at school, began sex early in a spirit of machismo, and used

[19]Julio Cortázar, *Hopscotch*, trans. Gregory Rabassa (New York: Pantheon Books, 1966).
[20]W. Y. Evans-Wentz, comp. and ed., *The Tibetan Book of the Dead; or, the After-Death Experiences on the Bardo Plane, According to Lama Kazi Dawa-Samdup's English Rendering* (London: Oxford University Press, H. Milford, 1927).

the crude language typical of their tribe. By finding the words they needed in the dreams and lyrics of rock, they entrusted their youth to the music.

While the rock experience was being thus "nationalized," the first counterculture generation began to dissolve. Police assaults on young people continued, and there was increasing evidence of the irreparable damage done by drug use; hippies got married, trimmed their hair and shaved their beards, and looked for security; communes disintegrated; rock concerts were confined to recordings; and, most important, mysticism evaporated. The great invention of Americanization, which was the youth culture, invigorated the consumer society and rockers returned to their regimented life.

How Do You Say "Honey" in English?

In retreat, or confined to its "impregnable" citadels, cultural nationalism was the link between the Left and Right with their different perspectives but very similar concerns. They were united in their warning against technology, in their complaints about the loss of traditions (the Right: respect for elders; the Left: the class struggle), in their homage to feudal family concepts, and in their puerile fear of the encroachment of "Spanglish."

Government after government tried to protect the Spanish language by means of coercion, laws and regulations, and fines and reprimands of businesses with names like "Jimmy's" and "Charlie's." Members and would-be members of the Academy of Language called for language purity and, without much success, they tried to isolate the language virus infecting speech. (For example, how many people started using *neblumo*, which was supposed to prevent the linguistic entrance of *smog*, and how many said *balompié* instead of *fútbol*?) This paternalism regarding the Spanish language was clearly a sincere and desperate action. During the administration of José López Portillo (1976–1982), a bureaucratic disaster was created called the Committee for the Defense of the Language, another implicit rebuke of those who failed even to protect the quality of what they were saying.

The hope of establishing an unappealable law that would treat language as a defenseless being ignored the obvious fact that the vast incursions of English into other languages were inevitable because of North American military, economic, and technological might, which generated a lingua franca throughout the world. Every day a word—*software* or *videoclip*—would be incorporated into the international dictionary, without any possible alternatives. Nevertheless, after a century of Americanization, Mexico's Spanish, both impoverished and enriched, keeps its vital rhythm.

Will There Come a Day When There Are More Youth Subcultures Than There Are Young People?

The counterculture (*la onda*) was only a part, the most radical and independent part, of the Mexican youth-culture universe. It was very closely tied to Americanization but, at the same time, capable of producing movements of considerable originality, especially on the northern border; in regions characterized by their outflow of immigrants (Jalisco, Sinaloa, Michoacán); and, in the case of *chavos-banda* (teenaged members of street gangs) and punks, in Mexico City.

The *chavos-banda*, who were very active in the 1980s, were a mixture of what had previously been the urban *palomillas* (bands of street kids) and the new spirit of owning a turf as expressed especially in two seminal movies—Walter Hill's *The Warriors* (1979) and George Miller's *Mad Max: The Road Warrior* (1981). The repercussions of *The Warriors* were collectivist and organizational, unlike those of *Rebel without a Cause* and the early films of Elvis Presley, which appealed to individualism and self-gratification. *Easy Rider*, so basic to the counterculture, was banned in Mexico. In *The Warriors*, New York was a city dominated by an underground network of teenaged street gangs, each one trying to be distinctive, beginning with its name. One of the gangs, the Warriors, unjustly accused of having murdered the leader of all the gangs, faced ambushes and persecution. During their attempt to return to their home turf, the Warriors lose some of their members, demonstrate their skills, and prove their innocence.

The growth of cult films had the immediate effect of speeding up the demographic explosion of street gangs, who were fanatic fans of Heavy Metal, the postapocalyptic squalor of *Mad Max*, and rock groups such as Kiss and the Police. The *chavos-banda*, who arose from the culture of urban poverty, combined Americanization (basically auditory) and the nationalism of survival. And this was also the case of the far less numerous punks, whose rebellion, in the sense that it was diluted in the megalopolis of Mexico City, was easier to tolerate. On the border, subcultures flourished for a while before their expansion was curbed by the enthusiasm for economic integration, which demanded well-behaved young people. In his book *¡A la brava ése!*, José Manuel Valenzuela Arce wrote about the main characters—*cholos* (street kids), low riders, punks and *chavos-banda*—as well as of a variety of secondary characters.[21] The first group, which reached its peak in the 1970s, vanished or retreated in the midst of self-destructive rites and a police persecution that made it very

---

[21]José Manuel Valenzuela Arce, *¡A la brava ése! Cholos, punks, chavos banda* (Mexico: El Colegio de la Frontera Norte, 1988).

dangerous to be or look like a *cholo*. In the way they evolved, Mexico's *cholos* confirmed that there was no such thing as a simple Americanization. From their counterparts in California, they derived their dress, their alphabet, their graffitis, their mural painting, and their musical tastes and attitudes. Nonetheless, this was not just a transplant; to the contrary. They were deeply attached to border life, and they saw in their barrio the image of their country and, incidentally, the synthesis of regional influences.

The first Mexican *cholos*, devotees of the Jefecita (Virgin) of Guadalupe, adored their tattoos and their "far-out" appearance. They longed for the identity of belonging to the ideal barrio; what was important to them was to be *carnales* (brothers) and *batos locos alivianados* (crazy laidback dudes) and not to be hassled by the pieties of official nationalism and the PRI. In Tijuana, Culiacán, Guadalajara, and Zamora the *chavos* of the poor neighborhoods were eager to undertake the adventure of migration. Even in their dress, they prepared for their journey to the promised land. They initiated their odyssey in old clothes, the rags of underemployment or of the fruit collector, which were all the baggage they needed for job hunting and for life in the barrios of Los Angeles.

After the *chavos-banda* and the *cholos*, pretensions of generational autonomy died down. What remained on the surface was the only youth culture left—the one promulgated by the consumer society.

Americanization: The Profoundly Superficial Integration

In the 1960s elite enthusiasm for everything North American began to spread to the Mexican masses. Although with less obvious repercussions in Mexico, the U.S. government's proposal of the Alliance for Progress was viewed by many as a failure because it did not diminish sympathy for the Cuban Revolution. Others, like the Utopian sociologist Ivan Illich, in his *Alternativas*, considered it a success:

> As an alliance for the progress of the consumer classes and for the domestication of the great masses, the Alliance has been a giant step in modernizing the consumer patterns of the Latin American middle classes. In other words, it has served as a means of integrating this colonial metastasis of the dominant culture of the North American metropolis. At the same time, the alliance has modernized the expectation levels of the great majority of the population and has directed their demand toward articles they will never be able to buy.[22]

Very probably, Illich exaggerated the role of the Alliance for Progress; but if we substitute "television commercials" for "Alliance," his description is flawless.

[22]Ivan Illich, *Alternativas*, 2d ed. (Mexico: Editorial Joaquín Mortiz, 1977).

The actions and speeches of nationalists to try to block Americanization did no good whatsoever and only facilitated and accelerated the process. They made a colossal mistake at one and the same time; they identified technological progress with North American ideology; they confused culture and consumerism; and their rallying cry to nationalism came close to requiring a rejection of all innovations. Those who accepted technology also believed, after suffering a few twinges of guilt, that they had become Americanized. And "globalization" as a technique of obedience was grounded in the foolish fears of a weak nationalism that unleashed nightmares of regression to autochthonous conditions. Therefore, Americanization was resisted mainly through declarations because its seduction was not based on an ideological but on a technological principle. Who was going to say "no" to comfort? And if the meaning of "contemporary" was to be decided in the United States (a statement that should itself be nuanced), when a Latin American asked himself, "How contemporary am I?", he was actually asking himself, "How do I measure up to the North American model?" What was national was a variation of lack of comfort—a mentality as colonized as it was inevitable.

Whether or not such an attitude was a conscious one, anything that did not closely follow North American paradigms was considered an anachronism. Other societies might be freer or less repressive (for example, the Scandinavian), but in Latin America it was widely believed that all progress was determined in the United States. Thus, shifts in ideology went along with changes in fashion (the bikini and the miniskirt responded to the fact that the desire of people to show off their bodies became stronger than their fear of what others would say); norms of family relations were relaxed; "effectiveness" sealed the fate of traditions ranging from the use of indigenous languages to adultery; areas of freedom were broadened for children, adolescents, and women; and there was a modicum of tolerance for previously unmentionable behavior.

Almost without exception, the dominant ideas of that period were those of the dominant class. The wealthy reasoned that imitating gringos was the only known strategy that would allow Mexicans to be included in what was worthwhile. The world revolved around a grand life-style. New York City, Houston, Dallas, and Los Angeles compensated for the knowledge that daughters would simultaneously enter puberty and lose their virginity, that marital infidelity was no longer unilateral, and that planned obsolescence applied to beliefs as well as to products. How much was forfeited by renouncing an individuality not so much nebulous as "diminished in market value"? Ivan Illich described the pathetic consequences of this position: "Underdevelopment as a state of mind appears when human needs are poured into the mould of a pressing demand for new brands of canned solutions that will always be beyond the reach of the majority."[23]

In the destruction of the natural and social resources of Mexico and Latin America, Americanization is the decisive instrument of control. It promotes depoliticization, consolidates economic denationalization, implants consumerism in social groups without purchasing power, and widens the distance between reality and expectations in an irrational and grotesque way. But its role is always changing. Until a short time ago, Americanization was the way to become "universal"—at the pace of the imitator country. Now it has become a meeting place for different social classes broadly defined in terms of technological impact and usually discussed in a tone of resignation or for rhetorical purposes. And working-class youth believe that, by becoming Americanized, they can exorcize their obvious lack of a future.

At the same time, in the face of this colorful deception, a growing number of Latin Americans have happily taken over the stupidity and degradation offered in the name of Americanization and transformed them into popular culture and nationalist sentiment. In some way, Americanization is Mexicanized or Peruanized, or whatever; and what is international is implacably melded into what is very local. One thing is clear: The principles and slogans of the culture industry are potentially true for the masses but inevitably false for each individual. And nationalist reaffirmation, even if ritualistic or incorrect from the viewpoint of the masses, is nonetheless indispensable to legions of individuals. For this reason, any final judgments on the mass media are risky. To be sure, the mind-control industry is concerned with the reproduction of the value codes of the relations of production—that is, that exploitation should be perpetuated through the collective internalization of dogmas and through acquiescence. But it is also certain that no one mechanically incorporates everything heard and seen into his or her life.

All Channels Transmit the Genesis and the Apocalypse

From the 1970s the transnationals, with no possibility of challenge and on an ever-widening scale, dictated the life rituals of the bourgeoisie and the middle classes—their children's entertainment, their youth culture, and the most prestigious way to spend their free time. Previously, fashions had taken time to cross commercial and psychological frontiers. Then the time was substantially reduced until—mainly thanks to cablevision and parabolic antennas—it became almost simultaneous for

[23]Ibid.

the social groups with purchasing power and the youthful vanguard. One after another, North American institutions of taste and consumption became the institutions of taste and consumption in Latin America: the award ceremonies for the Oscar, Grammy, Emmy; the hit parade; the cult films; the martial arts (viz., the Mexican Ninja); the avid interest in movie star gossip; rock as a generational language; Nintendo as a childish obsession.

Genuine internationalization and pathetic or brazen imitation coexisted and merged. A competitive mentality entered into the purchase of television sets, radios and transistors, blenders, tape recorders, washing machines, and computers. The greatest success of the process was that some social groups identified a given level of consumption as indispensable for a better life and rejected any idea of social justice. Such widespread subjugation meant that critics attributed to the cultural industry a greater influence than it actually had. It is true that in a mass society there is room only for the stentorian versions of attire, behavior, speech, sense of humor, and erotic visions; but the hegemony of the transnationals can never be complete as long as there are so many different ways to resist it. Television, for example, covers all of Mexico with its colonization patterns, but its reception in a working-class neighborhood is very different from the way it is received in a residential area.

The majority of the population see radio and television as the great interlocutors, not just entertainment but also life-styles that, by taking them into account and scorning any educative hierarchy—"I'm so interested in your watching me that I treat all of you like children"—compensate them for their social limitations. The message is crystal clear: You have no alternative, viewers; come closer to the paradigmatic mirror; see yourself reflected in these dramas, songs, phrases, and attitudes; by contagion you can acquire a globalized identity and a sentimental education. Who, in these circumstances, speaks of "cultural manipulation," which, to use half-truths, is correct but inadequate? The mass culture acts on those who are already conquered and, by channeling their defeat, makes exploitation the backdrop that sustains the victims' melodramatic dreams. One cannot use the idea of "manipulation" in such a consecrated and deterministic way without acknowledging that it is a tyranny that depoliticizes forever. But real life offers ample evidence to the contrary. In Mexico, we are called upon to protect "national identity" as an element that is always on the verge of wandering away or getting lost. Inasmuch as the concept is not clearly defined, the fear that it will vanish altogether is another result of excessive belief in the power of cultural imperialism. The extremes come together: The irrationalism of the solely defensive attitude, the nativist and the chauvinist "They shall not pass," is succeeded by the irrationality of the person who assumes that when one embraces the benefits of technology, the next and immediate step is to joyously accept the colonization mentality.

Irrationality is everywhere. Not only in middle-class residences but also in shacks and tenements, and in the vast marginal areas where there are few basic services and where multitudes live crowded together, there is no connection between personal achievement and the community. As for ideologies, feelings of well-being or of survival depend very much on the mass media. In this context, "ideologies of idiosyncrasy"—the belief in horoscopes, the practice of spiritualism, the police investigation of UFOs, the clientele of "witches," the fanatic support of a sports team, and the "religion of upward mobility"—all of these also operate in the culture of the masses in the manner of compensations, equivalencies, and conciliation. There is a secret rationality in those who choose the forms discarded by the educated minority and who outfit those forms with the official formulas of appeasement: You will have a job; you will be happy; you will have a good life; and your country will reward your sufferings with the opportunities offered to your children and grandchildren.

The Dawn of Globalization—Now Everyone Knows for Whom He Works

> I translate an *Esquire* article
> on a sheet of Kimberly-Clark paper,
> using an ancient Remington typewriter.
> I shall correct with an Esterbrook ballpoint pen.
> What I'm paid will go
> to add a few pesos to the coffers
> of Carnation, General Foods, Heinz,
> Colgate-Palmolive, Gillette,
> and the California Packing Corporation.[24]

Cablevision. Comics of super heroes. Humor rapidly and badly translated. Endless products that satiate, invent, and modify needs. Television programs glorifying the victory of the North American system of justice. Books in which sales pitches "construct" the reader's personality. Cutting-edge technologies. Videocassettes embodying the communitarian experience of the movies. Satellite communication. The ideology of Marshall McLuhan's global village. Music videos. Transnational control of telecommunications. Consumer strategies that reinvent the idea of control and the notion of the housewife. The "philosophy" of the biggest

---

[24]José Emilio Pacheco, *No me preguntes cómo pasa el tiempo (poemas, 1964–1968)* (Mexico: Editorial Joaquín Mortiz, 1969), 30.

seller in the world. Films created on the basis of detailed market research. Audiovisual software. International news agencies that combine information and release it with a single point of view. Disdain for each nation's history. Imposition—due to necessity or because of arrogance—of a world-wide language. The transmission circuit of ideologies ranging from commercials to the pedagogy of the news programs. Control of the "information revolution." Women's magazines that convert "femininity" into a shopping center. The reordering of living habits. Malls that function as basilicas with innumerable chapels.

A Mexican adjunct to this landscape of subjugation? The affinities between satire and reality: In the final scene of the movie *Born in East L.A.*, hordes of people resembling a population explosion stream from Tijuana to San Diego, California. And their headlong flight reveals, with the vividness of an allegory, that this is irreversible. Year after year, in never diminished numbers, hundreds of thousands of Mexicans, Salvadorans, and Guatemalans hurl themselves toward that obsessive goal (a modernity that is rooted in employment). They defy police brutality, the network of guides known as *polleros* (poulterers) who deceive and defraud undocumented workers, their peasant attachment to the soil, their feelings of inadequacy—cultural, linguistic, and technological. And in spite of everything, they persist.

In the twenty years from 1970 to 1990, Mexico's northern border area has been made over: It is no longer a way station; it has been "morally rehabilitated"; it is experiencing industrial development; it has been invaded by drug traffickers; it has expanded its university system and its cultural groups; its legendary small-scale vices have been forgotten; it both suffers and benefits from its *maquiladoras* (in-bond processing plants); it aspires to full employment; and although it is totally integrated into the North American economy, its intellectuals jealously ensure preservation of "national identity." The abuses of the national government continue; but the northern border categorically rejects its mythology as the waiting room for migratory dreams.

"I Am Mexican; My Land Is Barren."

Factors supporting allegations of determinism are the three-thousand-kilometer border with the United States; economic dependency (72 percent of transactions in Mexico are with the U.S. market); and the migration of workers directed chiefly, but not exclusively, to Texas and California. Previously, if those living in the provinces wanted to modernize themselves, they looked toward the capital; now that all of Mexico is becoming a single city, not only in appearance but also in its scattered flare-ups, would-be moderns turn their attention, which is influenced by the mass media and those "travel fantasies" that are the tales of the immigrants, away from the center of the country.

In the Mexican catalog of idealized images, the United States or, more precisely, Los Angeles, figures not as the only possible destination, but certainly as the urban monster that is thought to offer by far the most opportunities: a place already inhabited by millions of Mexicans, a paradise of freeways, and a multitude of ghettos. According to the Polish author Rykzsard Kapucinsky, Los Angeles fulfills the prophecy of the "cosmic race," the universal *mestizaje* (mixing of races) foreseen by José Vasconcellos in 1925: "The different races of the world tend to become more and more mixed until they form a new human type, composed from the selection of each one of the existing peoples."

Mexicans, Nicaraguans, Salvadorans, and Hondurans in Los Angeles are already "Hispanics," members of a minority that by the year 2000 will be the largest in the United States. It is there that they hope to find the jobs denied to them in their own countries, the house or apartment furnished with modern appliances, the school that will take their children out of the service sector, and the contemporary resonance impossible to obtain in their village or in their working-class neighborhood. Immigrants pay for this by the experience of being violently uprooted, which involves abandoning their essential identity based on the knowledge of their exact place in the community, having to adjust to learning foreign words, making their first contact with a technology that will end up as their second skin, and trying to recreate a rural setting in postmodernist conditions.

Everything is new and seems to be accessible; in the end everything is unattainable. Everything is taken on with willingness to work and suspension of disbelief. Undocumented workers, "wetbacks," illegal aliens, use a surprising tactic. They venerate the customs they leave behind to more easily shed the mental habits that make it difficult for them to belong to their new surroundings, which are hostile, racist, repressive, and also rewarding in various ways. This could be the immigrant's prayer:

> Thank you, Little Virgin of Guadalupe, because you allow me to be the same as always. But I have to tell you, in case you haven't noticed, My Holy Patron, I've become much more tolerant of what I do not understand or share. I can be faithful to you, for you are Mexico. I may be a Pentecostal, or a Jehovah's Witness, an Adventist, Baptist, or Mormon, but I'm determined not to change, even though I may look very different and I listen to this gigantic radio—I think it's called a ghetto blaster—that plays songs I never thought I'd be so crazy about. I swear to you, Little Virgin, I'm the same as always, although I don't even recognize myself when I look in the mirror.

"Americanization, Professor, Means That We Mexicans, Instead of Thinking in Spanish the Way We Used To, Think in Spanish the Way We Are Now."

Conjectures on the cultural consequences of Mexico's economic integration with the United States—fears of loss of identity and destruction of individuality, for example—are somewhat belated and alarmist. The process will take a while and even when it intensifies, its essential features can already be clearly seen: The continent, and Mexico, will continue to be Americanized and, depending on how close or how far a Latin American country is from high-level technology, the way it views the world will be modified (who can, in all seriousness, define what being a Mexican or a Peruvian means?), without having its fundamental values affected. These values include the Spanish language, whose vitality and powers of assimilation do not need government supports that are alien to the educative process itself.

As Americanization is extended, the many aspects of the term become evident. On the one hand is the Americanization that renounces all national traditions because they stand in the way of personal and family modernity; on the other is the Americanization that consists of a search for keys to understanding, a defense against what is not well understood due to the method used, which is an imitation that will become nationalized. To this is added the oppressive fact that at the same time that its influence modifies rigidities and intolerance, North American society—as a whole, profoundly racist and classist—sets the pattern for new racist and classist attitudes in Latin America.

To what extent does the force of Americanization affect prevailing definitions of "sovereignty" and "national culture"? A well-thought-out response should begin by eliminating the alarmism and conditioned reflexes of chauvinists and those who would assimilate at any price. It should take into account the obvious: Americanization, at its various levels, is already a substantial part of Latin American culture. And according to the logic of survival, sovereignty cannot be renounced, either in theory or in practice.

A new commonplace: In Mexico, the border with the United States is found everywhere, and as regards our culture and our economy, all Mexicans live on the border. Thus, for example, Mexico's migratory waves have established their own national identity without paying too much attention to their country's "great history." What they have is different: loyalty to Mexican food (without being fanatic), faithfulness to styles of religious piety (with or without lifetime commitment), and enthusiasm for songs and legends that serve as collective autobiographies and bring back memories. Furthermore, they have added something new to the ongoing melting pot of regional traditions—the invention of a northern spirit that is self-confident, sincere, audacious, and immoral as long as it does not land them in jail, and honest out of fear and conviction. They are also inveterate party goers—in short, they do not take themselves too seriously.

How do the migratory currents proceed from Mexico to the United States? In *The Current Situation in Mexican Immigration*, Georges Vernez and David Ronfeldt provide figures. In 1920, Mexican immigration represented 11 percent of legal immigration; in 1942, because of the Second World War, a treaty was signed between the two countries that assured the entrance of an unlimited number of seasonal workers (braceros), and by the time the Bracero Program ended in 1964, more than 4.5 million Mexicans had taken advantage of it. The 1965 Immigration Reform Act set quotas that in 1976 reduced immigration to 20,000 per country, without counting close family members, and which meant that every year 66,000 people could enter legally. But the number of illegal immigrants is extremely high, and hundreds of thousands are expelled every year. The result is that by 1988 the Mexican-origin population in the United States had passed the 12 million mark.[25]

Mexico evolved from a sedentary to a nomadic country. Villages are emptied every six months, and those remaining—women, children, and the elderly—maintain their traditional identity, consisting of tedium and resignation. And the emigrants, shouldering their wealth of cheap labor, arrive exhausted from their trip in rickety buses or trailers to make the difficult and hasty border crossing. Because it requires so much effort and there are so many obstacles in the way, for millions of Mexicans life in the United States represents personal accomplishment. Even though they know about the mistreatment and the ghettos, they hope to become third-class citizens of the future and not of the past.

Perhaps this partially explains the results of a survey showing that there is a sector of Mexico's population that no longer boasts of its patriotism, is disgusted with nationalism, and wants integration no matter how it comes about. But they are a minority, and Mexico has not decided to stop being Mexico. What has happened is that the new patriotism is concerned with raising living standards in response to the "lost decade" of the 1980s and the ruthlessness of the current neoliberalism.

"Watcha Ése" (From Ghetto to Nation)

Will Mexico be a nation of Chicanos in the future, of Mexican Americans? The question is, of course, rhetorical, but it is certain that the sub-

---

[25]Georges Vernez and David Ronfeldt, *The Current Situation in Mexican Immigration* (Santa Monica, CA: Rand, 1991).

stantial presence—not to say influence—of Chicano culture in Mexico is explained by various factors: strength in an educated sector of painting, theater, performance art, cinema; relationships stimulated by the continuous migratory flows; cultural intermediation between a traditional culture—in many parts of the country already symbolic—and the different degrees of Americanization. Chicanos are well aware of what an identity, whether national or regional, means in a world that regards identities as variations of the picturesque. Over a period of one or several generations, they have seen their traditions and native language endure and weaken; they are masters of both hanging on to their identity and taking advantage of the cultural and work benefits of integration.

I do not propose that Chicanos be viewed as convenient interpreters of the "American way of life," whatever that means. I am aware of the inevitable differences between the two communities, beginning with the obvious fact that Mexicans live in Mexico, which is reflected in an Americanization that, more often than not, fails or is skin-deep; this is what leads to the various methods used to "Mexicanize" Americanization. But during the stage of changes that will be to a great extent definitive transformation, at a time when the deepest attachment to Mexico may be expressed in a form of nomadism, there is growing interest in tactics of resistance and adaptation. In reconstituting nationalism, which survives in spite of everything, the Chicano cultural version is an indispensable object of observation.

Tomorrow's Nationalism Will Be Bilingual

At the beginning of the 1900s, a phrase attributed to Porfirio Díaz— "Poor Mexico, so far from God, so close to the United States"—became one of the slogans of the Mexican century. Later, there were variations such as "Poor Mexico, so far from God, so far from the United States," but basically these words would remain as the final verdict on Mexico and its nationalism. Nonetheless, in the administrations of José López Portillo (1976–1982), Miguel de la Madrid (1982–1988), and Carlos Salinas de Gortari (1988–1994), Mexican society was presented with economic integration as imperative to the country's welfare and as a major project of the government that could no longer be postponed.

Everything at once. Computers have changed the pace of progress; the bourgeoisie want to maintain part-time residences in the United States—La Jolla, Coral Gables, Miami Beach, Padre Island, MacAllen, the Olympic Towers in New York City; Yuppies take over the social scene; homogeneity advances; "Third World" becomes an insult; female beauty is judged by the Miss Mexico contest; Houston is the mecca of the ill; and if there's a McDonald's in Moscow, why can't there be one in the mountains of Oaxaca? Competitive ardor redefines ambitions and professions—even their names indicate new psychologies: "entrepreneurs," "junior executives," "first is first, and second is nobody." And many are of the opinion that nationalism has changed from a defining way of life to a "show" that can be entered or exited at will.

An extraordinary photo taken by Graciela Iturbide sums up the process: A Tarahumara Indian woman climbing a mountain is seen from behind; she is carrying what will neutralize or conquer her solitude—a huge radio. Defenders of indigenous identity will censure her for her predilection, but they are not there in the mountains to relieve her of the immense monotony of her life. For reasons similar to those of the Tarahumara woman, young girls from indigenous ethnic groups abandon their native attire, and young men adopt the type of clothes worn by punks or laid-back *chavos*. Communities continue, adversely affected or benefited— according to the way one looks at it—by the need to draw nearer to centers of modernity; and everything remains the same, except that it is all very different.

In an era of imports, of privatizations at all costs, of the "unipolar world," one prediction is possible: The great majority of Mexicans, confronted by the drive toward Americanization, each in his or her own way, will heed the advice of Sedar Senghor: Assimilate without being assimilated.

Writing the Border: The Languages and Limits of Representation

Norma Klahn

THE DIVERSE, COMPLEX, AND CONTRADICTORY WAYS in which Mexico, its culture, and its people have been imagined, portrayed, glorified, or vilified by the people of the United States have a long history. They began with the conflicts between the two colonizing powers, Spain and England. And they continued as the young United States expanded into territories occupied by the Indians and possessed first by Spain and later Mexico. In the process, a cultural and physical space known as "the border" emerged in the nineteenth century. Ultimately, it resulted in both a physical and a psychological distancing during and because of the U.S. nineteenth-century expansion and its conquest of what is now the U.S. Southwest. For political, cultural, and psychological purposes this movement or displacement rendered the region's former owners, the Mexicans, as "other," that is, constructed a different identity seen as dissonant to monolithic Western discourses of power.[1] The dynamics of "othering" finally become self-serving, for it affirms an ongoing process of, in this case, Anglo identity. Constituted as a cultural contestant, the Mexican became everything the Anglo was not.

In their studies of Anglo attitudes toward Mexicans, Carey McWilliams and Arnoldo de León present the U.S. expansionist project as an acquisition of territory justified by the mission Anglos assumed as civilizers of the hinterlands, with a need to control all that was seen as

---

[1]See Edward Said, *Orientalism* (New York: Vintage Random House, 1978); Tzvetan Todorov, *The Conquest of America: The Question of the Other* (New York: Harper and Row, 1982); Michel de Certeau, *Heterologies: Discourse on the Other* (Minneapolis: University of Minnesota Press, 1986); Michael Taussig, *Mimesis and Alterity: A Particular History of the Senses* (New York: Routledge, 1993).

barbaric—sexuality, vice, nature, and people of color.[2] The initial constructions were racist; that is, essential characteristics of personality, intelligence, and morals were attributed to physical appearances. Mexicans were perceived in light of their differences from Anglos. Americans carried to the Southwest values constructed by the founding fathers, who were of English descent, male, white, and Protestant—self-reliance, a puritanical morality, the erasure of the past, and a work ethic. They saw Mexicans as racially impure, descended of the Spaniards, who were contaminated by Moorish blood, and of the "bloodthirsty" Aztecs. "They are of mongrel blood, the Aztec predominating," asserted Gilbert D. Kingsbury, writing about the Mexicans of Brownsville in the early 1860s.[3] Positioned in relation to their differences to Anglos, Mexicans appeared to be dependent, resigned, complacent, committed not to improvement or progress but to fun and frolic. For these expansionists "to have accepted anything other than 'white supremacy and civilization,' " says De León, "was to submit to Mexican domination and to admit that Americans were willing to become like Mexicans. The prospect of being dominated by such untamed, uncivil, and disorderly creatures made a contest for racial hegemony almost inevitable."[4] Descriptions of Mexicans throughout the nineteenth century, some inoffensive, most virulent, all are grounded on the trope of difference, a rhetorical construct founded on paradigms of dissimilarity.

The border was the line established both to delineate and to inscribe that difference. Where the line is delimited, the "other" begins. The boundary was sacred, not to be transgressed. Yet, paradoxically, bridges and crossing passages are created as legitimate spaces where separation is established, precisely because the frontier, as Michel de Certeau says, is created by contacts where "the points of differentiation between two bodies are also their common points."[5] In the case of the U.S.-Mexican border, the "contact zone" has become a "combat zone" where crossings and/ or transgressions are the rule, rather than the exception.[6] Constructions,

[2]Carey McWilliams, *North from Mexico: The Spanish-Speaking People of the United States* (Philadelphia: J. B. Lippincott, 1949); Arnoldo de León, *They Called Them Greasers: Anglo Attitudes toward Mexicans in Texas, 1821–1900* (Austin: University of Texas Press, 1983).

[3]Quoted in De León, *They Called Them Greasers*, 15.

[4]Ibid., 13.

[5]Michel de Certeau, "Spatial Stories," in *The Practice of Everyday Life*, trans. Steven Rendall (Berkeley: University of California Press, 1984), 127.

[6]I use the term "contact zone" as defined by Mary Pratt in *Imperial Eyes: Travel Writing and Transculturation* (New York: Routledge, 1992), 6, that is, "a space of colonial encounters, the space in which peoples geographically and historically separated come into contact with each other and establish ongoing

concrete and imaginary, are established to distance the "other," at least symbolically, and, in this example, south of the delimitation.

The inhabitants of the United States continue to wrestle with this "alien territory." "South of the Borderism" is what I have called, borrowing from Edward Said, the way that the United States and its peoples have come to terms with Mexico as they continuously invent an "other" image and define and defend their own. In their writings, and in contrast to the ways they constructed or invented themselves (stereotypically, as morally superior, hardworking, and thrifty), Anglos portray Mexicans at best as mysterious, romantic, fun-loving, laid-back, and colorfully primitive; alternatively, Mexicans are seen as conniving, highly sexualized, disorderly, lazy, violent, and uncivilized.[7] Hollywood appropriated all of the images, from "greaser" and violent bandit to Latin lover and Mexican spitfire.[8]

This essay concentrates on the way Anglo Americans have invented and constructed both Mexicans and themselves textually over the last 150 years, taking the border as a point of departure and in its widest definition: a literal, figurative, psychological, cultural, and ever-changing constructed space. It follows the invented images that arise from such texts and registers the changes that these constructions undergo as interpretations of the border zone increasingly depict it as a space of confrontation.

"South of the Border, Down Mexico Way"

As soon as a boundary is established, the other side becomes desirable, the threshold to cross into the unknown, the yet-unexplored landscape where the "self" is discovered and the "other" is invented. The trope of difference becomes the figure most utilized by travelers and novelists writing about their adventures "south of the border." This trope, established from the initial moment of encounter and still prevalent today, opposes U.S. "civilization" to Mexican "barbarism." It seems, however, an encounter of images where language, as a code of communication, is never or seldom mentioned, stressing and acknowledging that writers cannot (or choose not to) cross one of the main borders: the spoken code. Anthropologically we could say that such literature remains etic and not emic;

---

relations, usually involving conditions of coercion, radical inequality, and intractable conflict."

[7]Said, *Orientalism.*

[8]See George Hadley-García, *Hispanic Hollywood: The Latins in Motion Pictures* (New York: Carol Publishing Group, 1990). For representation of Mexicans in the arts, see James Oles, *South of the Border: Mexico in the American Imagination, 1914–1947* (Washington, DC: Smithsonian Institution Press, 1993).

that is, the perspective is established as outside and above the culture. Paradoxically, and because of that positioning, the attraction to a regenerative vitality conceived as present within "barbarism" continues to seduce the traveler to the point of demarcation, both physically and psychologically, where the "other" is found. The adventure can be positive or negative. Many times it becomes a place appropriated as material to feed the imagination back home, perceived as devoid of adventure.

In *Another Mexico*, Graham Greene describes the passing of the threshold with positive yearnings:

> The border means more than a customs house, a passport officer, a man with a gun. Over there everything is going to be different; life is never going to be quite the same again after your passport has been stamped and you find yourself speechless among the money-changers. The man seeking scenery imagines strange woods and unheard-of mountains; the romantic believes that the women over the border will be more beautiful and complaisant than those at home; the unhappy man imagines at least a different hell; the suicidal traveler expects the death he never finds. The atmosphere of the border—it is like starting over again; there is something about it like a good confession: poised for a few happy moments between sin and sin. When people die on the border they call it "a happy death."[9]

For Paul Theroux, the crossing resembled a descent into hell.

> Looking south, across the river, I realized that I was looking toward another continent, another country, another world, . . . the frontier was actual: people did things differently there. . . . No people, but cars and trucks were evidence of them. Beyond that, past the Mexican city of Nuevo Laredo, was a black slope—the featureless, night-haunted republics of Latin America. . . . Laredo required the viciousness of its sister city to keep its own churches full. Laredo had the airport and the churches; Nuevo Laredo, the brothels and basket factories. Each nationality had seemed to gravitate to its own level of competence. The frontier was more than an example of cozy hypocrisy; it demonstrated all one needed to know about the morality of the Americas, the relationship between the puritanical efficiency north of the border and the bumbling and passionate disorder—the anarchy of sex and hunger—south of it.[10]

He does not stop there. Theroux's racism is rampant. Mexicans are naturally corrupt, lawless, unhygienic; they are a brutal and beaten people, who "cruelly beat their animals." Laredo becomes a microcosm of all the United States; Nuevo Laredo, not just of Mexico, but of all Latin America. Mary Pratt sees Theroux's writing as exemplifying "a discourse of nega-

---

[9]Graham Greene, *Another Mexico* (New York: Viking Press, 1939), 13.

[10]Paul Theroux, *The Old Patagonian Express: By Train through the Americas* (Boston: Houghton Mifflin, 1979), 40–41.

tion, domination, devaluation and fear that remain in the late 20th century, a powerful ideological constituent of the West's consciousness of the people and places it strives to hold in subjugation."[11] In both Greene's and Theroux's writings, a distancing occurs, either by idealization or by denigration.

The journeys into Mexico say more about the travelers, their desires, fears, ideologies and worldviews, than about Mexico or its inhabitants. The voyages are, finally, quests for self-definition, self-indulgence, or self-affirmation. Some journeys are evasions, flights from the law or from unspoken societal codes, searches for spaces where rules can be broken. For other travelers, the displacements become rites of initiation, crossings of thresholds toward the unexplored. For Stephen Crane (1871–1900), the other side became the last frontier, a place where the Anglo hero could be tested and could prove his strength, usually against a weakly constructed Mexican. For Ambrose Bierce (1842?–1914), it represented a "crossing of the bar," the quest for a romantic and heroic death. For Jack London (1876–1916), who initially supported the Mexican Revolution in his short story "The Mexican" (written before he had been to Mexico), the country became a moveable feast of horses, bullfights, and heavy drinking. His stories about trials and tribulations pit the "good" American against the "bad" Mexican. Only the fittest survive in London's fiction, and one may well imagine whom they were. Exceptions did exist. There were also writers who established a dialogue based on mutual exchange and common goals for humanity. For John Reed (1887–1920), the other side of the border was a revolutionary fiesta, a place where his ideas were put into practice. His writings had a political agenda, to convince the U.S. public of the Revolution's legitimacy.[12] Another such traveler to Mexico was John Kenneth Turner (1879–1948), who wrote an exposé of the atrocities of the Porfirio Díaz regime.[13]

Katherine Anne Porter (1890–1980) considered Mexico her second home, one where she found her humanistic, accepting, and magnanimous self. In "Hacienda," the protagonist, Porter's alter ego, differs from ethnocentric Anglos, accepting the brown faces of the inhabitants. The story, however, is grounded on the displacement of the "other" as subaltern. The Indian is initially represented as a marginal character, living within a class-based and racist Mexican system, unchanged by the Revolution. The character is then positioned as the stoic figure whose fantastic worldview renders her or him a passive protagonist in life, lacking agency in the

[11]Pratt, *Imperial Eyes*, 219.

[12]John Reed, *Insurgent Mexico* (New York and London: Appleton and Co., 1914).

[13]John Kenneth Turner, *Barbarous Mexico* (Chicago: C. H. Kerr and Co., 1911).

construction of her or his future. The controlling protagonist speaks with the voice of authority and knowledge: "In the Indian the love of death had become a habit of the spirit. It had smoothed out and polished the faces to a repose so absolute it seemed studied, though studied for so long it was held now without effort: and in them all was a common memory of defeat. The pride of their bodily posture was the mere outward shade of passive, profound resistance; the lifted, arrogant features were a mockery of the servants who lived within."[14] Besides perceiving the "Indian" as a homogeneous entity, Porter's authoritative positioning leaves no space for her or her contemporary readers to go beyond the monolithic and essentialist construction of the "other."

Edna Ferber was denied entrance to Mexico in 1933 by the Mexican government for her story "They Brought Their Women," a tale of three individuals whose journey to Mexico is not that of travelers toward the unknown but of tourists toward the cliché.[15] As they cross the border at Laredo, one protagonist says, "Look. Those are the peons Rivera's been painting."[16] Ferber's story can be read as an excellent depiction of the way tourists experience the commodified Mexico as it has been advertised or re-created by the Mexicans themselves. Xochimilco, Teotihuacán, curios, and the Casa de Azulejos become reified. The characters and language deployed to capture that touristy reality are accordingly stereotypical.

For the children of the sixties, Jack Kerouac, and William Burroughs, Mexico was a place of flight, a hallucinogenic trip where adventure and sex became heightened experiences. Certainly, it was a place in which to play, as is evident in this passage from Kerouac's *Lonesome Traveler*:

> The moment you cross the little wire gate and you're in Mexico, you feel like you just sneaked out of school when you told the teacher you were sick and she told you you could go home, 2 o'clock in the afternoon. . . . You look around and you see happy smiling faces, or the absorbed dark faces of worried lovers and fathers and policemen, you hear cantina music from across the little park of balloons and popsicles. . . . You walk thirsty through the swinging doors of a saloon and get a

---

[14]Edward Simmen, ed., *Gringos in Mexico: An Anthology* (Fort Worth: Texas Christian University Press, 1988), 140.

[15]Paul Fussel differentiates three types of voyagers: explorers, travelers, and tourists. "The explorer seeks the undiscovered, the traveler that which has been discovered by the mind working in history, the tourist that which has been discovered by entrepreneurship and prepared for him by the arts of mass publicity." *Abroad: British Literary Traveling between the Wars* (New York: Oxford University Press, 1980), 39. See James Clifford, "Notes on Travel and Theory" in *Inscriptions* 5 (1989): 177–188, who takes Fussel's definitions as a point of departure for theorizing about postcolonial displacement.

[16]Simmen, *Gringos in Mexico*, 205–206.

bar beer, and turn around and there's fellas shooting pool, cooking tacos, wearing sombreros, some wearing guns on their rancher hips, and gangs of singing businessmen. . . . It's a great feeling of entering the Pure Land, especially because it's so close to dry faced Arizona and Texas and all over the Southwest—but you can find it, this feeling, this fellaheen feeling about life, that timeless gayety of people not involved in great cultural and civilization issues.[17]

In a short story by Kerouac, "A Billowy Trip in the World," the protagonist spends a day in a whorehouse living out his sexual fantasies; it is a place where rules and laws are not in effect, where you can let it all hang out. At the end of the orgiastic rituals, he and his male friend (serious bonding has just occurred) symbolically "got towels and jumped right into ice cold showers inside and came out refreshed and new" before heading back home.[18] For Kerouac, as for William Burroughs and other refugee "hippies," Mexico became a haven from U.S. law. Burroughs, in *Junky*, writes about his adventures with peyote in Mexico, after having "jumped bail in the States."[19] The goal of the trip—to trip.

Latin American writing of recent decades has exerted an undeniable influence on American and world literature. Courses on Latin American literature at U.S. universities and the so-called Latin American boom literature in translation over the last ten years not only show Americans the complexities of Mexican culture but also give readers a view from the inside. Cross-fertilization is certainly at work at the level of discourse. A story written in 1980 by Eugene Garber, "An Old Dance," is reminiscent of *The Plumed Serpent* by D. H. Lawrence and of *A Change of Skin* by Carlos Fuentes who, following Lawrence, continued to unearth the Toltec and Aztec pantheon in literature. In Garber's story, a couple takes their son to Mexico, the necessary space for his initiation into manhood. Rituals at the corridas, at the pyramids, and at the local market, the Mercado Libertad, will make him the macho he might not have become in the United States, where he might have been considered "a cringing, hypersensitive, maybe gay persona."[20] In most cases, at the conclusion of such an adventure, the traveler will cross back, returning to the safety of home initiated and transformed but secure in his identity and place in the world. "Tomorrow," says the wife in Garber's story, "back to the good ol' USA."[21]

The neonationalism of the last decade in America has accentuated the return sequence. Oscar Mandel in his 1985 story "From Chihuahua to

---

[17]Jack Kerouac, *Lonesome Traveler* (New York: McGraw-Hill Book Co., 1960), 21–22.
[18]Simmen, *Gringos in Mexico*, 280.
[19]William Burroughs, *Junky* (New York: Penguin, 1977), 142.
[20]Simmen, *Gringos in Mexico*, 339.
[21]Ibid., 367.

the Border" no longer narrates the crossing of the threshold or the call to adventure, but registers the return from Mexico. Mexico taught the protagonist nothing; there was no transformation. The apotheosis occurred when he crossed back.

> And then, unbelievable, Texas— . . . And that time only, never before and never after—an exaltation of patriotism swelled in my rib cage. I could have kissed the asphalt. We halted at a bright chromium-and-plastic 'Eats,' drank the water, spread the butter, poured the milk, and marveled after three months at the smiles and the cleanliness. Ah, those Indians are not a cheerful race. . . . Here was my white-toothed America again, "Hi folks, what'll it be?"[22]

Drewey Wayne Gunn's book on U.S. and British writers who had written about Mexico from 1556 to 1973 appeared in 1974. It was published in Spanish by Fondo de Cultura Económica in 1977. Written when a new sensibility in questions of ethnicity, class, and gender was emerging, this book, although valuable, makes an anachronistic reading all too possible. However critical, the author finally positions himself as an outsider along with the authors and protagonists who felt "excluded" from an "alien world" that inspired "fear" in the visitor (traveler or tourist).[23] The reason, Gunn discovers, that Anglos find Europe a more familiar and shareable place is that Mexico is 30 percent pure Indian and 60 percent mestizo. At San Cristobal de las Casas, he says, "I faced an alien world from which I was forever excluded and that was therefore somewhat frightening."[24] Lawrence's *The Plumed Serpent* and Oscar Lewis's *The Children of Sanchez*, as he read them in the United States, were exactly how he remembered Mexico: obscure and with death and brutality all around. He quotes Henry Bamford Parkes's *A History of Mexico* (1938) to clarify his point further: " 'The Mexicans more than most other people were a race who always lived close to death, a closeness which had belonged both to those who worshipped Huitzilopochtli and to those who had introduced the Inquisition and the bullfight.' "[25]

In 1974, Gunn reelaborated the discourse of "civilization and barbarism" so prevalent in the nineteenth century on the American continent, the distancing trope continuously rewritten since the first encounter. Let us not forget that in the Zoot Suit Trials of the 1940s the accused were introduced as descendants of the bloodthirsty Aztecs, that is, as biologi-

---

[22]Oscar Mandel, "From Chihuahua to the Border," in *New Directions in Prose and Poetry 49*, ed. J. Laughlin (New York: New Directions, 1985), 63. I would like to thank Gaspar Rivera for bringing this story to my attention.

[23]Drewey Wayne Gunn, *American and British Writers in Mexico, 1556–1973* (Austin: University of Texas Press, 1974), 255.

[24]Gunn, *American and British Writers*, 254.

[25]Quoted in ibid.

cally predisposed to criminal behavior.[26] This image is still selling copies of Gary Jennings's book *Aztec*, a "remembrance of things past." The back cover reads thus: "This is the story of a man and his people. It is the story of Mixtli. . . . With Mixtli we experience blood-drenched but awesomely grand sacrificial ceremonies; we encounter other blood curdling forms of violence."[27] Gerald Jonas, in his review in the *New York Times* Book Review Section, is especially fond of the book's descriptions of cannibalism and the way Mixtli describes his first taste of baby stew, "tender white meat flaking off delicate bones."[28]

An event proving that reality is stranger than fiction seems to mark a continuity. In April 1989 fifteen bodies were discovered at the Rancho Santa Elena, twenty miles west of Matamoros by the Rio Grande. The killings involved drug traffickers practicing occult and sacrificial rituals. Four books narrating the gruesome horror story of the Matamoros killings quickly followed. In 1989 three nonfiction novels hit the market: 275,000 copies of *Cauldron of Blood* by Jim Schutze, 250,000 copies of *Across the Border* by Gary Provost, and 50,000 copies of *Hell Ranch* by Clifford L. Linedecker. In 1991, *Buried Secrets*, by Pulitzer Prize-winner Edward Humes, was added.[29] The true crime genre exemplified by Truman Capote's *In Cold Blood* was now placed at the not-so-romantic "south of the border."

The anthology *Gringos in Mexico*, compiled in 1988 by Edward Simmen, with stories written from the late 1800s to 1980s, is even more disturbing. The introduction presents many of the stories anthologized as timeless narratives capturing the unchanging essence of Mexico and its peoples. The foreword, written by the author John Graves, once again conceptualizes the project of this anthology within the trope of difference. Graves draws the line as he states that "Mexico for deep and ancient reasons is an especially, emphatically foreign country, one that has always rebuffed easy familiarity from outsiders except of a surface sort."[30]

[26]D. Tuck Ruth, "The Zoot Suit Riots," *Survey Graphic* 43 (1943): 333–336, among others during this period, reported on the trial. This scene is re-created in the play *Zoot Suit* (1979) and in the movie of the same name, both by Luis Valdés.

[27]Gary Jennings, *Aztec* (New York: Avon, 1980).

[28]Gerald Jonas, "Before Cortés," *New York Times Book Review* 14 (December 1980): 11.

[29]Jim Schutze, *Cauldron of Blood* (New York: Avon, 1989); Gary Provost, *Across the Border: The True Story of the Satanic Cult Killings in Matamoros, Mexico* (New York: Pocket Books, 1989); Clifford L. Linedecker, *Hell Ranch: The Nightmare Tale of Voodoo, Drugs, and Death in Matamoros* (Austin, TX: Diamond Books, 1989); Edward Humes, *Buried Secrets: A True Story of Serial Murder, Black Magic, and Drug Running on the U.S. Border* (New York: Dutton, 1991).

[30]Simmen, *Gringos in Mexico*, xxii.

These stories, written over the last hundred years, are an attempt at comprehension, he affirms. Literature as mediated language is positioned and, for most of the stories, that positioning assumes the "other" as object, thus impeding the creation of a space where dialogue is possible. For Tzvetan Todorov this is possible if "after having spent some time with the 'other,' the 'specialist' doesn't return to the original point of departure; but rather makes an effort to find a space of common understanding, of creating a discourse that not only takes advantage of the outsider position, but that speaks *to* the others and not only *about* the others."[31] The asymmetrical positioning in these stories, however, continues to mark the differences as irreconcilable.

El Norte, Upward Mobility, or "Push Them Back, Way Back"

Whereas Anglos considered the nineteenth-century displacement of the Mexicans as natural, they perceived the Mexicans' twentieth-century movement to the north as transgressive—an invasion. After the 1846–1848 war, a limited migration of Mexicans back and forth across the border appeared natural given that the territory once had belonged to Mexico and that (as is still true today) existing blood relations motivated many of the trips. Americans believed that Manifest Destiny sanctioned their journeys to the south, but, from the beginning, they branded Mexican incursions into the north, whatever their cause, as transgressions that must be punished. Juan N. Cortina's efforts to recuperate land marked him a bandit; Pancho Villa's raids into New Mexico are remembered as sacrilege.

The transgressors from the south were labeled "greasers," "wetbacks," "*bandidos*" (bandits), "invaders," "illegal aliens." But because the boundary was established by the Anglos, many believed that they could cross it at will. For example, entering Mexico to kidnap a suspected murderer during the presidency of George Bush was perceived as appropriate, as we witnessed with the seizure of Alvarez Machain. And in some cases, Anglo crossings were perceived to have been sanctioned by those "others" in power, such as in the search for Villa: says the famous *corrido* of the Revolution, "En nuestro Mexico Febrero 23, dejó Carranza pasar Americanos" ([President] Carranza allowed Americans to come into our Mexico on February 23). By 1912 an article in *The Survey* by Samuel Bryan of Stanford University warned that the Mexicans, and with them

[31]Tzvetan Todorov, "El cruzamiento entre culturas," in *Cruce de culturas y mestizaje cultural* (Madrid: Ediciones Júcar, 1988), 30: "Luego de haber pasado una temporada entre lo 'otro', el 'especialista' no regresa al mismo punto de partida; se esfuerza por encontrar un terreno de entendimiento común, de crear un discurso que saque partido de su exterioridad pero que al mismo tiempo hable *a* los otros y no sólo *de* los otros."

numerous social problems, were invading American territory. The author warned, "Although the Mexicans have afforded an efficient, cheap and elastic labor supply for the southwestern U.S., the evils they bring to the community have to be considered."[32] His analysis, without regard for economic, political, or racial realities, established that the "evils" of the Mexicans, due to "their low standards of living and of morals, their illiteracy, their utter lack of proper political interest, the retarding effect of their employment upon the wage scale of the more progressive races and finally their tendency to colonize in urban centers, with evil results, combine to stamp them as a rather undesirable class of residents."[33]

By 1914 the racism is clearly spelled out by E. L. C. Morse in *The Dial*, a semimonthly journal of literary criticism published in Chicago: "An inarticulate, amiable and immature race have unlimited aspirations for mezcal, gambling, cockfighting, robbery and murder when drunk and no aspiration for representative government, just and impartial judiciary, civil service reform and community altruism."[34] Neither did the Good Neighbor policy of the late 1930s alleviate the fear of the brown invasion, although certainly articles in the press became more culturally sensitive.

A short story, "Fiesta in St. Paul," written by Grace Flandrau and published in 1946 in the *Yale Review*, although seemingly not racist, registers a concern about the increasing migration and presence of Mexicans and the changing landscape that these now not-so-distant neighbors provide. "A number of people, all Mexicans and mostly in native costume, had, however, arrived . . . and it was odd to have them there. An American city on the upper Mississippi does not seem quite the background for Mexicans—especially these full-blooded Mexican Indians who, for the most part, make up St. Paul's Mexican population."[35]

The story, about the celebration of Mexico's Independence Day at a public park in St. Paul, re-creates the festivities of the afternoon and the willingness of the protagonist to participate in this pageant of international goodwill. The Mexican characters are portrayed again and again, with the same adjectives. Although described individually, they are also collectively signaled as "very dark." Cultural traits and behavior patterns are essentialized, seen as static. "In spite of their American clothes, they might have been any of the Indians who used to come down from their high villages to work on our Mexican plantation in the coffee picking

---

[32]Samuel Bryan, "Mexican Immigrants in the United States," *The Survey* 28 (1912): 726–730.

[33]Ibid., 730. In an article, earlier Bryan estimated that "some 15,000 persons of this race are residents of L.A. and vicinity."

[34]E. L. C. Morse, *The Dial* 57 (1914): 11.

[35]Grace Flandrau, "Fiesta in St. Paul," *Yale Review* 33, no. 1 (1946): 69.

seasons."[36] The female protagonist continues: "Tonight on this Minnesota picnic ground were the same dark, naive faces, the same feeling of zest, amenity, and good manners that did not in the least preclude the ever-present hint of sleeping violence. And just as on the plantation there had seldom been a ball without its stabbing or shooting, so this St. Paul fiesta produced at least one minor knifing."[37]

The narrator wishes to see the Indians as unchanged in this new territory, but in fact the tone of uneasiness that persists throughout the story belies her affirmations. Back in Veracruz, the Indians were servants with little possibility of upward mobility. As the protagonist looks back on her time in Veracruz, she remembers another fiesta where she could distance herself from the "natives" and "their" events. As an outsider partaking in the ceremony in Mexico, the "other" seemed to belong to that landscape, its natural extension, albeit "barbaric" at times. In the United States, the Indian's difference is emphasized, not against the American, but against nature itself—in this case a park where the Mexican's presence seems incongruent, unnatural. Throughout the story, the narrator's nostalgic and ongoing reminiscing imaginatively transports the Mexicans back to their original habitat south of the border. It seems wishful thinking in the face of a rapidly changing America and the anxiety this produces.

The Border Zone, or There's a Place for Us

With the continuous diaspora from the south forming communities in the United States with cultures that maintain strong ties to their original homelands and thus establish regular circuits of communication, the original line of demarcation—the borderline—becomes less clear. The one line separating north from south has expanded, mixing and blurring what were once seen as distinct cultures. The traveler's itinerary is diffuse. The crossings are multiple and complex.

By 1979, Joel Garreau, in *The Nine Nations of North America*, saw a third country emerging. He named it MexAmerica, a nation within a nation. It's where the gumbo of Dixie gives way to the refried beans of Mexico. The land looks like northern Mexico. And the sound of Spanish in the supermarkets and on the airwaves is impossible to ignore. The news stories it produces highlight the trouble Anglo institutions have in dealing with enormous cultural strain. It's a place where the cops sometimes shoot third-generation Americans of Mexican descent for very controversial reasons, a region faced with the question of whether the American Dream applies to innocent kids born of people who have crossed the bor-

[36]Ibid.
[37]Ibid., 75.

der illegally. It's hot and dry. It has more big dreams per capita than any other place you will ever know. Its capital is Los Angeles, but it stretches all the way to Houston. The politicians have difficulty comprehending it because it ignores political boundaries. But it's there, it's there.[38]

To the north, according to Garreau, MexAmerica extends as far as San Francisco, Sacramento, and Santa Fe; to the east as far as Austin and Houston; and to the south it reaches Hermosillo, Chihuahua, and Monterrey. By 1988, MexAmerica, as mapped by Lester D. Langley, had further expanded its territory: north to Chicago and Pittsburgh and south to Mexico City. Langley's intent was to show that American culture and politics are heavily influenced by their Mexican-American content and that MexAmerica from Chicago to Mexico City is shaping its values: "We can measure the U.S. imprint on Mexico and on Mexican Americans. Until now we have been loath to recognize the effective reach of Mexico north of the Rio Bravo, but the Mexicano imprint is deeper than we want to admit."[39] Indeed, Los Lobos, Doctor Loco, Flaco Jiménez, Linda Ronstadt, and Frida Kahlo, having claimed their Mexican roots, are celebrated as icons of the broad tapestry and the often redefined American folklore.

The imprint began to be acknowledged after the civil rights movements of the sixties when black Americans shattered the image of a homogeneous America by contesting the racism that had pushed them to the margins of society and discourse. Blacks and later Mexicanos, Chicanos, Latinos, women, Native Americans, and other previously marginalized groups proclaimed their right to be recognized as participants in and contributors to the history of the United States. In her excellent book *America Revised* (1979), Frances FitzGerald shows how racist textbooks that were written early in the century proclaiming an Anglo worldview to which all had to be integrated were forced to change their master story. In the 1920s, European immigration had accentuated the assimilationist position, and textbooks, says FitzGerald, presented immigrants as outsiders. A quote from David Sayville Muzzy's *An American History* (1911) represents the period's preoccupation: "Can we assimilate and mold into citizenship the millions who are coming to our shores, or will they remain an ever-increasing body of aliens, undigested, an indigestible element in our body politic and a constant menace to our free institutions?"[40] In the twenties, the textbooks expressed a good deal of pessimism about assimilation, says

[38]Joel Garreau, *The Nine Nations of North America* (Boston: Houghton Mifflin, 1981), ix, x.

[39]Quoted in Lester D. Langley, *MexAmerica: Two Countries, One Future* (New York: Crown, 1988), 7

[40]Quoted in Frances FitzGerald, *America Revised: History Schoolbooks in the Twentieth Century* (Boston: Little, Brown and Co., 1979), 78.

FitzGerald, quoting an example from that decade that warns that "great racial groups especially such as speak a foreign language or belong to races which we do not readily intermarry do add to the difficulty of solving certain social problems."[41] In the 1930s, Harold Rugg introduced the theory of America as the "melting pot," where millions of people of foreign speech and customs are thrown in with native colonial stock to be fused into a new type of American.

By the sixties, however, the melting pot had become, in Américo Paredes's words, a "sizzling fry pan." The "immigrants" talked back and have not stopped. Films such as *Salt of the Earth* were finally released. Revisionist scholars recorded and rewrote the history of the country to include resistance acts omitted previously. These scholars, many of them Chicanos, published books and articles in the United States that contested the stereotypical images of the Mexicans. Latin American, Mexican, and Chicano/Latino studies programs sprang up in universities. This time, Mexicans presented the view from across the Rio Bravo. Carlos Fuentes, for example, was one of the writers who responded to the accounts of the Anglo travelers. In *The Old Gringo* he redrew the border. In his novel, unlike the Anglo writers who direct their writings to an American audience, Fuentes implicitly erases the border as he addresses both nations. Although his writing is also marked by the trope of difference, he chooses characters, themes, and contexts from both sides of the border and maliciously places them in a space where confrontation, dialogue, and eye-to-eye contact become inevitable. "The general and the gringo looked at each other in silence, communicating from opposite sides of a deep chasm."[42] The "other" meets the "other," and everyone is unmasked. "Americans always moved West, but until the Revolution, Mexicans had never moved at all."[43] "Yes, the gringos did. They spent their lives crossing frontiers, theirs and those that belonged to others, and now the old man had crossed to the south because he didn't have any frontiers left to cross in his own country."[44]

Whereas *The Old Gringo* captures U.S.-Mexican relations in the past, Fuentes's *Christopher Unborn* addresses the present and future of that relationship in a sacrilegious and sarcastic form. The fear of silent invasion that Americans secretly, and sometimes not so secretly, harbor is voiced through one of the characters: "We've got to terminate this country that exports greasers who are invading us like the plague of locusts

---

[41]Quoted in ibid., 79.
[42]Carlos Fuentes, *The Old Gringo*, trans. Margaret Sayers Peden (New York: Farrar, Straus, and Giroux, 1985), 28.
[43]Ibid., 109.
[44]Ibid., 13.

that destroyed Pharaoh's power! Michigan is not growing, South Carolina is not growing, Georgia isn't growing, not even your own home state
Texas is growing, Professor, we aren't having kids but all these greasers
grow and grow and cross over and cross over and they'll end up coupling
with our own daughters and mothers and wives."[45] In the novel the north-
south border has disappeared, and the characters have no choice but to
inhabit and interact in a cross-cultural, interlingual space. Futuristic and
nightmarish, it is finally a criticism of both the U.S. and Mexican official
nationalisms, whose symbols have become commodified objects or empty
rhetoric devoid of any signifying process that might viably address the
problems facing the two nations. Both rhetorics are captured as
anachronistically behind the reality around them. Within its new, redrawn
borders, MexAmerica has become an independent state.

The erosion of unifying concepts of national identity in the United
States and in Mexico has made the border zone, once the periphery of
both nation-states, the center and the main item on the agenda. A hybrid
culture has emerged that is rejected by both hegemonic centers, which
are still holding to, on the one hand, the "American assimilationist dream"
and, on the other, the concept of "the *raza cósmica.*" The "cosmic race"
imagined by José Vasconcelos is privileged, a hybrid race, a *mestizaje*
that recognizes the indigenous make-up of the Mexican.[46] In effect,
Vasconcelos's postrevolutionary discourse helped consolidate a nationalist assimilative construct of the nation that defined itself as homogeneous
and essentialist and was founded on an inclusionary politics that erased
difference.[47] Post-1968 Mexican literature spoke to the heterogeneity of
the Mexican people and explicitly and implicitly attacked the reified symbols of official Mexico used to maintain hegemony in that country. Those
have been the images exported as folklore to the United States: revolutionary heroes, *charros*, mariachis, sarapes, pre-Columbian gods,
mestizaje, cacti, Virgins of Guadalupe, or, the more recently arrived icon,
Frida Kahlo. In themselves, their value is not disputed; it is their use that
is questioned. Many of these images, however, were creatively appropriated and recycled by Chicanos and Mexicanos in the seventies and eight-
ies. Symbols that homogenize Mexicans thus are used by some Chicanos
to undermine and resist racist Anglo nationalist agendas, such as the
English-only movement. Transculturated, or "transcreated," as Juan Flores

---

[45]Carlos Fuentes, *Christopher Unborn*, trans. Alfred MacAdam (New York:
Farrar, Straus, and Giroux, 1989), 493.

[46]José Vasconcelos, *La raza cósmica* (Mexico: Espasa Calpe-Mexicana,
1948).

[47]See Roger Bartra, *La jaula de la melancolía: Identidad y metamorfosis del
mexicano* (Mexico: Grijalbo, 1987).

and George Yudice would say, these images open a space where identities within the nation-state are being recreated and transformed.[48]

Literarily and figuratively, Chicanos also crossed the border to Mexico and were mainly disillusioned. There was no going back to the Old Country that had originally invited them to abandon its oppressive conditions. In the 1940s the cognitive dissonance of the Chicano translated into questions of "Where do I belong?" and "How do I balance two worlds that reject me?" which gave birth to the pachuco—the zoot suiter—an aesthetic imagining that became an ethic, as Carlos Monsiváis has said, a search for and the creation of a new and radical identity, rejected and repressed in the United States and in Mexico.[49] Octavio Paz, in *El laberinto de la soledad* (The labyrinth of solitude), first published in 1950, sees the pachuco as an aberration; he is unable to understand the process of ethnic self-valorization implied in this early social movement of contestation.[50] The spaces created by this identity crisis, however, became the antecedents to the Chicano movements of the seventies. The search for identity took many forms. In their search for origins, some crossed spatial borders and found little or nothing; many then crossed temporal borders reaching to the past and finding and founding Aztlán, a utopian space from where a new identity could be constructed—perhaps problematic, but certainly establishing a point of departure. Others crossed and made a U-turn. However, the crossing back over the threshold did not provide the same feeling of coming home as for the Anglo traveler.

Because Chicanos are searching for an identity they believe they have left behind, their journeys are more painful. The horizontal crossing did not provide any answers, but problematized further an already complex identity crisis. The protagonist in Oscar Zeta Acosta's *The Autobiography of a Brown Buffalo* crosses the border at Juarez. Reminiscent of our Anglo travelers, he finds two prostitutes and spends some time engaged in gaiety, tequila, tacos, and twin playmates. He gets arrested, is put in jail, and, not speaking Spanish, is told to go home and learn his father's language. But he thought he *was* home. Upon crossing back he is told he does not look American. "My single mistake has been to seek an identity with any one person or nation or with any part of history. . . . What I see now . . . is that I am neither a Mexican nor an American. I am neither a

---

[48]Juan Flores and George Yudice, "Living Borders/Buscando América," *Social Text* 24 (1990): 69.

[49]Carlos Monsiváis, "The Culture of the Frontier: The Mexican Side," in *Views Across the Border: The United States and Mexico*, ed. Stanley R. Ross (Albuquerque: University of New Mexico Press, 1978), 63.

[50]Octavio Paz, *El laberinto de la soledad* (Mexico: Fondo de Cultura Económica, 1972).

Catholic nor a Protestant. I am Chicano by ancestry and a Brown Buffalo by choice."[51] In Zeta Acosta's second autobiographical novel, *The Revolt of the Cockroach People*, the protagonist goes to Acapulco and learns not only about the struggle for land reform but also that the fight against oppression is not a national one; it is a transnational class struggle. Ethnic identity becomes class conscious.[52] In Gloria Anzaldúa's *Borderlands*, the crossings are further complicated by gender and sexuality.[53]

The attempts in literature to erase borders somehow cannot compete with the images in the newspapers and magazines. As it is wonderfully portrayed in the final scenes of *Born in East L.A.*, the fear of the brown and/or silent invasion is generating the most virulent attacks since cultural hegemony and political control were in question in the 1840s. The two-part article in the *Atlantic Monthly* by William Langewiesche (May and June 1992) registers what many believe is a lack of control. "Inevitably, there are calls to seal the border. This could be done, but only with enormous manpower—for instance, with a large-scale deployment of the U.S. armed forces and the creation of free-fire zones. It would not require much killing: the Soviets sealed their borders for decades without an excessive expenditure of ammunition. The simple fact that there existed a systematic policy of shooting illegal immigrants would deter most Mexicans."[54] Even granting the irony in Langewiesche's piece and his acknowledgment that obviously most Americans would be against his proposal is not sufficient to erase the bad taste of the verbal aggressiveness permitted. The English-only movement, the steel fences, the lighting up of the border, the rounding up of Mexicans during the L.A. riots are certainly phenomena indicative of what Miriam Davidson had anticipated in *The Nation* in 1990 and called "The Mexican Border War."[55] The construction of another wall, one between north and south, now that the Berlin Wall is no longer, seems urgent. The Republicans included such a wall in their platform for the 1992 election year. Reflecting mirrors and headlight beams at the border, however, provide an imagery of metaphoric contestation, wherein the border becomes that state of siege within the nervous system

[51]Oscar Zeta Acosta, *The Autobiography of a Brown Buffalo* (San Francisco: Straight Arrow Books, 1972), 199.

[52]Oscar Zeta Acosta, *The Revolt of the Cockroach People* (San Francisco: Straight Arrow Books, 1973).

[53]Gloria Anzaldúa, *Borderlands/La Frontera: The New Mestiza* (San Francisco: Spinsters/Aunt Lute, 1987).

[54]William Langewieshe, "The Border," *Atlantic Monthly* (May 1992): 53–92; and (June 1992): 91–108.

[55]Miriam Davidson, "The Mexican Border War: Immigration-Bashing," *The Nation* 251, no. 16 (November 12, 1990): 557–560.

to which Michael Taussig alludes—a "state of emergency," not the "exception but the rule," "where order is frozen, yet disorder boils beneath the surface," and "tension lies in repose."[56]

This end of the millennium is one of epistemic crisis, when polemical words such as "multiculturalism" and "pluralism" are eroding concepts of homogeneity generated by official nationalism in the United States and in Mexico. The backlash is strong. The American dream of assimilation has become Anglophilic and ethnocidal. In *Harper's Magazine* (January 1992), Lewis H. Lapham insists that hyphenated Americans should finally become assimilated to the American Dream to end the jumble of confused or mistaken identities.[57] Eric Hobsbawm answers, "Development in the modern world economy, because it generates vast population movements, constantly undermines ethnic-linguistic homogeneity. Multiethnicity and plurilinguality are quite unavoidable, except temporarily by mass exclusion, forcible assimilation, mass expulsion or genocide, in short, by coercion."[58]

Epilogue, or the Myth of the Eternal Return

The translations of the works of the Mexican writers Carlos Fuentes, Octavio Paz, Rosario Castellanos, Carlos Monsiváis, José Emilio Pacheco, Elena Poniatowska, Roger Bartra, and, more recently, of Angeles Mastreta, Laura Esquivel, Arturo Azuela, Homero Aridjis, Luis Zapata, Paco Ignacio Taibo II, and Barbara Jacobs, when added to the literature that the Chicanos are producing and to the new Mexican cinema that entered the popular culture market in the nineties (*Danzón, Cabeza de Vaca, Like Water for Chocolate*), deconstruct the invented images of the past that held Mexicans in a culturally and morally disadvantaged position. Together they create, from across the border, the complex images of Mexico today, and, on the U.S. side of the border, the images of a creative and struggling people reaching self-affirmation and assertiveness.[59] After 1968 this literature implicitly has proposed a postnational identity based on pluricultural and democratic forms of civic life. Somehow, however, one gets the feeling that we are engaged in *un diálogo de sordos* (a dialogue

---

[56]Michael Taussig, *The Nervous System* (New York: Routledge, 1992), 10.

[57]Lewis H. Lapham, "Who and What Is American," *Harper's Magazine* 284, no. 1700 (January 1992): 43–49.

[58]Eric Hobsbawm, "The Perils of the New Nationalism," *The Nation* 253, no. 15 (November 4, 1991): 537–538.

[59]This convergence is indicative of the creation of spaces of dialogue that have been emerging in the last five years. Chicano and Mexicano intellectuals, and in particular Chicana and Mexicana writers, are talking with each other. See the interview with Richard Rodríguez, David Torres, and Joseph Trevino, "De la

of the deaf). It is not a problem of literacy but a problem of communication: no one is reading, no one is talking, language barriers are not crossed; it is a problem of listening.

otra memoria a los días de obligación," *La Jornada* (July 24, 1994): 18–21; and Aralia López, Amelia Malagamba, and Elena Urrutia, eds., *Mujer y literatura mexicana y chicana: Culturas en contacto* (Mexico: El Colegio de México, 1990).

Beyond Myths and Borders in Mexican and North American Literature

Luis Leal

BEYOND ITS BASIC MORAL AND AESTHETIC VALUES, a work of literature also entails certain social and historical functions that have been recognized by critics the world over. In his essay "Breve reseña histórica de la crítica" (Brief historical review of criticism), Alfonso Reyes clearly states that literature must inevitably fulfill a social role "not merely by reason of its origin, but because of the essential unity of the spirit." Reyes adds that "the ancillary nature of literature is made more apparent during times of crisis when, with all the resources at its disposal, human intelligence is attempting to provide remedies; and also it is emphasized in proportion to the increase in the human transcendence of the work in question."[1]

One of the social functions that literature fulfills is that of creating personal or social paradigms that serve as models for the reader. Whether directly or by means of translations, readers are made aware of a community's ways of living, thinking, and being, of the behavior of a nation's inhabitants, their aspirations and ideals, their attitudes and values, as well as their myths, legends, and prejudices, even though the particular community may be physically unknown to the reader. And in cases where the reader can claim a prior knowledge, the experience of reading is often much more effective than other ways of learning and interpreting the history of a nation. In the book *En tierra yankee* (In Yankee territory), in which Justo Sierra gives his impressions of a trip he made to the United States and Canada in 1895, we find the following rather interesting

An earlier Spanish version of this work appeared in *Mexican Studies/Estudios Mexicanos* 9, no. 1 (Winter 1993): 95–118. It is published here with permission from The Regents of the University of California.

[1]Alfonso Reyes, *Obras completas*, vol. 14 (Mexico: Fondo de Cultura Económica, 1962), 337.

statement: "All this pessimism of mine is 'bookish' and derives from what I have read about North American society. I didn't observe well."[2]

Furthermore, literature recognizes no boundaries. It is not limited to verifiable facts, because it can encompass events in imaginary lives. Literature finds its characters among the most obscure beings and can give them a voice. Carlos Fuentes has observed that "there are many things that history, reason and logic don't see, but that perhaps novelists do see. There are some things that only Dostoyevsky has seen."[3]

No less important for literature is the presence of myths, both old and new. Myths are firmly established as a way of interpreting human nature and culture. According to Mircea Eliade, myths have not disappeared. He claims that the presence of certain symbols in society may be interpreted as the persistence of collective thought, a form of thought that has not altogether disappeared and within which myths are the principal form.[4]

The North American writer Ambrose Bierce, in his satirical book *The Devil's Dictionary* (1911), published two years before his death in Mexico, defines mythology as the combined beliefs relating to the origin, early history, heroes, gods, and other concepts that are found among primitive peoples in contrast to the true beliefs that are invented nowadays. As we know, these "true beliefs" of modern man are of capital importance to the social groups that invent them; however, we also know that those beliefs and myths are often damaging in their effect on other communities and therefore contribute to dissolution rather than to the unity of nations. Such is the case of the myth of the racial and cultural superiority of the Anglo American and the inferiority of Hispanic and indigenous races. These harmful concepts, negative beliefs, and historical and cultural myths are what literature helps history to overcome.

From this perspective, it seems to me that literature affords an excellent means of international exchange, because it can help to correct errors and prejudices and thereby reduce tensions and conflicts, especially between neighboring countries that have different cultures, as in the case of Mexico and the United States. In the nineteenth century, Ignacio Manuel Altamirano was aware that literature had the power to project the cultural wealth of a nation beyond its geographical borders. He tells us that the

[2]Justo Sierra, *Viajes (En tierra yankee, en la Europa latina)*, ed. José Luis Martínez (Mexico: Universidad Nacional Autónoma de México, 1948), 192.

[3]Bill Moyers, "The Many Worlds of Carlos Fuentes," interview, *Bill Moyers' Journal* (June 19, 1980): 4.

[4]Mircea Eliade, *Myths, Dreams, and Mysteries* (New York: Harper and Row, 1967), 24.

novels of Sir Walter Scott brought the attention "of the entire world to his country, which previously had been so unknown."[5]

According to this view, literature has the power to transcend artificial national borders in order to circulate and make known in other countries a truer vision of the people and the culture that produce it and thereby to promote a better understanding among nations. By literature, we mean works of fiction such as novels, short stories, dramatic works, essays, and poetry. We also can include here the works of some historians when they refer to literature or when they express ideas related to the theme of the present discussion.

Although there are numerous historical and political studies of the relations between Mexico and the United States, the literatures of these two neighboring countries have not been studied from such a perspective, with the aim of documenting the contributions of each. The only exceptions are the books of Cecil Robinson (*Mexico and the Hispanic Southwest in American Literature*) and Stanley T. Williams (*The Spanish Background of American Literature*), which, however, do not concern themselves with the other side of the coin, which is the presence of the United States in Mexican literature.[6]

For the purposes of the present essay, we will be able to just briefly examine the nature of some of the myths that occur most frequently in literature and that have been the source of conflicts between representatives of the two great cultures that settled in the New World. The emphasis will be on the myths that appeared among the people of the United States and Mexico, for it was these two nations that confronted one another, face to face, in North America.

The Roots of Euro-American Conflict

During the colonial period, the conflicts that developed between Anglos and Hispanics, whether in Europe or in the New World, were primarily the result of religious and racial antagonisms. In Europe the wars between Protestants and Catholics were very intense. The racial struggles grew out of the pseudoscientific myth that held that America was a continent on which both nature and human beings had degenerated.[7]

[5]Ignacio Manuel Altamirano, *La literatura nacional*, ed. José Luis Martínez (Mexico: Editorial Porrúa, 1949), 1:12.

[6]I have dealt in part with an aspect of this issue in "El norteamericano en la literatura mexicana," *The Bilingual Review/La Revista Bilingüe* 6, no. 1 (1979): 31–38.

[7]See Antonello Gerbi, *Viejas polémicas sobre el nuevo mundo: En el umbral de una conciencia americana*, 3d ed. (Lima: Banco de Crédito del Perú, 1946), ch. 1.

According to the theories of the celebrated French naturalist Georges-Louis Leclerc de Buffon, who was the author of *Histoire naturelle* (1749–1789), the climate of the New World was malignant and caused the degeneration of both plants and animals. The philosopher Corneille de Pauw, author of *Recherches philosophiques sur les Américains* (Philosophical research on the Americans) (1771), extended the theory to include the native peoples of the Americas, while the Scottish historian William Robertson, author of the *History of America* (1777), accepted the idea and caused it to be spread throughout the English-speaking world. The ideas that Robertson expressed were taken up by other authors who wrote about Mexico and the Latin American countries.[8] Stanley Williams indicates that Robertson's book was responsible for the almost century-long popularity of various types of prose and verse narratives about South America and Mexico. It also influenced romantic historians such as Washington Irving and William H. Prescott.[9] Raymund Paredes, in his study of the origins of anti-Mexican sentiment in the United States, adds that the popularity of Robertson's work "served to bring into play the final component necessary to form an ideological prism through which Americans would view contemporary Mexicans in the 19th century."[10]

The theory of the supposed inferiority of America and Americans was contested by, among others, Thomas Jefferson and Benjamin Franklin. The Italian scholar Antonello Gerbi notes that Jefferson defended the inhabitants of America, who had been slandered by De Pauw, and that he attempted to confound Buffon by ordering that a moose be sent to him from America. Gerbi also writes that Franklin invited the abbot Guillaume Raynal, who was a popularizer of the ideas of De Pauw, to a dinner attended by five very short Frenchmen and five gigantic Americans, in order to give the abbot an object lesson.[11]

Among the Mexicans of the period who most forcefully attacked the ideas of De Pauw and Robertson were Francisco Javier Clavijero and Fray Servando Teresa de Mier. While in Italy, Clavijero wrote an entire book (the *Disertaciones*, a supplement to his *Historia antigua de México*) (1780) to rebut the theories of the degeneration of the Mexican people but primarily to oppose the ideas of De Pauw, whose book, which Clavijero

[8]See the study by Frederick S. Stimson, "William Robertson's Influence on Early American Literature," *The Americas* 14, no. 1 (July 1957): 37–43.

[9]Stanley T. Williams, *The Spanish Background of American Literature*, 2 vols. (New Haven, CT: Yale University Press, 1955), 1:26.

[10]Raymund A. Paredes, "The Origins of Anti-Mexican Sentiment in the United States," in *New Directions in Chicano Criticism*, ed. Ricardo Romo and Raymund A. Paredes (Santa Barbara: University of California, Santa Barbara, Center for Chicano Studies, 1984), 157.

[11]Gerbi, *Viejas polémicas*, 99.

calls a collection of blunders, attempted to convince the world that everything in America had degenerated. According to Clavijero, his refutation is based on direct, personal knowledge of the Mexicans, on his extensive study of their culture, on having known and dealt intimately with the Americans, on having personally observed their character, their genius, their predilections, and their habits of thought, and on having very carefully studied their ancient history, their religion, their government, their laws and customs, all of which qualified him to dispute De Pauw's contentions. Clavijero considered the souls of the Mexicans in no way inferior to those of Europeans, for Mexicans were capable of mastering all the sciences, even the most abstract, if only serious attention were given to their education. "Never," he states, "have Europeans done a greater disservice to their own reason, than when they question the rationality of the Americans."[12]

Fray Servando Teresa de Mier is much more aggressive in his objections than is Clavijero. Mier was firmly convinced that the Spanish had made available to De Pauw negative reports about the New World. Therefore, in the first of his *Cartas de un americano, 1811–1812* (Letters of an American, 1811–1812), Mier wields his combative style, asserting that the Consulado (Merchants' Guild) of Mexico had sent an account to the Cortes (Parliament) of Cádiz that was a compendium of the nonsense that the Spanish had communicated to De Pauw, the very same nonsense that was carelessly repeated by Robertson, Raynal, and Juan Bautista Muñoz.[13]

Manifest Destiny and the Myth of Anglo-American Superiority

In 1816, Fray Servando traveled from London to the United States in the company of General Xavier Mina. They carried with them a printing press with which they planned to issue proclamations in favor of independence for New Spain. Mier returned to the United States in 1821 and, under a variety of influences, among them Thomas Paine's *Common Sense*, he wrote the *Memoria político instructiva*, a work that favored a republic instead of the empire that Agustín de Iturbide was establishing. The six thousand copies he published and sent to Mexico became a source of republican ideals,[14] but not of the Anglo-American belief in the mythic origin of their culture, a belief that would lead to the expansionist policies

[12]Francisco Javier Clavijero, *Historia antigua de México*, 4 vols. (Mexico: Editorial Porrúa, 1945), 4: 258–259 and 1:167.

[13]Fray Servando Teresa de Mier, *Cartas de un americano, 1811–1812* (Mexico: Partido Revolucionario Institucional, 1976), 42.

[14]*La formación de un republicano*, vol. 4 of *Obras completas de Servando Teresa de Mier*, ed. Jaime E. Rodríguez O. (Mexico: Universidad Nacional Autónoma de Mexico, 1988).

of Manifest Destiny. Animated by this myth, the North Americans undertook the territorial expansion of the United States to the south and west as they initiated a process that began with the Louisiana Purchase of 1803, continued with the annexation of Texas, yielded bountiful rewards with the Treaty of Guadalupe Hidalgo in 1848, and culminated with the Spanish-American War of 1898, thus completing a series of historical events that revolve around a myth of origin.

Shortly after the Louisiana Purchase, the United States had begun to expand toward the southern and western regions of the continent, first with the intention of establishing commercial ties, and, shortly afterward, to settle the area. In 1807, Commander Zebulon Montgomery Pike, while exploring the western frontier of Louisiana, inadvertently found himself in territory of New Spain, where he was made a prisoner and taken to Santa Fe.[15] In 1810 he published an account of his adventures, which stirred the interest of North Americans in that world, which they had heretofore ignored. After 1821 they began to invade the vast and largely undefended territory of Mexico. This gave rise to the first conflicts, as the Mexicans resented the new invaders and their myth of racial superiority. The historian David J. Weber observes that the stereotype of the inferior Mexican appears as a result of the arrogant sense of cultural and political superiority known in U.S. history as Manifest Destiny.[16] It was perhaps in an effort to combat this myth that in 1823, during Mexico's First Empire, the secretary of state and foreign affairs, José Cecilio del Valle, published in his newspaper *El Amigo de la Patria* an article that quotes Alexander von Humboldt. The Prussian scholar discredited those who drew "frightful portraits of this beautiful half of the earth," and he defended Mexicans against the attacks of De Pauw. In his masterpiece, *Kosmos*, Humboldt would later deny the existence of superior or inferior races of human beings.[17]

During the first decades of the nineteenth century, myths are prevalent in nearly all North American literary works that dealt with Mexico. Even in the work of Zebulon Pike, one finds a superior attitude (moral, however, rather than racial, Pike being a good Puritan) that is critical of the Mexican way of life: their treatment of women; their dances, which he considers indecent; and their priests, whose conduct he finds deplor-

---

[15]See Cecil Robinson, *Mexico and the Hispanic Southwest in American Literature* (Tucson: University of Arizona Press, 1977), 23–24.

[16]David J. Weber, *Myth and the History of the Hispanic Southwest* (Albuquerque: University of New Mexico Press, 1988), 166.

[17]Gerbi, *Viejas polémicas*, 180. For a negative assessment of Humboldt's ideas regarding Mexico and the Mexicans, see Raymund A. Paredes, "The Image of the Mexican in American Literature" (Ph.D. diss., University of Texas at Austin, 1973), 61–67.

able. In the first North American novel about Mexico, *Francis Berrian; or the Mexican Patriot* (1826), by Timothy Flint, the protagonist takes the side of the insurgents and fights for the independence of Mexico in the armies of Morelos. In this work, the criticism of the Mexican is expressed through the character of Doña Martha, the daughter of the governor of Durango and Berrian's fiancée. The young woman praises the North Americans: "What a noble people! What a difference it is to compare their faces and persons with those of people here!"[18]

One might say that Doña Martha's exclamation gives literary form to the myth of the supposed inferiority of the Mexican.[19] Doña Martha considers the North Americans superior to the Mexicans in their physical appearance as well as in their nobility. Doña Martha is a fictional character created by a North American novelist. Her words reflect the thinking of the author. On the other hand, Lorenzo de Zavala's *Viaje a los Estados Unidos del Norte América* (Trip to the United States of North America) (1834) compares the character of the North Americans and the Mexicans without showing prejudice.[20] The book gave Mexican readers an opportunity to form a clearer notion of their neighbors' way of life, which is captured well by Zavala. Justo Sierra was familiar with the book, as it was reissued in Mérida, Yucatán, in 1846, with an introduction by his father.

Not all North American writers of the period credited the myth of Mexican inferiority, however. Although Zebulon Pike and Albert Pike, another traveler of the period (author of a book entitled *Prose Sketches and Poems*, 1834) criticize the culture of the New Mexicans, they occasionally—in a very few instances—praise certain characteristics, such as the hospitality of the people. This was not the case, however, of the authors of popular novels, such as the so-called dime novels and Westerns, whose central theme was border conflict. For writers of these works, no aspect of Mexican culture was worthy of praise, and their view would prevail in North American literature well into the twentieth century. In his novel *Legends of Mexico* (written in 1846 and published in 1847),

---

[18]Quoted by Robinson, *Mexico and the Hispanic Southwest*, 73. On the life and work of Flint, see John E. Kirkpatrick, *Timothy Flint* (Cleveland: Arthur H. Clark Co., 1911); Lennie M. Walker, "Picturesque New Mexico Revealed in Novel as Early as 1826," *New Mexico Historical Review* 13 (1938): 325–328; and Paredes, "Image of the Mexican in American Literature," 141–148.

[19]A Mexican view of this myth can be found in the work of Samuel Ramos, *El perfil del hombre y la cultura en México*, 2d ed. (Mexico: Editorial Pedro Robredo, 1938); Peter G. Earle, trans., *The Profile of Man and Culture in Mexico* (Austin: University of Texas Press, 1962).

[20]Lorenzo de Zavala, *Viaje a los Estados Unidos del Norte América* (Paris: Imprenta de Decourchant, 1834); reissued by Sierra O'Reilly in Mérida, Yucatán, 1846.

George Lippard predicts the conquest of Mexico with the following words: "Just as the Spaniards conquered the Aztecs, so the mongrel race will be conquered by the northern race of steel."[21]

Lippard and other authors of sensationalist fiction were responsible for the mythification of the historical events of 1836 through 1848. The great myth of Texas began with the dream of Moses Austin and reached its apotheosis at the Alamo, where a handful of "brave men" defended the now-sacred site against the "powerful" army of Santa Anna. Today the Alamo is a shrine that preserves the cult of William Travis, Davey Crockett, Jim Bowie, and the other heroes who, according to the myth, were sacrificed there for Texas independence. The historian Walter Lord, who has traced the development of the Texas myth from its origins, writes that in spite of the zeal with which Texans defend the myth of the Alamo, the heroes who died there were not native Texans. Two-thirds had just recently arrived from other states, and only half a dozen of them had been in the territory more than six years. Still others claim that some had come from Europe to aid the cause of liberty.[22] Lord's statements are supported by the inscriptions on the walls of the Alamo, which indicate the place of origin of each of the heroes. According to those plaques, the only real Texans were the Mexicans who died there.

The myth of the Alamo, which has been so widely popularized by North American novelists and filmmakers, is only one manifestation of a larger myth that is fundamental to North American nationhood, and that is the myth of the frontier. This larger myth was given great importance by Frederick Jackson Turner in his famous essay on the significance of the frontier in American history (1893). Turner attributed the democratic character of North Americans to their struggle to tame the frontier.[23] The defeat of Santa Anna at San Jacinto, which resulted in the independence of Texas, gave great hope to the desires of Anglo Americans who wished to conquer the entire Southwest and establish a nation that extended from the Atlantic to the Pacific.

In spite of efforts by historians to demythify the Alamo, the myth has persisted and has become stronger over time. Novels have had an especially corrosive effect, which at times has carried over into the historical record. Walter Lord notes that Amelia Williams, who made the first attempt to demythify the Alamo legend, built her case on one of the worst

[21]Quoted by Paredes, "Image of the Mexican in American Literature," 158.
[22]Walter Lord, "Myth and Realities of the Alamo," *The American West* 5, no. 3 (May 1968): 20.
[23]On the theory of the frontier in U.S. history, see Weber, *Myth and the History of the Hispanic Southwest*, ch. 3.

novels to depict the historic battle: *Margaret Ballantine, or the Fall of the Alamo.* Williams obtained biographical information from this novel that later was found to be false.[24]

In Mexican literature, the demythification of the Alamo occurs in *Julia* (1868), a novel by Manuel Martínez de Castro that takes place during the Texas revolution and in which the hero easily defeats the Anglo Americans. However, that work was published after the events of 1846–1848, when Mexican attitudes toward the United States and toward North Americans had changed completely. In the United States, another version of the physical superiority myth had been created: that of the Marines who defeated the Mexicans and, according to the Marines' Hymn, advanced to "the halls of Montezuma." The North American invasion produced a Mexican myth as well, that of the "Niños Héroes" (young heroes) of Chapultepec who uselessly gave up their lives in defense of their country.[25]

In the poem *Los niños mártires de Chapultepec* (The young martyrs of Chapultepec), Amado Nervo composes the following verses that present the historical event in a mythic light:

> Their death was no Phoebean conjunction
> nor Diana's melancholy setting,
> but Vesper's eclipse which re-creates
> the heavens with twinkling illumination
> and yields to the brilliance of morning.[26]

Hilarión Frías y Soto attempted something similar in his "Discurso," an address delivered in 1874 on the occasion of the twenty-seventh anniversary of the battle of Chapultepec, in which he decrees that "there the fighting was sublime; for it had a majesty that even Homer couldn't have imagined for his heroes."[27] On the other hand, in 1875 Guillermo Prieto ("Fidel") published a Sunday piece about the very same battle as seen from the point of view of a student named Martín Zapatilla, undoubtedly a fictional character, whom Fidel "quotes." The student lived to write his picaresque memoirs, including an eyewitness account of the famous battle. According to Zapatilla, he is a bit of a poet and he writes the following verses to his beloved Cuca:

---

[24]Lord, "Myth and Realities of the Alamo," 19.

[25]See the brief, anonymous work, Mexico, Departamento del Distrito Federal, *El asalto al Castillo de Chapultepec y los Niños Héroes* (Mexico: Talleres Gráficos de la Nación, 1983).

[26]Ibid., this and the poetic citations that follow.

[27]Ibid.

> The cannon explodes
> the clamor quickens
> and I scream and curse the pitiless Yankee,
> and in order to restore my valor,
> I remember the eyes of my Cuca.

Zapatilla adds a critical statement to his own composition: "But this consonant rhyme in 'uca' disturbs me, perturbs me, sets my wig to bristling, that is, if I were a wigged gentleman." Zapatilla is not a hero like the martyred youths of Chapultepec. According to Fidel, the memoirs end with the following confession: "As I had no funds, nor a gallant figure, like a deer I slipped away as soon as the general was secure."[28]

Joaquín Murrieta, History or Myth?

One of the results of the War of 1847 was the conflict that arose for the Mexicans who remained in the territories that were ceded by Mexico to the United States. The conflict was most intense in California because of the discovery of gold there in 1849, an event that attracted new immigrants from Mexico. The injustices committed against these newcomers caused them to react violently and form small groups of armed marauders who traveled on horseback throughout the state.[29]

These groups are represented in history and legend by Joaquín Murrieta's small band. Despite Murrieta's short life and brief career as the avenger of the wrongs suffered by the Californios, his name has provided historians, novelists, playwrights, and poets with a subject for a good number of works. Many California historians mention his name, many poets sing of him, and many novelists have made him into a mythic hero.[30] And although the historical record on Murrieta is scanty, he is the protagonist of many novels,[31] as well as of other artistic forms, such as theater and films.[32]

[28]Ibid.

[29]See the text edited by Pedro Castillo and Albert Camarillo, *Furia y muerte: Los bandidos chicanos* (Los Angeles: University of California, Los Angeles, Chicano Studies Center, 1973).

[30]For a bibliography on Murrieta, see the Introduction by Joseph Henry Jackson to the novel by John Rollin Ridge, *The Life and Adventures of Joaquín Murrieta, the Celebrated California Bandit* (Norman: University of Oklahoma Press, 1955).

[31]Those with the greatest impact have been Ridge's novel and one by Walter Noble Burns, *The Robin Hood of El Dorado* (New York: Coward-McCann, 1932).

[32]Among the dramatic works, one by Pablo Neruda, *Fulgor y muerte de Joaquín Murrieta, bandido chileno injusticiado en California el 23 de julio de 1853* (Santiago de Chile: Empresa Editorial Zig-Zag, 1967), which was translated into English by Ben Belitt (*Splendor and Death of Joaquín Murieta* [New York: Farrar, Straus, and Giroux, 1972]); and among the films, the 1936 production based on Burns's novel and featuring Warner Baxter as Joaquín.

In the case of Murrieta, history and fiction have become so interwoven that it is impossible to separate them. As an example, in the *Breve historia de México*, José Vasconcelos contributed to spreading the North American version of the myth when he derived his information not from the historical texts, nor even from the first novel, *The Life and Adventures of Joaquín Murieta*, by John Rollin Ridge ("Yellow Bird")—the source of all information about the hero—but from a motion picture, *The Robin Hood of El Dorado* (1936), which was based on a novel of the same name by Walter Noble Burns. Vasconcelos accepted the movie version of Murrieta's life without question, giving a step-by-step description of his adventures, while interjecting his own comments on Mexican politics. He states, for example: "But even with [the presence of] Murrieta the bandits are without a program. They are like Mexican politicians who shout slogans from this or that manifesto without either understanding what they mean or how to implement them if chance should concede them the victory."[33]

Although Vasconcelos declares that the film is "an extraordinarily significant work of fiction," he adds, almost immediately, that Murrieta was a "historical character who was more or less modified in the film version, yet was eminently representative [of reality]."[34] He then describes the key scenes of the film: "Murrieta was robbed of his land, his bride was raped, a generous Yankee friend offered to support his claims. . . . A short time later, Murrieta was beaten by a lynching party. Finally, a bandit came to his aid and made him the leader of a small band that terrorized the district. . . . One night, Murrieta assaulted, not the North Americans, but a group of Mexican property owners who were meeting in an attempt to save their lands from the Yankee businessmen who were usurping their properties."[35]

The film narrated by Vasconcelos does not transform the protagonist as far as Joseph E. Badger's novel, *Joaquín the Saddle King* (1881), in which Murrieta becomes a young blond Spaniard who supported the Texas revolutionaries and later fought on the side of the North Americans in the Mexican War of 1847. When someone asks him why he loves the Americans, Joaquín says: "Oh! because they are very manly: I have lived with them, I have eaten, fought and ridden with them. I am proud that they are my friends. How I wish that they were my countrymen as well!"[36] Thus, in Badger's novel, Murrieta becomes a hero for all North Americans by rejecting his own culture.

[33]José Vasconcelos, *Breve historia de México*, 5th ed. (Mexico: Ediciones Botas, 1944), 386.
[34]Ibid., 385.
[35]Ibid., 385–386.
[36]Paredes, "Image of the Mexican in American Literature," 182.

Despite Mexico's resentment of the United States, the French invasion of Mexico in 1862 presented the United States with an opportunity to recover the goodwill of the Mexican government by helping Benito Juárez in his struggle against Maximilian. Abraham Lincoln, the liberator of the slaves and a friend of Juárez, became the new symbol of his country. When former secretary of state William H. Seward visited Mexico, the journal *El Renacimiento*, under the direction of Ignacio Manuel Altamirano, praised the United States. Nonetheless, the War of 1847 had not been completely forgotten. In the same journal, the poet Julián Montiel commemorated the twenty-second anniversary of the battle of Churubusco by publishing a poem in which the Mexican eagle—so despised by North American writers—awoke from its slumber and repelled the barbaric invasion.

North American Views of Mexican Literature

Shortly after the war, the North American poet William Cullen Bryant, who had shown an early interest in demythifying the pernicious belief in Mexican cultural and racial inferiority, was a guest of the Mexican government. In fact, Bryant was the first writer in his country to recognize that Mexicans possessed a culture that was capable of producing a literature of great merit. By 1827, Bryant had reviewed the novel *Jicotencal*, which, although written by an anonymous author, dealt with the conquest of Mexico.[37] That review was the first critical work on a literary text dealing with a Mexican subject to appear in the United States. In addition, Bryant somehow obtained José Rosas Moreno's *Fábulas* (Fables), which he adapted for the North American public. According to Stanley T. Williams, one stanza by Rosas Moreno, a poet who was hardly known outside of Mexico, affected Bryant more deeply than all of Lope de Vega's comedies.[38] Unlike Longfellow and Lowell, Bryant was immensely interested in Mexican poetry. In 1872, at the age of seventy-eight, Bryant traveled to Mexico, where he was received with high honors and recognized as a great friend. In one of six lengthy letters that recorded his impressions and appeared in the New York *Evening Post*, Bryant referred to Mexican literature in the following terms: "Mexico has her men of science, her eloquent orators, her eminent researchers, her historians, her

---

[37]The review by Bryant appeared in Boston, in *The United States Review and Literary Gazette* 1, no. 5 (February 1827): 336–346. See my article, "*Jicotencal*, primera novela histórica en castellano," *Revista Iberoamericana* 25 (1960): 9–31.

[38]Williams, *Spanish Background of American Literature*, 2:145.

excellent novelists, and numerous poets who write in the melodious language spoken in this country."[39]

It is a fact that even American literary figures of international reputation, such as Washington Irving, James Fenimore Cooper, Walt Whitman, and Richard Henry Dana, accepted the myth of Anglo-American cultural superiority and Manifest Destiny. In 1846, Whitman, who was admired in Latin America for his poetry, wrote the following in a moment of patriotic fervor: "What has miserable, inefficient Mexico, with its superstition, its burlesque upon freedom, its tyranny by the few over the many—what has Mexico to do with the great mission of peopling the New World with a noble race? Be it ours, to achieve that mission!"[40] This assertion is in contrast with what the Old Gringo—the title character of Carlos Fuentes's novel *Gringo viejo* (1985), who represents the writer Ambrose Bierce—tells another American character, the schoolteacher Harriet Winslow, about what he believes to be the superiority of the Mexican *mestizaje* over the myth of racial purity advanced by the North Americans. He declares, "Now open your eyes, Miss Harriet, and recall that we killed our redskins and lacked the courage to fornicate with Indian women and thus produce at least a nation of half and half. We are trapped in this business of forever killing people of a different skin color. Mexico is the proof of what we could have been, so do keep your eyes open."[41]

The United States in Mexican Literature

In the first half of the nineteenth century, Mexican literature had reflected a different attitude toward its neighbor to the north. Only rarely did North Americans appear in the literature during the first decades of the century. When one did, it was in the stereotype of the businessman, the rich merchant interested only in making money, thus giving birth to the myth of North Americans as unscrupulous men who exploit weaker nations.

[39]William Cullen Bryant, *Prose Writings*, ed. Parke Godwin (New York: Russsell and Russell, 1964), 2:179.

[40]Quoted by Robinson in *Mexico and the Hispanic Southwest*, 26, from the collection of Whitman's prose writings published between 1846 and 1847 in Whitman's newspaper, the *Brooklyn Daily Eagle*, and collected by Cleveland Rogers and John Black in *The Gathering of the Forces* (New York: G. P. Putnam and Sons, 1920).

[41]Carlos Fuentes, *Gringo viejo* (Mexico: Fondo de Cultural Económica, 1985), 77. This novel has been translated into English by Margaret Sayers Peden and the author under the title *The Old Gringo* (New York: Farrar, Straus, and Giroux, 1985).

Well before 1900, the year in which José Enrique Rodó expounded
that myth in his transcendental work *Ariel*, the North Americans were
already seen as the representatives of materialist positivism. In Mexico,
the North American businessman appears in literature from the earliest
decades of the nineteenth century. One finds him in José Joaquín Fernández
de Lizardi's novel, *La quijotita y su prima* (1819), in the character of
Jacobo Welser, a Washington businessman. However, in contrast to the
Mexican characters in North American novels, who are all bandits, in
Lizardi's novel the North American Welser is a gentleman who appreci-
ates Mexican culture. Jacobo changes his name to Agustín, gives up his
Anabaptist religion, embraces Catholicism, and marries Carlota. Lizardi,
who was formed in the intellectual climate of the late eighteenth century,
admired the revolutionary movements of France and the United States, as
well as the people who built the first independent nation on the American
continent.

The stereotype of the North American businessman in Mexican literature continues to the present. One finds him in the novel *El monedero*
(1861), by Nicolás Pizarro, in which he appears as a ruthless exploiter
devoid of moral principles. That all North Americans are considered expert businessmen is evident in what the protagonist of *Los caciques* (1917),
a novel by Mariano Azuela, says to a group of merchants: "Gentlemen,
your oracle is the Yankee, the only definition of the word business that
you will ever need is the one that he has taught you."[42] In the play *La
hora de todos* (1949), Juan José Arreola created a character named Harrison
Fish, who may be considered the epitome of the obnoxious businessman.
In Arreola's short stories one finds another stereotype of the North American, the inventor of absurd gadgets. In the story "Baby H.P.," mothers
can purchase a small machine that, when attached to their child's back,
stores the energy produced while the child is playing for later use in the
home—an extremely useful appliance, if it really worked. Another inventor decided to manufacture a plastic woman and advertised her as the
perfect mate. In the novel *Las vueltas del tiempo* (1973), by Agustín Yáñez,
a self-described "nosey gringo" named Max Goldwyn is a caricature of
the American. He finds a way to infiltrate the upper circles of the Mexican political establishment by becoming an inside player. These characters, especially the ones in Arreola, confirm what Octavio Paz has said
about North Americans in *El laberinto de la soledad*. According to Paz,

---

[42]Mariano Azuela, *Los caciques, novela de la Revolución Mexicana, precedida de Las moscas, cuadros y escenas de la Revolución* (Mexico: Ediciones
de "la Razón," 1931), 102.

Americans are credulous and optimistic, they are open and active, they believe in hygiene, work and happiness, and they enjoy their inventions.[43]

In the narrative literature of the Mexican Revolution, one finds several American characters. In *El águila y la serpiente* (1928), by Martín Luis Guzmán, there is a beautiful spy who was working for the Mexican government; there is also a lawyer in San Antonio who helped the Revolution, as well as several adventurers in Villa's army. In general, Guzmán's attitude toward the Americans is a favorable one, except in the case of government officials and representatives. In the same novel by Guzmán, one reads: "It is fortunate—he told me—that the Yankees, except for a few rare exceptions, are persons with whom one can speak frankly. What a great country it would be if the nation were like its individuals!"[44]

Both Guzmán and Rafael Muñoz had lived in the United States, but Muñoz showed less sympathy for the Yankees. In his short story "Un asalto al tren" (1936), he satirized various American archetypes, such as the Hollywood movie cowboy, the elderly female tourist, the big game huntress, the summer school coed, and the newspaper correspondent. The movie star Tom Mix recounts his amazing adventures to his fellow passengers as they travel through Mexico on vacation. But when the train is stopped by a group of revolutionaries (whom the passengers consider to be bandits), the brave cowboy becomes paralyzed with fear. The stereotype of Mexico as a country whose only industry is the manufacture of "Mexican curios" is seen in the question that a tourist wearing a parrot-green sweater asks of a fellow traveler when the train stops at a station: "¿Saber osté qué Mexican curiosities vender aqui?"[45] The huntress, a daughter of one of Theodore Roosevelt's guides, has killed lions and tigers in both Africa and India but faints when the revolutionary appears. The newspaperman is no less of a caricature. He is a representative of the Great Alliance of American Dailies (GAAD), an association whose membership includes ten thousand newspapers and one hundred forty-two magazines. After interviewing the passengers about the rebel assault on the train, the journalist reports exactly the opposite of what they told him. When asked, "What did the attackers look like?" the coed answered: "A tall man, very handsome . . ." but the correspondent writes: "The interior of the cars has been overrun by what appears to be a horde of cave men, heavily armed with pistols in each hand, a knife thrust between their teeth

---

[43]Octavio Paz, *El laberinto de la soledad* (Mexico: Fondo de Cultural Económica, 1959), 21–22.

[44]Martín Luis Guzmán, *El águila y la serpiente*, 4th ed. (Mexico: Editorial Anáhuac, 1941), 5.

[45]Rafael F. Muñoz, *Fuego en el Norte: Cuentos de la Revolución* (Mexico: Libro Mex, 1960), 40.

and letting out terrifying screams . . . their hairy manes and unshaven beards gave them the appearance of savage beasts."[46]

The characters that appear in the works of Muñoz are caricatures. The same is true of Rodolfo Usigli, the creator of Oliver Bolton, a character in Usigli's play *El gesticulador* (1937). Bolton is a professor of history at Harvard University who goes to Mexico in search of the truth about a certain revolutionary figure. He represents the stereotypical rich American. In the town of Allende, in Nuevo León, César invites Bolton to spend the night in his house. Elena, César's wife, tells him: "You shouldn't have received him that way. We have no idea who he is . . . one never knows with these Americans: they all dress well, they all dress the same, they all have automobiles."[47]

During World War II, Mexico fought alongside the United States against the Axis powers. This may account for the change in the attitude of some North American writers toward Mexico. Their tone is no longer as hostile as in the past, and at times it almost seems benevolent. Nowadays, there is not a single North American writer who would dare to print the denigrating expressions that were used so naturally by the writers of the last century. But Professor Cecil Robinson observes that "without a doubt, the great sympathy that some American intellectuals have for Mexico is not reciprocated by their Mexican counterparts."[48] This observation, however, cannot be applied to writers such as Alfonso Reyes, Xavier Villaurrutia, Octavio Paz, and Carlos Fuentes, among others, who have expressed favorable opinions about many aspects of North American life. The interest in North American literature is due, in part, to the influence of Pedro Henríquez Ureña, who introduced a very significant change in Mexican letters when he recommended to the members of the Ateneo de la Juventud (Atheneum of Youth) that they read U.S. literature, with which he was quite familiar, as may be seen in his essay "Viente años de literatura de los Estados Unidos" (Twenty years of literature in the United States).[49]

The study of North American letters was one of the values that the generation of the "Contemporáneos" (1930s) inherited from the "Ateneístas" (1910s), and this influence is reflected in the work of the younger writers. I will mention only one of them, the poet Xavier Villaurrutia,

[46]Ibid., 47.

[47]Rodolfo Usigli, *El gesticulador*, 2d ed. (Mexico: Editorial Stylo, 1947), 24–25. This character has the same surname as a famous Berkeley historian, but there seems to be no relation between the fictional and historical characters. Although Oliver Bolton is a professor at Harvard, Usigli nevertheless characterizes him as "blond and deeply tanned by long years in the sun," 23.

[48]Robinson, *Mexico and the Hispanic Southwest*, 175.

[49]Pedro Henríquez Ureña, "Viente años de literatura de los Estados Unidos," *Obra crítica* (Mexico: Fondo de Cutural Económica, 1960), 309–323.

who published "Guía de poetas norteamericanos" (Guide to North American poets) and completed studies of Elmer Rice, George Santayana, and Walt Whitman. It is thus understandable that the work of Villaurrutia receives more attention in the universities of the United States than anywhere else outside of Mexico.[50]

The interest in North American literature that was first shown by the "Ateneístas" and the "Contemporáneos" has continued to the present. Octavio Paz has published translations of several poets; Carlos Fuentes has written critical studies of C. Wright Mills, Ernest Hemingway, Oscar Lewis, William Styron, and others.[51] Salvador Elizondo, José Emilio Pacheco, and many others have continued to study the literature of the United States. And the same thing is happening in the United States, where the influence of Mexican literature has reached a peak, partly due to the popularity of the writers of the Latin American literary "boom" and also because of the participation of Chicano writers and readers.

Mythical Modes in Chicano Literature

Let us now examine the case of various Chicano writers, who are the product of a synthesis of the two cultures of Mexico and the United States. In general, although their work is written primarily in English, it is evident that a Mexican cultural background is always present in their writing. Especially after the decade of the sixties, as a result of the Chicano Movement, they searched for their roots in the country of their ancestors. They found those roots in Indian mythology and in the heroes of the War of Independence and the Revolution. A profound nationalism moved them to create a myth of their origins, of Aztlán, the land abandoned by the Aztecs and reclaimed by the Chicanos. The myth of Aztlán unites Chicanos with the past, especially with the Aztecs, with the Seven Caves, and with the creative deities Coatlicue and her son, Huitzilopochtli, as well as with the mythic journey and the no less mythic founding of the Aztec Empire in Lake Texcoco.

The Aztlán myth, whose Mexican origins go back to the sixteenth century, has evolved over time.[52] Its recent rebirth must be attributed to

[50]See Luis Mario Schneider, "Bibliografía de Xavier Villaurrutia," in *Obras de Xavier Villaurrutia*, ed. Miguel Capistrán, Alí Chumacero, and Luis Mario Schneider (Mexico: Fondo de Cultura Económica, 1966), xxxiii–lxxi; and Merlin H. Forster, *Fire on Ice: The Poetry of Xavier Villaurrutia* (Chapel Hill: University of North Carolina, 1976).

[51]See Carlos Fuentes, *Casa con dos puertas* (Mexico: Editorial Joaquín Mortiz, 1970).

[52]See *Aztlán, Essays on the Chicano Homeland* (Albuquerque, NM: Academia/El Norte Publications, 1989), a collection of essays and articles edited by Rudolfo A. Anaya and Francisco Lomelí.

Chicanos and, in particular, to the poet Alurista, although, as he himself stated in his study of three Chicano novelists, myths are not the product of individuals but of generations of people who share a common space over a considerable period of time.[53] But it is Alurista who, in fact, identified Chicanos with the myth of Aztlán. His "Plan espiritual de Aztlán," which he presented in Denver in March 1969, declares the following: "We are a nation, we are a union of free peoples, we are AZTLAN."[54] The impact of the myth is clearly evident in the work of the principal Chicano writers of the seventies, a decade in which poems, novels, and anthologies appeared with the word "Aztlán" in the title. For example, the journal *Aztlán*, which began publication in 1970; the poems "Floricanto en Aztlán" (1971), by Alurista; the novels *Peregrinos de Aztlán* (1974), by Miguel Méndez M., and *Heart of Aztlán* (1976), by Rudolfo Anaya; and the anthology *Aztlán* (1972), by Luis Valdéz.

Of fundamental importance to the creation of that and other myths is the epic poem, "Yo soy Joaquín" (1967), by Rodolfo "Corky" Gonzales, in which the hero is identified with a mythic Joaquín. One may ask, Who is Joaquín? The most obvious answer would be Joaquín Murrieta. But Joaquín as a historical/mythical character is transformed in the poem into a symbol of and for Chicanos. Joaquín becomes a synthesis of various popular heroes and antiheroes in Mexican and Chicano cultures. However, the poetic subject is personified by the figure of Joaquín Murrieta:

> I rode the mountains of San Joaquín.
> I rode to the East and the North
> as far as the Rocky Mountains
> And men feared the pistols
> of Joaquín Murrieta.[55]

Joaquín, as a symbol of Chicanos, is, for the first time in the literature of his people, identified with Mexicans and their culture, which are exalted and praised for their merit and values. He is directly identified with various mythic Mexican heroes. Some are Indians from the period before the conquest; another, Juan Diego, is also an Indian who belongs to the colonial period. Finally, two are twentieth-century revolutionaries. The voice of Joaquín declares:

---

[53]Alurista, "Myth, Identity and Struggle in Three Chicano Novels: Aztlán . . . , Anaya, Méndez and Acosta," ibid., 220.

[54]This poem was published in the first issue of the journal *Aztlán, a Journal of Chicano Studies* (Spring 1970): ix. On the poetry of Alurista, see Gary Keller's Introduction to the poet's book, *Return, Poems Collected and New* (Ypsilanti, MI: Bilingual Press/Editorial Bilingüe, 1982), xi–xlix.

[55]*I Am Joaquín/Yo soy Joaquín* (New York: Bantam Books, 1972), 45. All of the quotations that follow are from this edition.

> I am Cuauhtemoc
> majestic and noble
> a leader of men . . .
> I am Netzahualcoyotl,
> the renowned chief of the Chichimecas.[56]

> I am the loyal, the humble Juan Diego
> I am . . . the apostle of Democracy
> Francisco I. Madero.[57]

However, there is never a direct identification with Pancho Villa. It is clear that Joaquín is not Villa, for he calls himself a companion of the rebel chief, who remains at a distance:

> I am Joaquín
> I rode with Pancho Villa,
> so coarse and charming.[58]

On the other hand, there is total identification with Zapata, who had fought to reclaim the land. Joaquín allows the Hero of the South to speak:

> I am Emiliano Zapata.
> "This land,
> this earth, is OURS."[59]

This identification with popular Mexican heroes, whether direct or indirect, represents only one of Joaquín's two faces; the other is formed by antiheroes and despots like Hernán Cortés, Porfirio Díaz, and Victoriano Huerta.[60] The connection in the case of Cortés, however, is not to the conqueror himself, but to his sword, the symbol of the destruction of the indigenous cultures:

> I am the sword and the flame
> of Cortés, the despot.[61]

To counteract the shock of the identification with the Conqueror, there is an immediate reference to the symbol that unites the Aztecs that Cortés conquered with the Mexicans of today:

> I am the eagle and the serpent
> of the Aztec civilization.[62]

---

[56]Ibid., 16.
[57]Ibid., 41–42.
[58]Ibid., 34.
[59]Ibid.
[60]Ibid., 41.
[61]Ibid., 16.
[62]Ibid.

While the poem foregrounds the identification of Joaquín with Mexican heroes, antiheroes, and symbols, that is not the only association, for there is also a natural association with popular Chicano heroes such as Elfego Baca and the Espinoza brothers of the San Luis Valley, who, in a parallel structure, are identified with Mexican heroes. But the main association that structures the entire poem is, of course, a mythical synthesis with Murrieta:

> Hidalgo! Zapata!
> Murrieta! Espinozas![63]

The syncretic cultural images of the poem give form to another type of identity that involves the gods, the people, and the symbols of the nation and of nature. The antithetical images and concepts are multiplied, and Joaquín becomes a Mayan prince, but he is also Christ; he is a pagan and also a Christian; he is the sword of Cortés and also the Aztec's eagle and serpent; he is a tyrant as well as a slave; he is the Virgen de Guadalupe and also Tonántzin; he is a member of the rural police and also a revolutionary; he is Indian and also Spanish; he is a mestizo and also a criollo; he is a soldier and also a *soldadera*; he is a farm laborer and also a farm owner. But most of all, he is the Chicano people, the outcome of a racial, social, and cultural synthesis. Chicanos are the descendants of racial mixtures; they are the representatives of that mythical cosmic race of which Vasconcelos spoke. Joaquín is a Yaqui, a Tarahumara, a Chamula, a Zapotec, a mestizo, a Spaniard, a Mexican, a Latino, a Hispano, a Chicano,

> or whatever I may call myself,
> I will look the same
> I will feel the same
> I cry and I sing the same.[64]

Of all the mythical Mexican heroes, the figure of Zapata is the one that has most influenced Chicano writers, artists, and leaders. Among the younger generation, however, there already is an apparent desire to demythify the great hero. An example of this is found in "The Eyes of Zapata," a short story by Sandra Cisneros, from her collection *Woman Hollering Creek.*[65] In the story, Zapata appears not as the mythical hero of the *corridos* and the narrative literature of Mexico and Aztlán but as he is seen by one of his numerous lovers, a woman named Inés Alfaro, with whom he had children but did not wish to marry. According to the character of Inés, Zapata is a legend, a myth, and a god to other women. But to

---

[63]Ibid., 48.
[64]Ibid., 98.
[65]Sandra Cisneros, *Woman Hollering Creek and Other Stories* (New York: Random House, 1991).

her, Miliano (as she calls him) is the young man she met at the fair of San Lázaro; he is not a peasant who dresses in the white linen trousers and blouse of Diego Rivera's Cuernavaca murals. No, he is a horseman who wears the tight pants, the short jacket, and the large, braided sombrero of the *charro*. Although the peasants may follow him, they know that he is not of their social class, that he is not one of them.

Another myth demythified by Sandra Cisneros is that of la Llorona—a story as popular among Mexicans as among Chicanos—in her short story "Woman Hollering Creek." The demythification consists, first of all, in the name change from woman crying (la Llorona) to woman hollering. Furthermore, the story is no longer the lament of a woman in search of her lost children, but the triumphant shout of a woman who is liberated from the man who abused her. Before Cisneros's short story, Rudolfo Anaya had tried to demythify la Llorona by identifying her with a historical character, Doña Marina, who killed her children rather than permit Hernán Cortés to take them away to Spain.[66]

In Chicano literature, Luis Valdéz demythified the Spanish conquest of Mexico in an *acto*, a play based on the historical events, in which he uses irony and satire to demythify the heroes, now seen from a Chicano perspective. The conquistadores are characterized as ordinary men who are more interested in finding gold than in the redemption of the Indians. The satiric, demythifying effect is obtained by means of various linguistic devices, such as translating proper names into English: Herman Cortez [*sic*], Pete Alvarado; and also by attributing modern-day negative characteristics to the principal characters: Cortés is a bearded *coyote* (smuggler of undocumented persons); Fray Bartolo is Cortés's chief witch doctor; la Malinche (Cortés's Indian mistress) is the first traitor. The only character that is not demythified is Cuauhtemoc, who opposes the Aztec emperor, Moctezuma. He attempts to convince the emperor that the Spaniards are not gods and calls on him to defend his empire. In the final speech of the *acto*, Cuauhtemoc blames the Mexicans, saying that they were defeated because they lacked unity. But he is already speaking from a contemporary perspective, given that the *acto* is directed at farmworkers who lose their fight against the owners because of the same lack of unity. Cuauhtemoc says, "We Mexicans of ancient times lost because we were not united with our *raza* brothers, because we believed that those white men were powerful gods and because we never wised up."[67]

[66]Rudolfo A. Anaya, *The Legend of la Llorona: A Short Novel* (Berkeley: Tonatiuh-Quinto Sol International, 1984).

[67]Luis Valdéz and the Teatro Campesino, *Actos* (San Juan Capistrano, CA: Menyah Productions, 1971), 65; the original text is in Spanish.

Luis Valdéz's characterization of Doña Marina (la Malinche) is consistent with the image of her that has prevailed in Mexico, which condemns her as a woman who betrayed her people. The voice of the Sun Stone, which presents the historical events in the *acto*, says of la Malinche, "She was destined to be an infamous figure in the history of Mexico. Not only did she turn her back on her own people, she joined the white men and assimilated, serving them as a guide and interpreter, and generally assisting in the process of the Conquest."[68]

The social myth of Doña Marina as a traitor to her people has been contested by Chicana writers who have created a countermyth of la Malinche as a heroine, as a feminist prototype, and as the creator of the "cosmic race." Adelaida R. del Castillo tries to rehabilitate la Malinche by asserting that "after all that Doña Marina suffered to give birth to a new world, few have recognized or appreciated her merit and her contributions. No one, not Cortés, the Catholic Church, her husband, not even history nor the mestizo nation that she created has realized what a great injustice has been committed by clouding her achievements and slandering her name."[69]

The influence of Mayan mythology on Chicano literature is evident in two short stories, "The Village which the Gods Painted Yellow," by Rudolfo Anaya, published in his 1982 collection *The Silence of the Llano*, and in "One Holy Night," by Sandra Cisneros, which is included in her previously mentioned book of short stories. Both stories are shaped by the well-known legend of the dwarf, Uxmal. Anaya recreates the mythical character of legend by giving him a new dimension (death and resurrection), whereas Cisneros attempts to demythify Uxmal by presenting him as a picaresque figure who uses the myth to seduce and deceive women.

Gonzalo, a tourist guide, is the reincarnation of Uxmal in Anaya's story. According to the myth, Uxmal constructed a palace (or a pyramid) overnight. Thus, Gonzalo, a lame, hunchbacked dwarf, wants to repeat Uxmal's feat, but when he fails to do so, he is sacrificed, and the same fate will await his successor. The rite, which is carried out "in honor of the dying sun," is reenacted annually on the day of the winter solstice.

Sandra Cisneros's character, on the other hand, is not a real dwarf representing Uxmal, but a vagrant who calls himself Chaq Chaq Uxmal Palonquín and says that he is a descendant of the Mayan kings. His name means "boy-child," which becomes "Boy Baby" in the story. Boy Baby says that when he was a child, he prayed in the Temple of Uxmal the

[68]Ibid., 58.
[69]Adelaida R. del Castillo, "Malintzin Tenépatl: A Preliminary Look into a New Perspective," *Encuentro Femenil* (1974): 143.

Magician (in other words, in the Temple of the Dwarf), where his father made him promise that he would restore the ancient Mayan traditions. The reader discovers, however, that Boy Baby is actually a bluebeard who uses the Uxmal myth to deceive and seduce women. There is a suggestion that he already has killed more than seven women. The two stories are good examples of the tendency in contemporary Chicano literature to both re-create and demythify some of the traditional Mexican myths.

Mutual Understanding through Literature

In general, it can be said that the fiction writer is able to create imaginary worlds in which history and myth work hand in hand to present a reality that transcends cultural frontiers. Yet one must also keep in mind that those works of fiction either may be the result of cultural and racial antagonisms or may represent a desire to bring peoples together. Although in the nineteenth century some fiction writers in the United States spread the myth of Mexican racial and cultural inferiority, others defended the Mexicans.

The image of Mexico current at the time—the result of a limited knowledge of Mexico's cultural values—was replaced during the twentieth century by a more balanced understanding. In some writers, this appeared as outright sympathy and admiration for Mexican culture, which previously had been considered exotic, distant, and incomprehensible. Although some critics may claim that sympathy is not mutual among Mexican writers, a more careful analysis reveals that Mexico too has experienced a change in the attitude of its writers toward North American culture, a change that tends to be much more favorable.

In conclusion, it is apparent that the study of literature helps to complement the historical view that the inhabitants of a given country may have of themselves and of their neighbors. Unfortunately, in the case of Mexico and the United States, critics have not taken into consideration the reciprocal influence that the two literatures have had on the development of political and cultural relations between the two countries. My hope is that this brief essay will encourage others to undertake further research, as the subject is a promising one that would undoubtedly help to improve relations between these neighboring countries, the representatives of the two great cultures of the American continent.

Bibliography

Archives and Special Collections

Universidad Iberoamericana, Mexico City
    Archivo Porfirio Díaz

Periodicals

Brooklyn Daily Eagle, 1846–1847
The Dial, 1914
Excélsior, 1949, 1992
El Imparcial, 1900
La Jornada, 1994
Los Angeles Times, 1993
Miami Herald, 1993
El Nacional, 1952
Noticias del Mundo, 1990
Novedades, 1944
La Opinión, 1987, 1990
El Pueblo, 1915
Semana Mercantil, 1895
El Tiempo, 1891, 1895
Unión Hispana, 1990

Secondary Sources

Acosta, Oscar Zeta. *The Autobiography of a Brown Buffalo*. San Francisco: Straight Arrow Books, 1972.
———. *The Revolt of the Cockroach People*. San Francisco: Straight Arrow Books, 1973.
Adams, John. *The Works of John Adams*. 10 vols. Boston: Little, Brown and Co., 1850–1856.
Alamán, Lucas. *Documentos diversos*. 4 vols. Mexico: Editorial Jus, 1945–1947.
Alessio Robles, Vito. *Coahuila y Texas desde la consumación de la independencia hasta el tratado de paz de Guadalupe Hidalgo*. 2 vols.

Mexico: Talleres Gráficos de la Nación, 1945–1946. Reprint, Mexico: Editorial Porrúa, 1979.

Altamirano, Ignacio Manuel. *La literatura nacional*. Vol. 1. Edited by José Luis Martínez. Mexico: Editorial Porrúa, 1949.

Alurista. "Poem in Lieu of Preface." *Aztlán, a Journal of Chicano Studies* (Spring 1970): ix.

————. *Return, Poems Collected and New*. Introduction by Gary Keller. Ypsilanti, MI: Bilingual Press/Editorial Bilingüe, 1982.

Anaya, Rudolfo A. *The Legend of la Llorona: A Short Novel*. Berkeley: Tonatiuh-Quinto Sol International, 1984.

Anaya, Rudolfo A., and Francisco Lomelí, eds. *Aztlán, Essays on the Chicano Homeland*. Albuquerque, NM: Academia/El Norte Publications, 1989.

Anzaldúa, Gloria. *Borderlands/La Frontera: The New Mestiza*. San Francisco: Spinsters/Aunt Lute Books, 1987.

Azcárate y Lezama, Juan Francisco de. *Un programa de política internacional*. Archivo Histórico Diplomático Mexicano, no. 37. Mexico: Publicaciones de la Secretaría de Relaciones Exteriores, 1932.

Azuela, Mariano. *Los caciques, novela de la Revolución Mexicana, precedida de Las moscas, cuadros y escenas de la Revolución*. Mexico: Ediciones de "la Razón," 1931.

Bancroft, Hubert Howe. *History of the Northwest Coast*. Vol. 1. San Francisco: A. L. Bancroft and Co., 1884.

Bartra, Roger. *La jaula de la melancolía: Identidad y metamorfosis del mexicano*. Mexico: Grijalbo, 1987.

Berninger, Dieter George. "Immigration and Religious Toleration: A Mexican Dilemma, 1821–1860," *The Americas* 32, no. 4 (April 1976): 553–563.

————. *La inmigración en México, 1821–1857*. Mexico: Secretaría de Educación Pública, 1974.

Billington, Ray Allen. *The Protestant Crusade, 1800–1860: A Study of the Origins of American Nativism*. Chicago: Quadrangle Books, 1964.

Blaisdell, Lowell L. *The Desert Revolution: Baja California, 1911*. Madison: University of Wisconsin Press, 1962.

Bolton, Herbert. *Rim of Christendom: A Biography of Eusebio Francisco Kino, Pacific Coast Pioneer*. New York: Macmillan Co., 1936.

Bosch García, Carlos, comp. *Documentos de la relación de México con los Estados Unidos*. Vols 2–4. Mexico: Universidad Nacional Autónoma de México, Instituto de Investigaciones Históricas, 1983–1985.

Bryan, Samuel. "Mexican Immigrants in the United States." *The Survey* 28 (1912): 726–730.

Bryant, William Cullen. *Prose Writings*. Vol. 2. Edited by Parke Godwin. New York: Russell and Russell, 1964.

————. Review of *Jicotencal*. *The United States Review and Literary Gazette* 1, no. 5 (February 1827): 336–346.

Burns, Edward McNall. *The American Idea of Mission*. New Brunswick, NJ: Rutgers University Press, 1957.

Burns, Walter Noble. *The Robin Hood of El Dorado*. New York: Coward-McCann, 1932.

Calderón Valdes, Sergio, comp. *Historia general de Sonora*. 3 vols. Hermosillo: Gobierno del Estado de Sonora, 1985.

Canny, Nicolas P. "The Ideology of English Colonization: From Ireland to America," *William and Mary Quarterly*, 3d ser., 30 (1973): 575–598.

Cárdenas, Lázaro. *Obras*. Vol. 1. Mexico: Universidad Nacional Autónoma de México, 1980.

Cardoso, Lawrence A. *Mexican Emigration to the United States, 1897–1931: Socio-Economic Patterns*. Tucson: University of Arizona Press, 1980.

Castillo, Pedro, and Albert Camarillo, eds. *Furia y muerte: Los bandidos chicanos*. Los Angeles: University of California, Los Angeles, Chicano Studies Center, 1973.

Cisneros, Sandra. *Woman Hollering Creek and Other Stories*. New York: Random House, 1991.

Clark, Victor S. "Mexican Labor in the United States." *Bulletin of Bureau of Labor*, no. 78 (September 1909): 467–522.

Clavijero, Francisco Javier. *Historia antigua de México*. Vols. 1 and 4. Mexico: Editorial Porrúa, 1945.

Clendenen, Clarence Clemens. *The United States and Pancho Villa: A Study in Unconventional Diplomacy*. Ithaca, NY: Cornell University Press, 1961.

Clifford, James. "Notes on Travel and Theory." *Inscriptions* 5 (1989): 177–188.

Collier, George A., with Elizabeth Lowery Quaratiello. *Basta! Land and the Zapatista Rebellion in Chiapas*. Oakland, CA: The Institute for Food and Development Policy, 1994.

Constitución Política Mexicana con reformas y adiciones. . . . Mexico: Ediciones Andrade, 1945.

Cortázar, Julio. *Hopscotch*. Translated by Gregory Rabassa. New York: Pantheon Books, 1966.

Cortés, Hernán. *Cartas y documentos*. Mexico: Editorial Porrúa, 1969.

Cosío Villegas, Daniel. *Historia moderna de México. El Porfiriato. Vida política exterior, segunda parte*. Mexico: Editorial Hermes, 1963.

———. *Historia moderna de México: La república restaurada vida social*. Mexico: Editorial Hermes, 1956.

Davidson, Miriam. "The Mexican Border War: Immigration-bashing." *The Nation* 251, no. 16 (November 12, 1990): 557–560.

Dávila Garibi, J. Ignacio. "El Padre Rositas." *Memorias de la Academia Mexicana de la Historia* 12, no. 2 (April–July 1953):113.

De Certeau, Michel. *Heterologies: Discourse on the Other*. Minneapolis: University of Minnesota Press, 1986.

————. *The Practice of Everyday Life*. Translated by Steven Rendall. Berkeley: University of California Press, 1984.

De la Peña, José Enrique. *La rebelión de Texas; manuscrito inédito de 1836, por un oficial de Santa Anna: Edición, estudio y notas de J. Sánchez Garza*. Mexico: Impresora Mexicana, 1955.

Del Castillo, Adelaida R. "Malintzin Tenépatl: A Preliminary Look into a New Perspective." *Encuentro Femenil* (1974): 143.

De León, Arnoldo. *They Called Them Greasers: Anglo Attitudes toward Mexicans in Texas, 1821–1900*. Austin: University of Texas Press, 1983.

Dorfman, Ariel, and Armand Mattelmart. *Para leer al Pato Donald*. 2d ed. Buenos Aires: Siglo Veintiuno Argentina, 1972.

Eliade, Mircea. *Myths, Dreams, and Mysteries*. New York: Harper and Row, 1967.

Esquivel Obregón, Toribio. *Apuntes para la historia del derecho en México: Relaciones Internacionales, 1821–1860*. 4 vols. Mexico: Antigua Librería Robredo de José Porrúa e Hijos, 1948.

Fernández de Navarrete, Martín, et al., eds. *Colección de documentos inéditos para la historia de España*. Vol. 4. Madrid: Imprenta de la Viuda de Calero [etc.], 1884.

Fernández MacGregor, Genaro. *El río de mi sangre: Memorias*. Mexico: Fondo de Cultura Económica, 1969.

Fernández Retamar, Roberto. *Calibán: Apuntes sobre la cultura en nuestra América*. Mexico: Editorial Diogenes, 1971.

FitzGerald, Frances. *America Revised: History Schoolbooks in the Twentieth Century*. Boston: Little, Brown and Co., 1979.

Flandrau, Grace. "Fiesta in St. Paul." *Yale Review* 33, no. 1 (1946): 69–76.

Flores, Juan, and George Yudice. "Living Borders/Buscando América." *Social Text* 24 (1990): 57–84.

Fogel, Robert W. *Without Consent or Contract: The Rise and Fall of American Slavery*. New York: W. W. Norton, 1989.

Forster, Merlin H. *Fire on Ice: The Poetry of Xavier Villaurrutia*. Chapel Hill: University of North Carolina Press, 1976.

Frost, John. *Pictorial History of Mexico and the Mexican War*. Philadelphia: Thomas Cowperthwait and Co, 1849.

Fuentes, Carlos. *Casa con dos puertas*. Mexico: Joaquín Mortiz, 1970.

————. *Christopher Unborn*. Translated by Alfred MacAdam. New York: Farrar, Straus, and Giroux, 1989.

————. *Gringo viejo*. Mexico: Fondo de Cultura Económica, 1985.

————. *The Old Gringo*. Translated by Margaret Sayers Peden. New York: Farrar, Straus, and Giroux, 1985.

Fussel, Paul. *Abroad: British Literary Traveling between the Wars*. New York: Oxford University Press, 1980.

Galbraith, John Kenneth. *The Affluent Society*. Boston: Houghton Mifflin, 1958.

Gamio, Manuel. *El inmigrante mexicano. La historia de su vida. Notas preliminarias de Gilberto Loyo sobre la inmigración de los mexicanos a los Estados Unidos de 1900 a 1967.* Mexico: Universidad Nacional Autónoma de México, 1969.

———. *Mexican Immigration to the United States: A Study of Human Migration and Adjustment.* Chicago: University of Chicago Press, 1930.

García Cantú, Gastón. *Las invasiones norteamericanas en México.* Mexico: Ediciones Era, 1971.

García Riera, Emilio. *México visto por el cine extranjero.* Mexico: Ediciones Era: Universidad de Guadalajara, Centro de Investigaciones y Enseñanzas Cinematográficas, 1987.

Garreau, Joel. *The Nine Nations of North America.* Boston: Houghton Mifflin, 1981.

Genovese, Eugene D. *Roll, Jordan, Roll.* New York: Pantheon Books, 1974.

Gerbi, Antonello. *Viejas polémicas sobre el mundo: En el umbral de una conciencia americana.* 3d ed. Lima: Banco de Crédito del Perú, 1946.

Gómez-Quiñones, Juan, and David Maciel. *Al norte del Río Bravo: Pasado lejano, 1600–1930.* Mexico: Siglo Veintiuno, 1981.

Gonzales, Rodolpho. *I Am Joaquín/Yo soy Joaquín.* New York: Bantam Books, 1972.

González Navarro, Moisés. *Anatomía del poder en México.* Mexico: El Colegio de México, 1983.

———. "Instituciones indígenas, en el México independiente." In *La política indigenista en México, métodos y resultados,* 2d ed., edited by Alfonso Caso et al., 209–233. Mexico: Instituto Nacional Indigenista, 1973.

———. *El Porfiriato: La vida social.* Mexico: Editorial Hermes, 1957.

Gordon, Lincoln. *A New Deal for Latin America: The Alliance for Progress.* Cambridge: Harvard University Press, 1963.

Greene, Graham. *Another Mexico.* New York: Viking Press, 1939.

Griswold del Castillo, Richard. *La familia: Chicano Families in the Urban Southwest, 1848 to the Present.* Notre Dame, IN: University of Notre Dame Press, 1984.

Guerin-González, Camile. "Repatriación de familias inmigrantes mexicanas durante la gran depresión." *Historia Mexicana* 35, no. 2 (October–December 1985): 245–272.

Gunn, Drewey Wayne. *American and British Writers in Mexico, 1556–1973.* Austin: University of Texas Press, 1974.

———. *Escritores norteamericanos y británicos en México.* Mexico: Fondo de Cultura Económica, 1977.

Gutiérrez Ibarra, Celia. *Cómo México perdió Texas: Análisis y transcripción del informe secreto (1834) de Juan Nepomuceno Almonte.* Mexico: Instituto Nacional de Antropología e Historia, 1987.

Guzmán, Martín Luis. *El águila y la serpiente.* 4th ed. Mexico: Editorial Anáhuac, 1941.

Hadley-García, George. *Hispanic Hollywood: The Latins in Motion Pictures.* New York: Carol Publishing Group, 1990.

Heizer, Robert F., and Alan J. Almquist. *The Other Californians: Prejudice and Discrimination under Spain, Mexico, and the United States to 1920.* Berkeley: University of California Press, 1971.

Henríquez Ureña, Pedro. *Obra crítica.* Mexico: Fondo de Cultura Económica, 1960.

Hernández, Fortunato. *Las razas indígenas de Sonora y la guerra del Yaqui.* Mexico: Talleres de la Casa Editorial "J. de Elizalde," 1902.

Hobsbawm, Eric. "The Perils of the New Nationalism." *The Nation* 253, no. 15 (November 4, 1991): 537–538.

Hofstadter, Richard. *Social Darwinism in American Thought.* New York: G. Braziller, 1959.

Horsman, Reginald. *Race and Manifest Destiny: The Origins of American Racial Anglo-Saxonism.* Cambridge: Harvard University Press, 1981.

Humes, Edward. *Buried Secrets: A True Story of Serial Murder, Black Magic, and Drug Running on the U.S. Border.* New York: Dutton, 1991.

Illich, Ivan. *Alternativas.* 2d ed. Mexico: Editorial Joaquín Mortiz, 1977.

Inman, Samuel Guy. *Intervention in Mexico.* New York: G. H. Doran, 1919.

Jennings, Francis. *The Invasion of America: Indians, Colonialism, and the Cant of Conquest.* Chapel Hill: University of North Carolina Press, 1975.

Jennings, Gary. *Aztec.* New York: Avon, 1980.

Jonas, Gerald. "Before Cortés." *New York Times Book Review* 14 (December 1980): 11.

Katz, Friedrich. *La guerra secreta en México.* 2 vols. Mexico: Ediciones Era, 1982.

Kerouac, Jack. *Lonesome Traveler.* New York: McGraw-Hill Book Co., 1960.

Kirkpatrick, John E. *Timothy Flint.* Cleveland: Arthur H. Clark Co., 1911.

Langewieshe, William. "The Border." *Atlantic Monthly* (May 1992): 53–92; (June 1992): 91–108.

Langley, Lester D. *Mexamerica: Two Countries, One Future.* New York: Crown, 1988.

Lapham, Lewis H. "Who and What Is American." *Harper's Magazine* 284, no. 1700 (January 1992): 43–49.

Leal, Luis. "*Jicotencal,* primera novela histórica en castellano." *Revista Iberoamericana* 25 (1960): 9–31.

———. "El norteamericano en la literatura mexicana." *The Bilingual Review/La Revista Bilingüe* 6, no. 1 (1979): 31–38.

León-Portilla, Miguel. *Aztec Thought and Culture: A Study of the Ancient Nahuatl Mind.* Norman: University of Oklahoma Press, 1991.

————. *Cartografía y crónicas de la Antigua California.* Mexico: Universidad Nacional Autónoma de México, 1989.

Linedecker, Clifford L. *Hell Ranch: The Nightmare Tale of Voodoo, Drugs, and Death in Matamoros.* Austin, TX: Diamond Books, 1989.

López, Aralia, Amelia Malagamba, and Elena Urrutia, eds. *Mujer y literatura mexicana y chicana: Culturas en contacto.* Mexico: El Colegio de México, 1990.

Lord, Walter. "Myths and Realities of the Alamo." *The American West* 5, no. 3 (May 1968): 18–25.

MacLachlan, Colin M. *Anarchism and the Mexican Revolution.* Berkeley: University of California Press, 1991.

MacLachlan, Colin M., and Jaime E. Rodríguez O. *The Forging of the Cosmic Race: A Reinterpretation of Colonial Mexico.* 2d ed. Berkeley: University of California Press, 1990.

Maltby, William S. *The Black Legend in England: The Development of Anti-Spanish Sentiment, 1558–1660.* Durham, NC: Duke University Press, 1971.

Mandel, Oscar. "From Chihuahua to the Border." In *New Directions in Prose and Poetry 49*, edited by J. Laughlin, 54–71. New York: New Directions, 1985.

Marín, Fausto Antonio. *La rebelión de la Sierra (Vida de Heraclio Bernal).* Mexico: Edición América, 1950.

McWilliams, Carey. *North from Mexico: The Spanish-Speaking People of the United States.* Philadelphia: J. B. Lippincott, 1949. Reprint, New York: Greenwood Press, 1968.

Menéndez, Gabriel Antonio. *Doheny el cruel: Episodios de la sangrienta lucha por el petroleo mexicano.* Mexico: Bolsa Mexicana del Libro, 1958.

Merk, Frederick. *Manifest Destiny and Mission in American History.* New York: Alfred A. Knopf, 1963.

————. *The Monroe Doctrine and American Expansionism.* New York: Alfred A. Knopf, 1966.

Mexico. Cámara de Diputados. *Diario de debates,* Mexico: Cámara de Diputados,1946.

————. Comisión de Limites. *Diario de viaje de la comisión de límites: Que puso el gobierno de la República bajo la dirección del Exmo. Sr. general de división D. Manuel Mier y Terán, lo escribieron por su orden los individuos de la misma comisión, D. Luis Verlandier y D. Rafael Chovel.* Mexico: Juan N. Navarro, 1850.

————. Comisión Pesquisidora de la Frontera del Norte. *Informe de la Comisión Pesquisidora de la Frontera del Norte al Ejecutivo de la Unión sobre depredaciones de los indios y otros males que sufre la frontera mexicana.* Mexico: Imprenta de Díaz de León y White, 1874.

————. Departamento del Distrito Federal. *El asalto al Castillo de Chapultepec y los Niños Héroes.* Mexico: Talleres Gráficos de la Nación, 1983.

————. Departamento del Trabajo. *Memoria*, 1933–1934.

————. Secretaría de Economía. *Memoria*, 1947–1948.

————. Secretaría de Estado. *Memoria presentada al congreso de la Unión por el Secretario de Estado y del Despacho de Fomento, Colonización e Industria de la República Mexicana, Olegario Molina, enero 1905–junio 1907*. Mexico: Imprenta y Fototipia de la Secretaría de Fomento, 1909.

————. Secretaría de Gobernación. *Memoria*, 1939–1940.

————. Secretaría de Relaciones Exteriores. *La diplomacia mexicana*. 3 vols. Mexico: Tipografía Artística, 1910.

————. *Memoria*, 1925–1926, 1926–1927, 1928–1929, 1931–1932, 1932–1933, 1942–1943, 1948–1949.

Mier, Fray Servando Teresa de. *Cartas de un americano, 1811–1812*. Mexico: Partido Revolucionario Institucional, 1976.

————. *Obras completas*. Vol. 4, *La formación de un republicano*. Edited by Jaime E. Rodríguez O. Mexico: Universidad Nacional Autónoma de México, 1988.

Monsiváis, Carlos. "The Culture of the Frontier: The Mexican Side." In *Views across the Border: The United States and Mexico*, edited by Stanley R. Ross, 50–94. Albuquerque: University of New Mexico Press, 1978.

Moquim, Wayne, with Charles Van Doren, eds. *A Documentary History of the Mexican Americans*. New York: Praeger Publishers, 1971.

Morales, Rebecca, and Paul Ong. "Immigrant Women in Los Angeles." *Economic and Industrial Democracy* 12, no. 1 (February 1991): 65–81.

Morefield, Richard H. "The Mexican Adaptation in American California, 1846–1875." Ph.D. diss., University of California, Berkeley, 1955.

Morgan, Edmund S. *American Slavery and American Freedom: The Ordeal of Colonial Virginia*. New York: W. W. Norton, 1975.

Moyers, Bill. "The Many Worlds of Carlos Fuentes." Interview. *Bill Moyers' Journal* (June 19, 1980): 4.

Muñoz, Rafael F. *Fuego en el Norte: Cuentos de la Revolución*. Mexico: Libro Mex, 1960.

Murray, Paul V. *Tres norteamericanos y su participación en el desarrollo del Tratado McLane-Ocampo, 1850–1860*. Colección de la Revista "Estudios Históricos" Cuaderno, no. 3. Guadalajara: Imprenta "Gráfica," 1946.

Neruda, Pablo. *Fulgor y muerte de Joaquín Murieta, bandido chileno injusticiado en California el 23 de julio de 1853*. Santiago de Chile: Empresa Editorial Zig-Zag, 1967.

————. *Splendor and Death of Joaquín Murieta*. Translated by Ben Belitt. New York: Farrar, Straus, and Giroux, 1972.

O'Connor, Kathryn Stoner. *Presidio La Bahía del Espíritu Santo de Zuñiga, 1721–1846*. 1966. Reprint, Victoria, TX: private printing, 1984.

Oles, James. *South of the Border: Mexico in the American Imagination, 1914–1947.* Washington, DC: Smithsonian Institution Press, 1993.

Ordóñez de Montalvo, García. *Las sergas del virtuoso caballero Esplandían, hijo de Amadís de Gaula.* 1510. Reprint, Madrid: Biblioteca de Autores Españoles, 1857.

Ortoll, Servando, "Turbas antiyanquis en Guadalajara en vísperas de la Revolución de Díaz." *Boletín del Archivo Histórico de Jalisco,* segunda época (second phase), 1, no. 2 (May–August 1983): 2–15.

Pacheco, José Emilio. *No me preguntes cómo pasa el tiempo (poemas, 1964–1968).* Mexico: Editorial Joaquín Mortiz, 1969.

Packard, Vance Oakley. *The Hidden Persuaders.* New York: D. McKay Co., 1957.

———. *The Status Seekers: An Exploration of Class Behavior in America and the Hidden Barriers That Affect You, Your Community, Your Future.* New York: D. McKay Co., 1959.

Paredes, Raymund A. "The Image of the Mexican in American Literature." Ph.D. diss., University of Texas at Austin, 1973.

———. "The Origins of Anti-Mexican Sentiment in the United States." In *New Directions in Chicano Scholarship,* edited by Ricardo Romo and Raymund A. Paredes, 157. Santa Barbara: University of California, Santa Barbara, Center for Chicano Studies, 1984.

Paz, Octavio. *El laberinto de la soledad.* Mexico: Cuadernos Americanos, 1950. 2d ed. rev. Mexico: Fondo de Cultura Económica, 1959. Reprint, Mexico: Fondo de Cultura Económica, 1972.

———. *The Labyrinth of Solitude: Life and Thought in Mexico.* New York: Grove Press, 1962.

Pellicer, Carlos. "Lineas por el Che Guevara." *Cuadernos Americanos* 157 (March–April 1968): 105.

Pitt, Leonard. *The Decline of the Californios: A Social History of the Spanish-Speaking Californians, 1846–1890.* Berkeley: University of California Press, 1966.

Pletcher, David M. *Rails, Mines, and Progress: Seven American Promoters in Mexico, 1867–1911.* Port Washington, NY: Cornell University Press, 1958.

Portelli, Alessandro. "¿Historia oral? Historia y memoria: La muerte de Luigi Trastulli." *Historia y Fuente Oral* 1 (1989): 27–68.

Powell, Philip Wayne. *The Tree of Hate: Propaganda and Prejudices Affecting United States Relations with the Hispanic World.* New York: Basic Books, 1971.

Pratt, Julius W. *Expansionists of 1898.* Gloucester, MA: P. Smith, 1959.

Pratt, Mary. *Imperial Eyes: Travel Writing and Transculturation.* New York: Routledge, 1992.

Provost, Gary. *Across the Border: The True Story of the Satanic Cult Killings in Matamoros, Mexico.* New York: Pocket Books, 1989.

Ramenofsky, Ann F. *Vectors of Death: The Archaeology of European Contact.* Albuquerque: University of New Mexico Press, 1987.

Ramos, Samuel. *El perfil del hombre y la cultura en México*. 2d ed. Mexico: Editorial Pedro Robredo, 1938.

———. *The Profile of Man and Culture in Mexico*. Translated by Peter G. Earle. Austin: University of Texas Press, 1962.

Reed, John. *Insurgent Mexico*. New York and London: Appleton and Co., 1914.

Reyes, Alfonso. *Obras completas*. Vol. 14. Mexico: Fondo de Cultural Económica, 1962.

Ridge, John Rollin. *The Life and Adventures of Joaquín Murieta, the Celebrated California Bandit*. Introduction by Joseph Henry Jackson. Norman: University of Oklahoma Press, 1955.

Riesman, David. *The Lonely Crowd: A Study of the Changing American Character*. New Haven, CT: Yale University Press, 1950.

Robin, Regina. "Literatura y biografía." *Historia y Fuente Oral* 1 (1989): 69.

Robinson, Cecil. *Mexico and the Hispanic Southwest in American Literature*. Tucson: University of Arizona Press, 1977.

Rodó, José Enrique. *Ariel*. Boston: Houghton Mifflin, 1922.

Rodríguez, Roberto. "Group Fights for Presence on Olvera St." *Hispanic Link Weekly Report* 8, no. 22 (June 1990).

Rodríguez O., Jaime E. "The Conflict between the Church and the State in Early Republican Mexico." *New World* 2, nos. 1 and 2 (1987): 93–112.

———. *The Emergence of Spanish America: Vicente Rocafuerte and Spanish Americanism, 1808–1832*. Berkeley: University of California Press, 1975.

Rogers, Cleveland, and John Black. *The Gathering of the Forces*. New York: G. P. Putnam and Sons, 1920.

Romero, Matías. *Estudio sobre la anexión de México a los Estados Unidos*. Mexico: Imprenta del Gobierno, 1890.

Ruiz, Ramón Eduardo. *The People of Sonora and Yankee Capitalists*. Tucson: University of Arizona Press, 1988.

———, ed. *The Mexican War: Was It Manifest Destiny?* New York: Holt, Rinehart and Winston, 1963.

Ruth, D. Tuck. "The Zoot Suit Riots." *Survey Graphic* 43 (1943): 333–336.

Said, Edward. *Orientalism*. New York: Random House, 1978. Reprint, New York: Vintage Books, 1979.

Schneider, Luis Mario. "Bibliografía de Xavier Villaurrutia." In *Obras de Xavier Villaurrutia*, edited by Miguel Capistrán, Alí Chumacero, and Luis Mario Schneider, xxxiii–lxxi. Mexico: Fondo de Cultura Económica, 1966.

Schutze, Jim. *Cauldron of Blood*. New York: Avon, 1989.

Seed, Patricia. " 'Are These Not Also Men?': The Indians' Humanity and Capacity for Spanish Civilization." *Journal of Latin American Studies* 25, no. 3 (October 1993): 629–652.

Shepherd, George W., ed. *Racial Influences on American Foreign Policy.* New York: Basic Books, 1970.

Sierra, Justo. *Viajes (En tierra yankee, en la Europa latina).* Edited by José Luis Martínez. Mexico: Universidad Nacional Autónoma de México, 1948.

Simmen, Edward, ed. *Gringos in Mexico: An Anthology.* Fort Worth: Texas Christian University Press, 1988.

Smith, Robert Freeman. "Estados Unidos y las reformas de la Revolución Mexicana, 1915–1928." *Historia Mexicana* 19, no. 2 (October–December 1969): 189–227.

Stimson, Frederick S. "William Robertson's Influence on Early American Literature." *The Americas* 14, no. 1 (July 1957): 37–43.

Taussig, Michael. *Mimesis and Alterity: A Particular History of the Senses.* New York: Routledge, 1993.

———. *The Nervous System.* New York: Routledge, 1992.

Teixidor, Felipe. *Viajeros mexicanos (Siglos XIX y XX).* Mexico: Ediciones Letras de México, 1939.

Theroux, Paul. *The Old Patagonian Express: By Train through the Americas.* Boston: Houghton Mifflin, 1979.

The Tibetan Book of the Dead; or, the After-Death Experiences on the Bardo Plane, According to Lama Kazi Dawa-Samdup's English Rendering. Compiled and edited by W. Y. Evans-Wentz. London: Oxford University Press, H. Milford, 1927.

Todorov, Tzvetan. *The Conquest of America: The Question of the Other.* New York: Harper and Row, 1982.

Todorov, Tzvetan, et al. *Cruce de culturas y mestizaje cultural.* Madrid: Ediciones Júcar, 1988.

Turner, Frederick C. *The Dynamic of Mexican Nationalism.* Chapel Hill: University of North Carolina Press, 1968.

Turner, John Kenneth. *Barbarous Mexico.* Chicago: C. H. Kerr and Co., 1911.

U.S. Congress. Senate. Committee on Foreign Relations. *Senate Document, Investigation of Mexican Affairs, Preliminary Report and Hearing of the Committee of Foreign Relations, United States Senate pursuant to S. Res. 106 directing the Committee of Foreign Relations to investigate the matter of outrages on citizens of the United States in Mexico.* 66th Cong., 2d sess., December 1, 1919–June 5, 1920. Vols. 9 and 10. Washington, DC: Government Printing Office, 1920.

Usigli, Rodolfo. *El gesticulador.* 2d ed. Mexico: Editorial Stylo, 1947.

Valdéz, Luis, and the Teatro Campesino. *Actos.* San Juan Capistrano, CA: Menyah Productions, 1971.

Valenzuela Arce, José Manuel. *¡A la brava ése! Cholos, punks, chavos banda.* Mexico: El Colegio de la Frontera Norte, 1988.

Vasconcelos, José. *Breve historia del México.* 5th ed. Mexico: Ediciones Botas, 1944.

———. *La raza cósmica.* Mexico: Espasa Calpe-Mexicana, 1948.

Venegas, Miguel. *Noticia de la California*. Vol. 3. Mexico: L. Alvarez y Alvarez de la Cadena, 1943.

Vernez, Georges, and David Ronfeldt. *The Current Situation in Mexican Immigration*. Santa Monica, CA: Rand, 1991.

Walker, Lennie M. "Picturesque New Mexico Revealed in Novel as Early as 1826." *New Mexico Historical Review* 13 (1938): 325–328.

Weber, David J. *Myth and the History of the Hispanic Southwest*. Albuquerque: University of New Mexico Press, 1988.

———, ed. *Foreigners in Their Native Land: Historical Roots of the Mexican Americans*. Albuquerque: University of New Mexico Press, 1973.

Weinberg, Albert K. *Manifest Destiny*. Chicago: Quadrangle Books, 1963.

Weston, Rubin F. *Racism in U.S. Imperialism*. Columbia: University of South Carolina Press, 1972.

Whyte, William H. *The Organization Man*. New York: Simon and Schuster, 1956.

Williams, Stanley T. *The Spanish Background of American Literature*. 2 vols. New Haven, CT: Yale University Press, 1955.

Zamacois, Niceto de. *Historia de Méjico desde sus tiempos más remotos hasta nuestros días*. 18 vols. Barcelona: Parres y Compañía, 1878.

Zavala, Lorenzo de. *Viaje a los Estados Unidos del Norte América*. Paris: Imprenta de Decourchant, 1834. Reprint, Mérida: Sierra O'Reilly, 1846.

Zorrilla, Luis G. *Historia de las relaciones entre México y los Estados Unidos de América, 1800–1958*. 2 vols. Mexico: Editorial Porrúa, 1965. 2d ed., Mexico: Editorial Porrúa, 1977.

Index

Latin American Silhouettes
Studies in History and Culture

William H. Beezley and
Judith Ewell
Editors

Volumes Published

William H. Beezley, Cheryl English Martin, and William E. French, eds., *Rituals of Rule, Rituals of Resistance: Public Celebrations and Popular Culture in Mexico* (1994). Cloth ISBN 0-8420-2416-6 Paper ISBN 0-8420-2417-4

Stephen R. Niblo, *War, Diplomacy, and Development: The United States and Mexico, 1938–1954* (1995). ISBN 0-8420-2550-2

G. Harvey Summ, ed., *Brazilian Mosaic: Portraits of a Diverse People and Culture* (1995). Cloth ISBN 0-8420-2491-3 Paper ISBN 0-8420-2492-1

N. Patrick Peritore and Ana Karina Galve-Peritore, eds., *Biotechnology in Latin America: Politics, Impacts, and Risks* (1995). Cloth ISBN 0-8420-2556-1 Paper ISBN 0-8420-2557-X

Silvia Marina Arrom and Servando Ortoll, eds., *Riots in the Cities: Popular Politics and the Urban Poor in Latin America, 1765–1910* (1996). Cloth ISBN 0-8420-2580-4 Paper ISBN 0-8420-2581-2

Roderic Ai Camp, ed., *Polling for Democracy: Public Opinion and Political Liberalization in Mexico* (1996). ISBN 0-8420-2583-9

Brian Loveman and Thomas M. Davies, Jr., eds., *The Politics of Antipolitics: The Military in Latin America*, 3d ed., revised and updated (1996). Cloth ISBN 0-8420-2609-6 Paper ISBN 0-8420-2611-8

Joseph S. Tulchin, Andrés Serbín, and Rafael Hernández, eds., *Cuba and the Caribbean: Regional Issues and Trends in the Post-Cold War Era* (1997). ISBN 0-8420-2652-5

Thomas W. Walker, ed., *Nicaragua without Illusions: Regime Transition and Structural Adjustment in the 1990s* (1997). Cloth ISBN 0-8420-2578-2 Paper ISBN 0-8420-2579-0

Dianne Walta Hart, *Undocumented in L.A.: An Immigrant's Story* (1997). Cloth ISBN 0-8420-2648-7 Paper ISBN 0-8420-2649-5

Jaime E. Rodríguez O. and Kathryn Vincent, eds., *Myths, Misdeeds, and Misunderstandings: The Roots of Conflict in U.S.-Mexican Relations* (1997). ISBN 0-8420-2662-2

Jaime E. Rodríguez O. and Kathryn Vincent, eds., *Common Border, Uncommon Paths: Race, Culture, and National Identity in U.S.-Mexican Relations* (1997). ISBN 0-8420-2673-8

William H. Beezley and Judith Ewell, eds., *The Human Tradition in Modern Latin America* (1997). Cloth ISBN 0-8420-2612-6 Paper ISBN 0-8420-2613-4

Donald F. Stevens, ed., *Based on a True Story: Latin American History at the Movies* (1997). ISBN 0-8420-2582-0

Jaime E. Rodríguez O., ed., *The Origins of Mexican National Politics, 1808–1847* (1997). Paper ISBN 0-8420-2723-8

Che Guevara, *Guerrilla Warfare*, with revised and updated introduction and case studies by Brian Loveman and Thomas M. Davies, Jr., 3d ed. (1997). Cloth ISBN 0-8420-2677-0 Paper ISBN 0-8420-2678-9

Adrian A. Bantjes, *As If Jesus Walked on Earth: Cardenismo, Sonora, and the Mexican Revolution* (1998). ISBN 0-8420-2653-3

Henry A. Dietz and Gil Shidlo, eds., *Urban Elections in Democratic Latin America* (1998). Cloth ISBN 0-8420-2627-4 Paper ISBN 0-8420-2628-2

A. Kim Clark, *The Redemptive Work: Railway and Nation in Ecuador, 1895–1930* (1998). ISBN 0-8420-2674-6

Joseph S. Tulchin, ed., with Allison M. Garland, *Argentina: The Challenges of Modernization* (1998). ISBN 0-8420-2721-1

Louis A. Pérez, Jr., ed., *Impressions of Cuba in the Nineteenth Century: The Travel Diary of Joseph J. Dimock* (1998). Cloth ISBN 0-8420-2657-6 Paper ISBN 0-8420-2658-4

Guy P. C. Thomson, *Patriotism, Politics, and Popular Liberalism in Nineteenth-Century Mexico: Juan Francisco Lucas and the Puebla Sierra* (1998). ISBN 0-8420-2683-5

ISBN 0-8420-2673-8

9 780842 026734

90000>